DAVID COBLEY

ALL BY HIMSELF

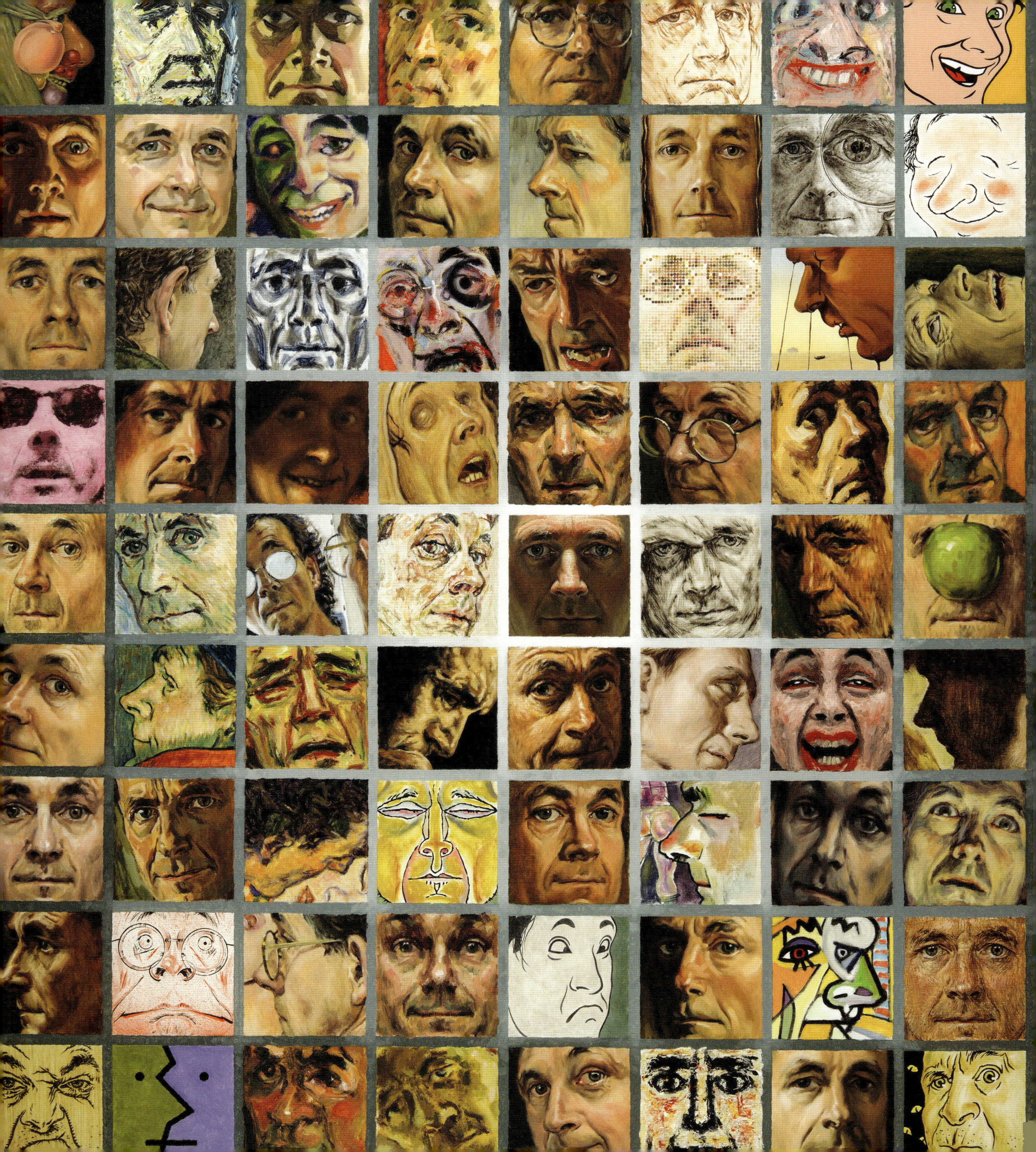

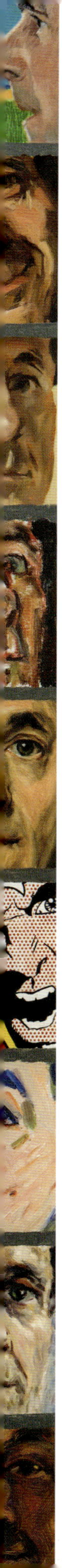

Peter Davies

DAVID COBLEY

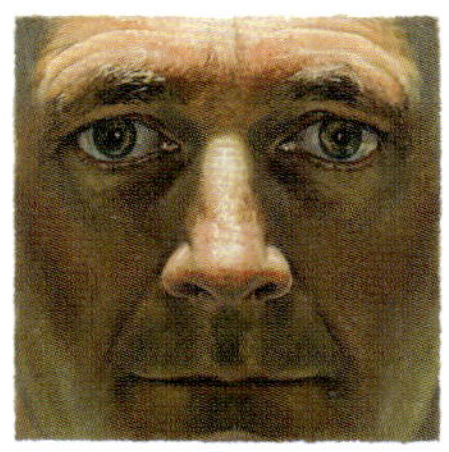

ALL BY HIMSELF

Sansom & Company

First published in 2019 by Sansom and Company,
a publishing imprint of Redcliffe Press Ltd.,
81g Pembroke Road, Bristol BS8 3EA
www.sansomandcompany.co.uk | info@sansomandcompany.co.uk

ISBN 978-1-911408-53-6

British Library Cataloguing-in-Publication Data:
A catalogue record for this book is available from the British Library.

Design and typesetting by E&P Design
Paintings photographed by Peter Stone, Tony Smith and David Cobley

Printed and bound by Akcent Media Ltd

FSC www.fsc.org MIX Paper from responsible sources FSC® C014138

Sansom & Co is committed to being an environmentally friendly publisher. This book is made from Forest Stewardship Council® certified paper.

front cover
What Are You Doing Here?
2010 | oil on linen | 61 x 61 cm
collection of the artist

back cover
In Bits
2019 | oil on linen | 122 x 106.5 cm
collection of the artist

frontispiece
All By Myself
1998 | oil on linen | 122 x 122 cm
collection of the artist

Contents

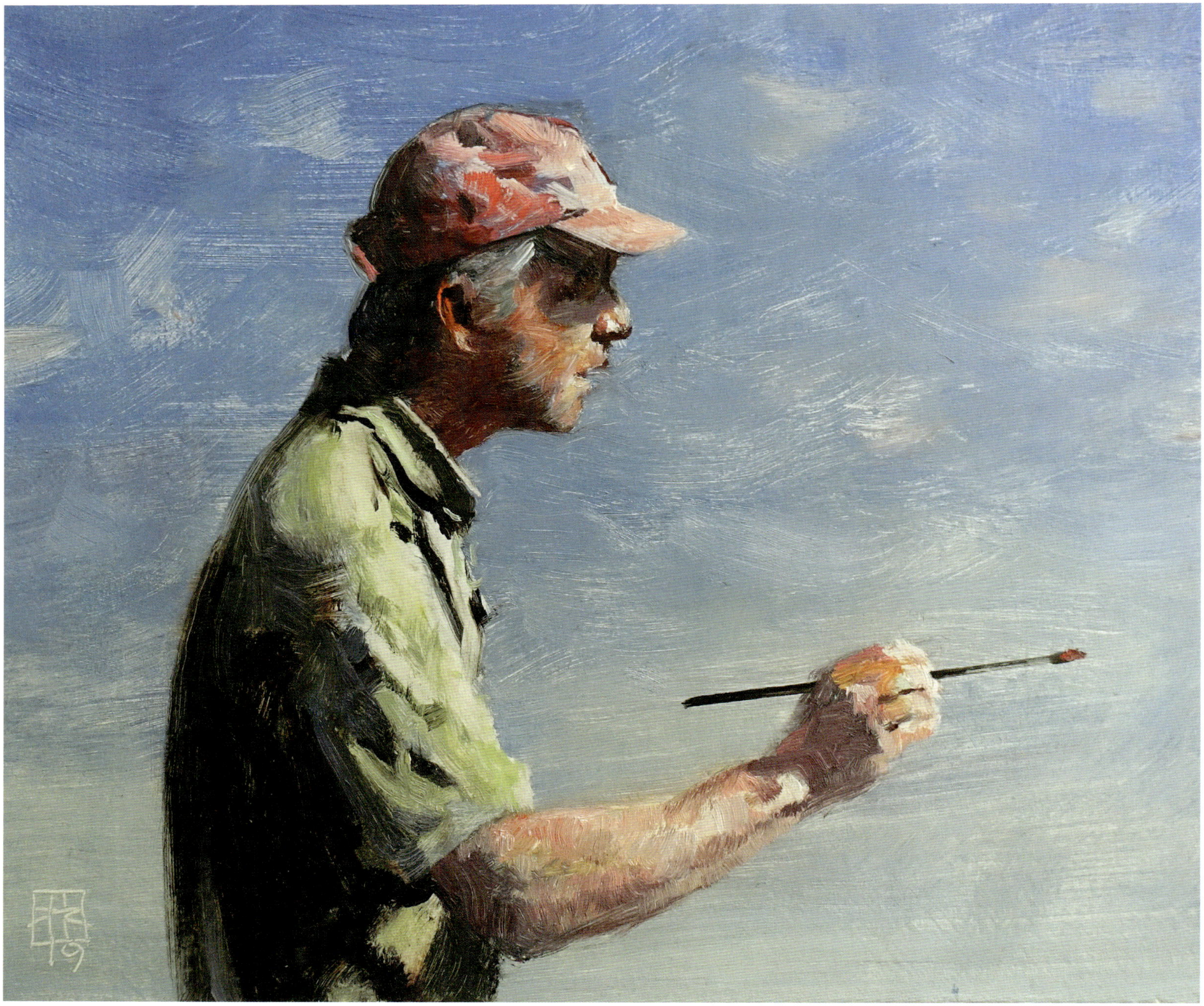

Going For It (Pete 'The Street' Brown) | 2019 | oil on panel | 20 x 24 cm

collection of the artist

Foreword

I first met my friend 'Cobo' while painting on the streets of Bath. He had a studio at Bath Artists' Studios and suggested I might need a studio space there. In 1999, while trying to paint a large commission, I decided to take him up on it and rented a studio. It was to change my life.

Other than the fact that we got on really well, I was amazed by his dexterity – his incredible eye and fluid brushwork. I had never met an artist of this ability before. I can remember simply wondering at it. When it came to seeing and recording, nothing seemed too ambitious for him. He'd work directly in pen, drawing bicycles chained to railings from above, nailing the complex perspective effortlessly.

Being so adept meant he was always looking for new angles. Suspending a large square mirror from the ceiling of his studio he painted himself looking up at the viewer. The resulting self-portraits painted in different lights, *Clutter I* and *Clutter II* (both p. 37), are etched in my mind. Then there was the remarkable painting *The Smell of Turps* (p. 130), bought by Bath's Victoria Art Gallery, that shows a palette and brush-washer catching the light of the fluorescent lamp in the studio. Later at Comfortable Place I can remember a group of us looking at a painting of bedsheets he had just started. We just couldn't understand how he did it.

Although his ability to see and manipulate oil paint is unquestionable, it is something he seems to struggle with because he doesn't like showing off. He would say: 'I hate it when people say "aren't you clever!"' Rather than dazzle, he prefers his work to pose questions.

Instead of trying to dictate how the world should be, he is open to different ways of looking at it. This childlike wonder means he rarely dismisses something as naïve, immature, slick or overly intellectual. It enables him to look at something unfamiliar as just a different way of seeing the world – in its own way as valid as any other. This approach means that everything is worth investigating and anything is possible.

A non-religious man, he has a deep spirituality that is a love of humanity: a fascination with the variety of human thought and the myriad of possibilities on offer. We all meet people who go through the motions in conversation but who are simply waiting for their turn to say what's in their head. Cobo listens and asks questions – a true observer in a self-obsessed world dominated by people who shout the loudest.

Pete 'The Street' Brown **PNEAC PS ROI RP Hon RBA**

Introduction

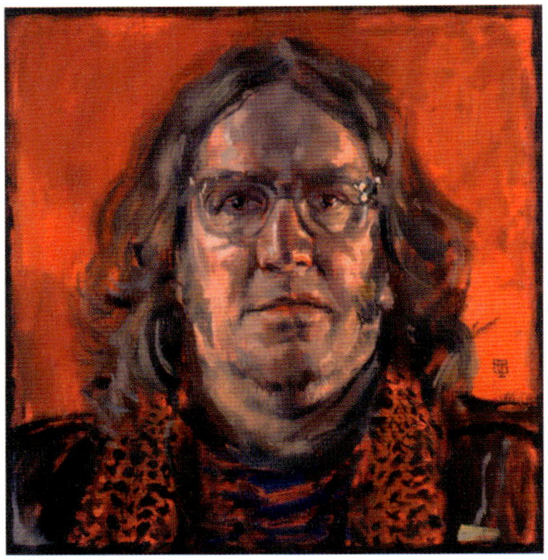

Peter Davies
2002 | oil on linen | 45.5 x 45.5 cm
author's collection

David Cobley RP NEAC is perhaps most celebrated as a professional portrait painter, counting among his sitters royalty and a host of well-known, distinguished public figures from many walks of life. Important though this bread and butter side of his *oeuvre* is, Cobley also uses his technically accomplished powers to pursue a private vision. In his independent, non-commissioned work he often has fun, letting his imagination run free and letting down his proverbial hair in the pursuit of speculative, symbolic or even metaphysical subjects reflecting an introspective, philosophical or religious mind-set. Here, the restrictions of portrait commissions are set aside. The voluminous self-portraits, nudes, still lifes or studio interiors that engage his able hands are not merely ancillary works using leftover oil paint from a royal, celebrity or VIP commission but are in fact integral to his main artistic interests.

In many respects these pictures are deconstructed from a grand portrait or conversation piece, which in itself may contain interior, still-life, or, via a window or door, landscape elements. The posed quietude and platonic intimacy of these interior situations allows the artist to explore not just

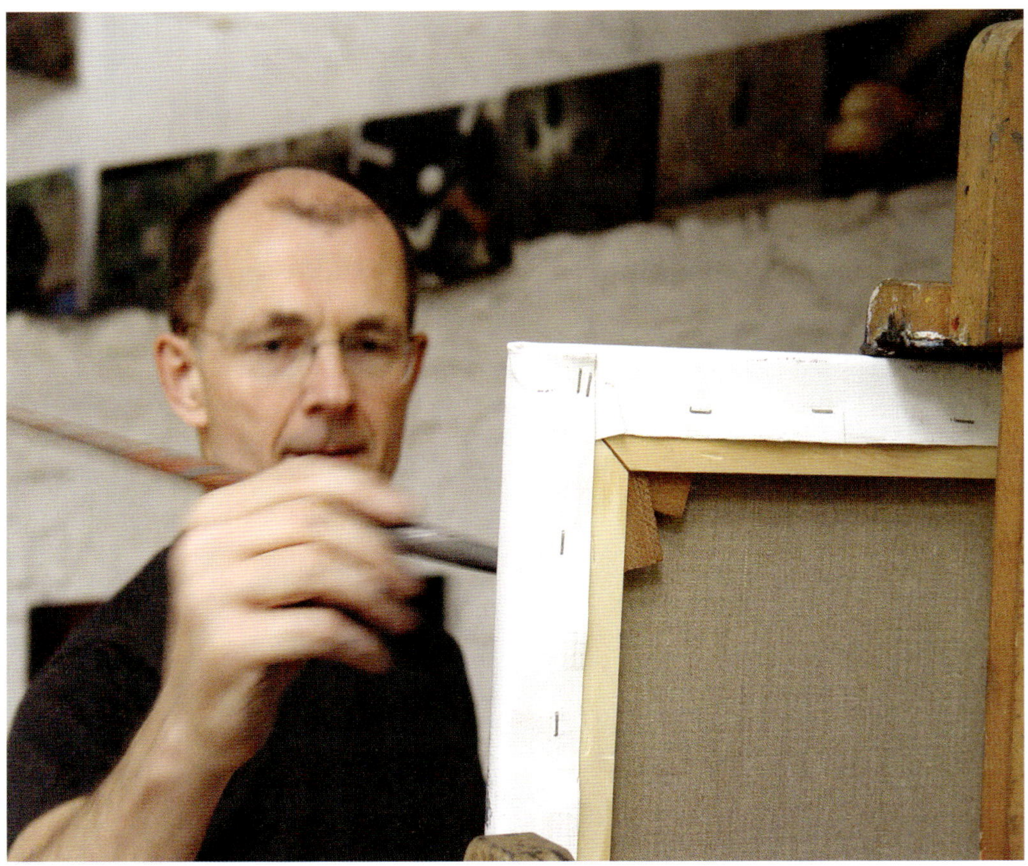

At work, 2007

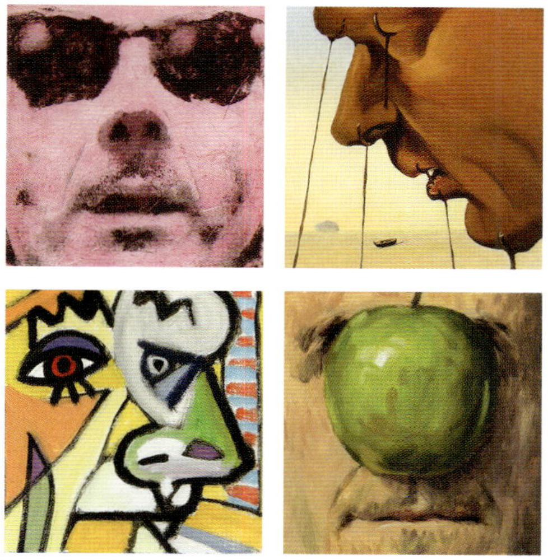

All By Myself (details)
1998 | oil on linen | 122 x 122 cm
collection of the artist

visually but psychologically, with Cobley probing the mysteries of appearance without the distraction of outside or cultural influences. The fecund symbolism of his art is to this extent discrete and implicit, a product of plastic and psychological discovery through the working process.

While Cobley's distinctive art does not easily lend itself to stylistic pigeonholing, there are occasions when a sardonic take on historical precedent and an awareness of style comes unobtrusively to the fore, as in the case of the precocious *All By Myself* (see title page and details, left). By parodying a host of celebrated old, modern and contemporary masters in terms of 81 self-portraits, Cobley's work advertises – boasts almost – his technical versatility, his ability to take on the garb of painters often very different to himself. As he is the first to admit, Cobley is not a connoisseur of abstract art, though major modern movements like cubism, fauvism, expressionism or photorealism are dextrously used 'off pat' by a versatile artist in showy, virtuoso mode. *All By Myself* may be his magnum opus, a visual equivalent of world music reflecting a broad cultural awareness developed from long periods spent in Japan. This picture celebrates the iconic significance of the self-portrait – that suitably introspective, self-revelatory subject for an artist of Cobley's temperamental disposition. *All By Myself* also slots seamlessly into a pluralist, 'anything goes' postmodern zeitgeist. And while Cobley's own style and brand of painting – the handmaiden of refinement of drawing, observational exactitude, mastery of tone, balance of composition and so on – may glibly be described as akin to Lucian Freud without the impasto, in the unique case of *All By Myself* Cobley becomes a hybrid styliser able to cross many divides.

Notwithstanding multiple mini allusions to Van Gogh, Lautrec, Picasso, Spencer, Close, Auerbach, Bacon, Warhol, Magritte, Dalí and a host of others, Cobley's art is personal and unique to him and spawned in a sober and serious academic environment in which prolonged study in the life room saw the virtues of objective scrutiny, observational naturalism, visual analysis and craftsmanly care prioritised. It is therefore no surprise to see in the artist's developing *oeuvre* a situation where the working studio is centre stage – the warts of dishevelled corners and paint-splattered floors 'n' all. The many depictions of his working studio contain the unmistakeable paraphernalia of cushions, armchairs, mirrors, easels, palette boards, unmade beds, paints, brushes and bottles of turps. Iconographically at least, this is art about art if only in a literal rather than plastic sense.

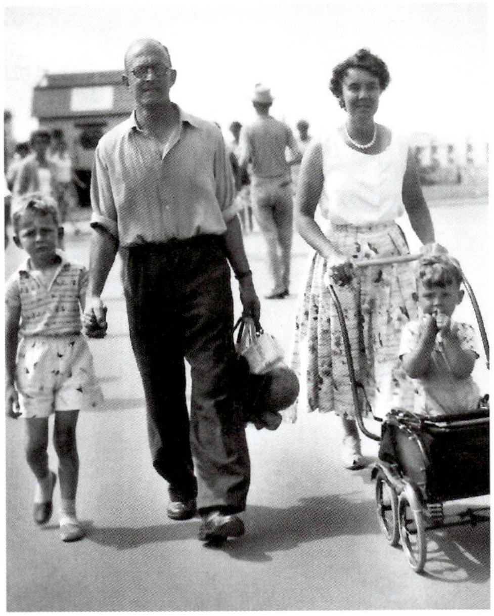

David (left) and family, Cliftonville, 1959

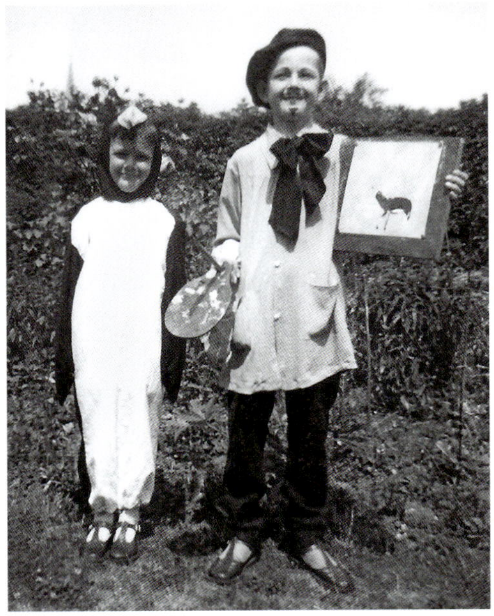

A portrait of the artist as a young man
with penguin/younger brother Andy, 1962

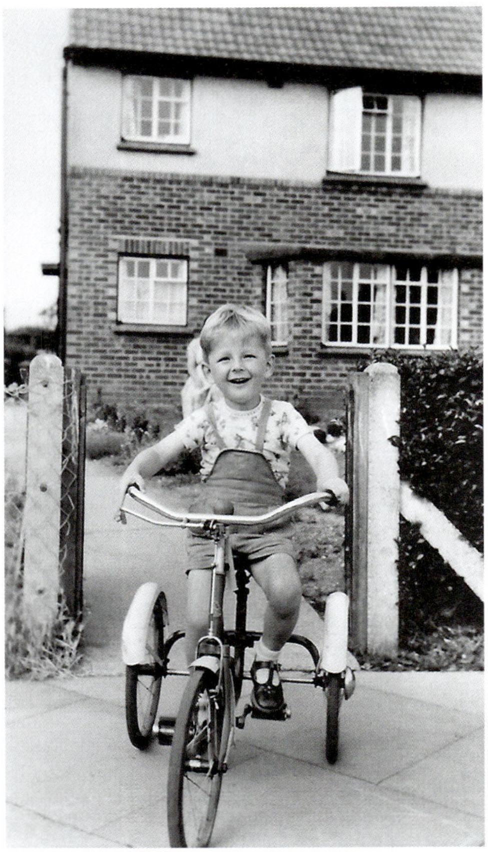

Riding the red tricycle, 1957

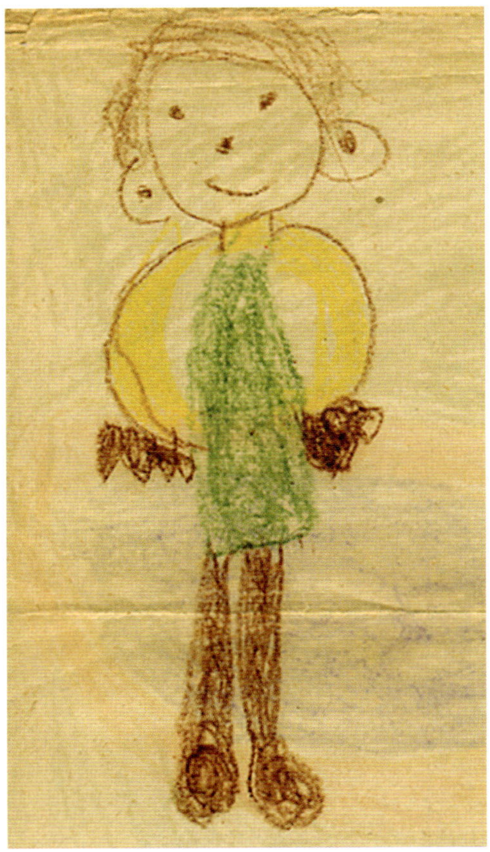

An early portrait, *c.*1958

The making of an artist

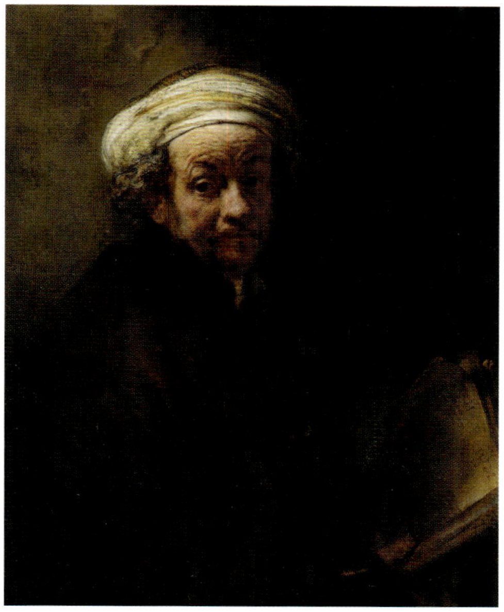

REMBRANDT
Self-Portrait as the Apostle Paul
1661 | oil on canvas | 91.5 x 77 cm
© Rijksmuseum, Amsterdam

David Cobley was born in June 1954 in Northampton, the elder of two brothers and the son of a shoe machinery mechanic. He grew up in Higham Ferrers, a market town about fifteen miles away. Early artistic proclivities were encouraged by an arty maternal uncle who correctly predicted young David would become a successful artist. His parents were liberal and encouraging. The humble circumstances of an ordinary council house were alleviated by a supportive family environment. Further encouragement came from a local grammar school where 'Eddie' Phillips was an inspirational art teacher, helping David achieve top grades in O- and A-level art. Art school was beckoning. The youth was moved by seeing Rembrandt's *Self-Portrait as the Apostle Paul* at a local shop selling Athena prints. He purchased the reproduction with money from his paper round and hung it in his bedroom, a talisman for his own direction in both an artistic and religious sense.

At this early stage Cobley took a big leaf out of George Bridgman's seminal *Constructive Anatomy*, which he saw among other books at the local library. A precise manual on the analytical disciplines of figure drawing could not fail to impress the budding artist, and he made copies of many of the drawings. An early fascination for Bosch and Brueghel anticipated his feeling for allegory and crowd scenes. During a Foundation year at Northampton College of Art Cobley experimented with many disciplines, though he remained most committed to the life room. Entering Liverpool College of Art during the autumn of 1972, Cobley fell under the tutelage of the Slade-trained Welsh expressionist Peter Prendergast, whom he described as a 'disciplinarian'. Further studies in the life room on Hope Street ensued, although he produced just one painting, *Cain and Abel*, (p. 13) during his solitary term at Liverpool.

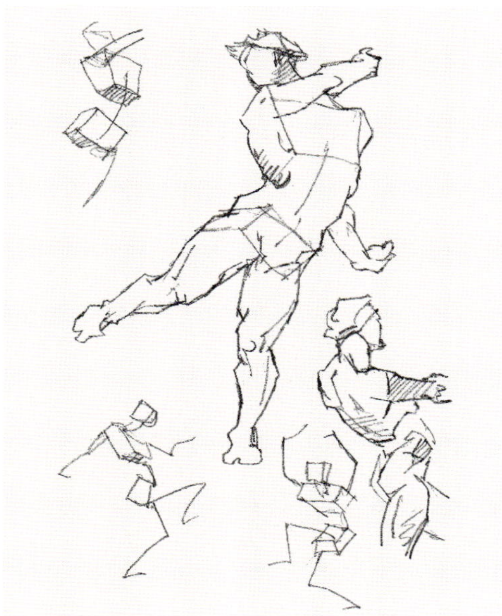

GEORGE BRIDGMAN
Constructive Anatomy (page 4)
published 1920
copy of page by David Cobley 1968

Liverpool College of Art was situated in a grand Victorian building midway between the Catholic and Anglican cathedrals in Hope Street. A centre of excellence for textiles, the College also famously had John Lennon and Stuart Sutcliffe as students during the late 1950s. Inspired by the charismatic Liverpool-born Arthur Ballard and the Royal College-trained Nicholas Horsfield, a de Staël cult developed at the College, in awe of the influential, if short-lived, Russian-born French painter. Prendergast and his friend Mike Knowles, on the other hand, followed the impasto realism of Frank Auerbach, who taught them in London. An outward-looking Liverpool art scene also included pop-inspired painters like the portraitist Sam Walsh and the poet Adrian Henri.

A Methodist upbringing had instilled in David a religious calling, one as strong as art. In the face of much criticism from Prendergast, who

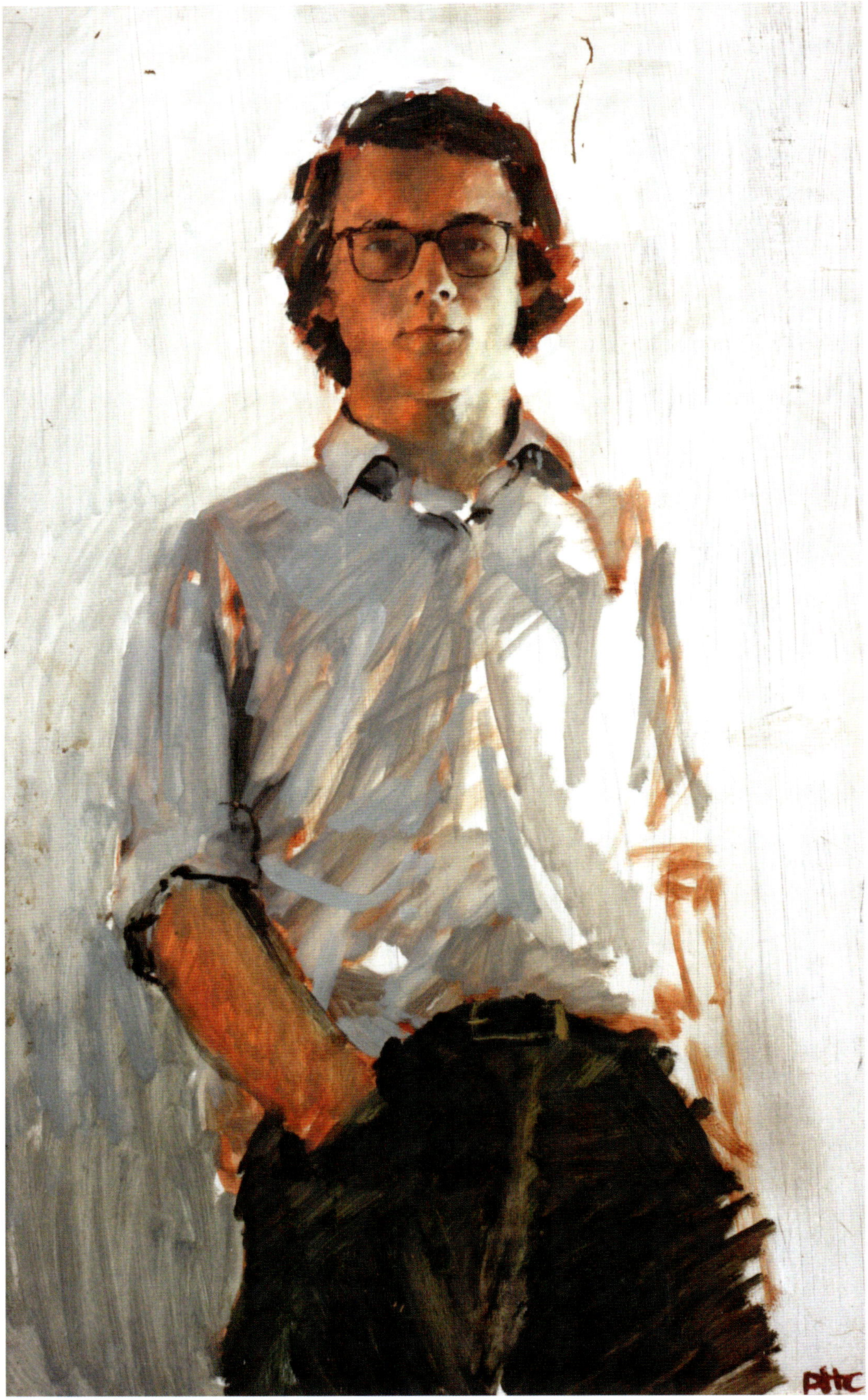

Summer '71 | 1971 | oil on board | 91.5 x 61 cm collection of the artist

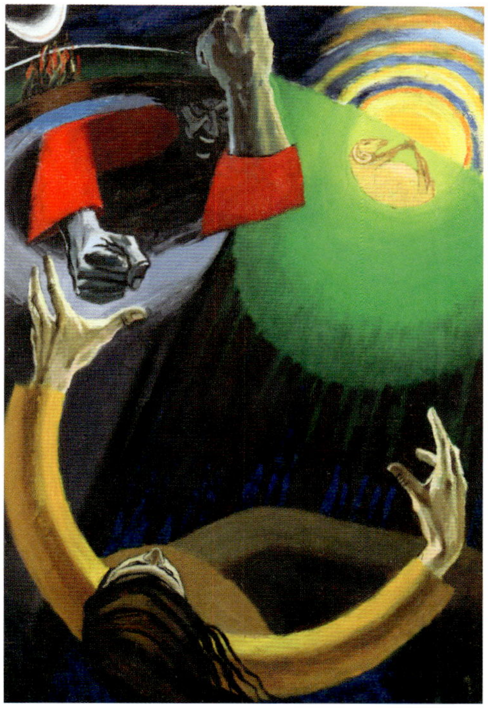

Cain and Abel
1973 | oil on canvas | 122 x 86.5 cm
collection of the artist

counselled him to pursue art, Cobley decided to put art on hold for the time being at least and follow the religious option.

What Cobley described as a 'pull towards a life of altruism, serving God and other people' saw him join the Rev. Moon's Unification Church and move to Japan, a departure that turned his world upside down. After five years with the organisation he stayed on in Japan and pursued a university course in philosophy, logic and literature. He also learnt the language and taught English. As if this engagement with a country he described as 'fascinating' was not enough, he married a Japanese woman, Masami (overleaf), in 1978, with whom he had three daughters – Selima, Melanie and Maya.

Though Cobley's time in the Far East was not artistically very productive, the effect of Japanese culture would prove subtle and enduring: a Zen-like feeling for emptiness, space and for a preoccupation with the self in his subsequent portraiture is evident in much of his later work. He exhibited paintings of rural shrines and farmhouses in a three-man show at the Yamagata Gallery, Tokyo in 1982 (overleaf).

Cobley and his young family returned to the UK in the mid-1980s, drawing to a close a near decade-long Japanese sojourn. He decamped *en famille* to West Wales, where his younger brother Andy lived, in Pembroke.

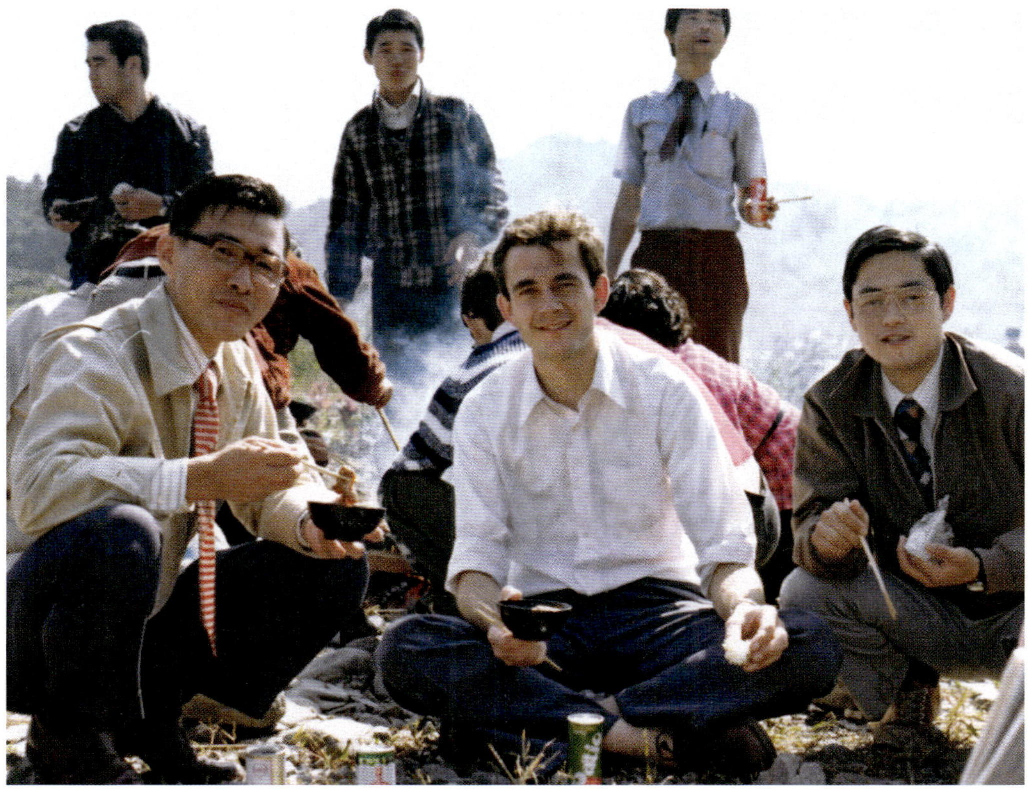

With the Moonies, Japan, *c.*1976

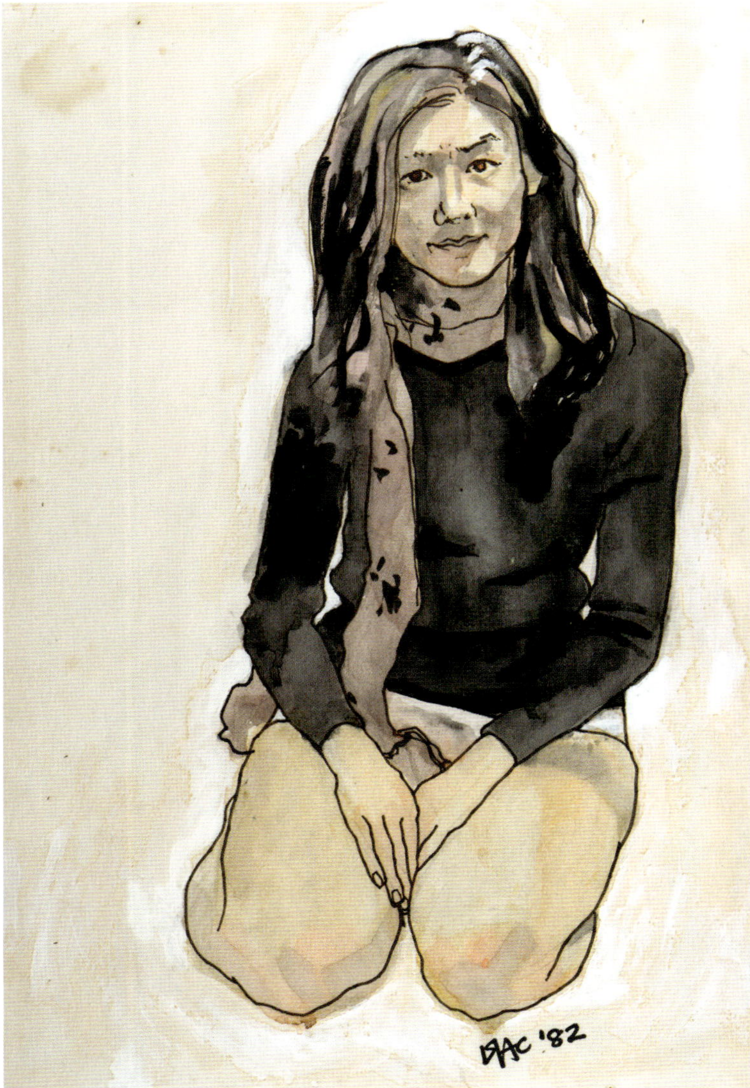

Masami Kneeling
1982 | pen and wash | 41 x 30 cm
collection of the artist

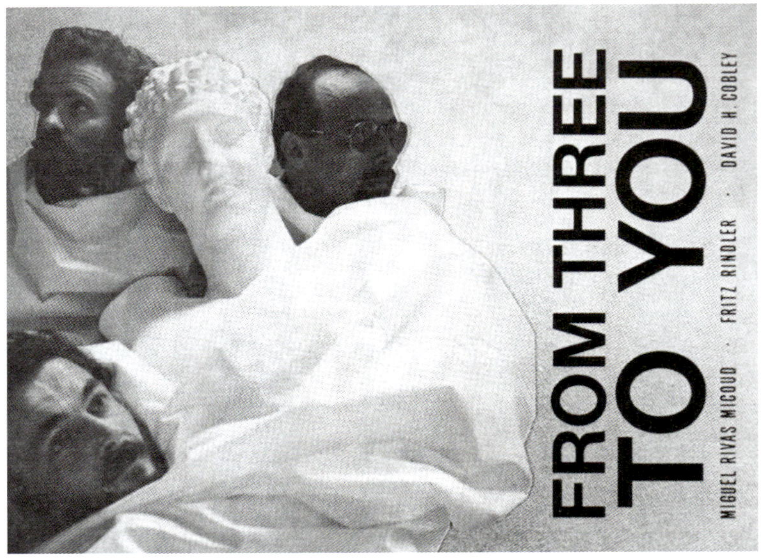

'From Three to You' invitation, Yamagata Gallery, Tokyo, 1982

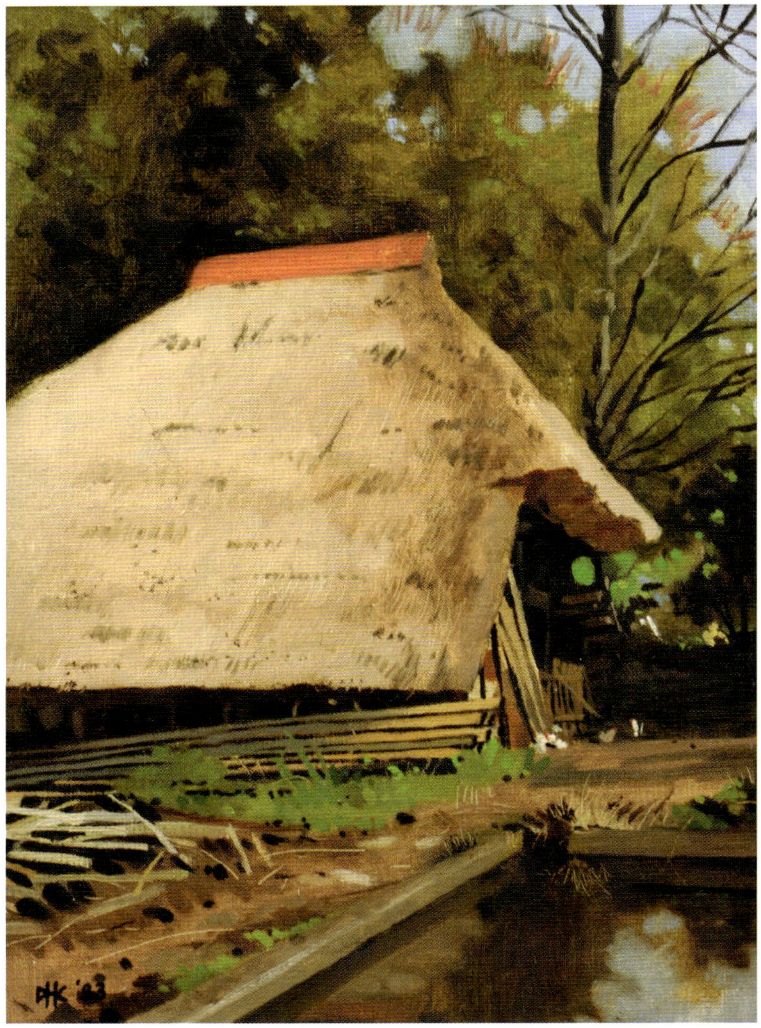

Farmhouse in Saitama
1983 | oil on linen | 40.5 x 30.5 cm
collection of the artist

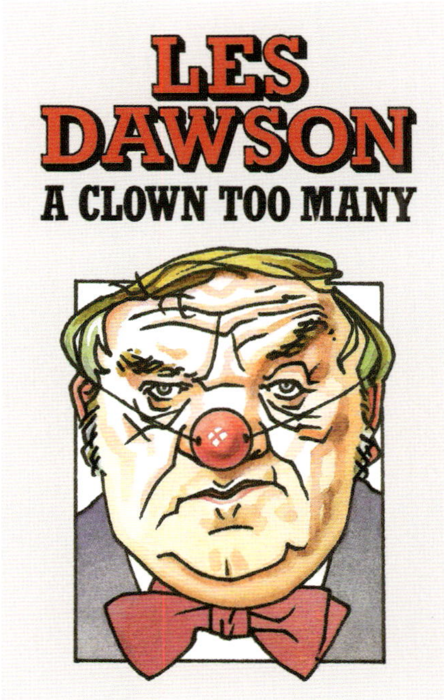

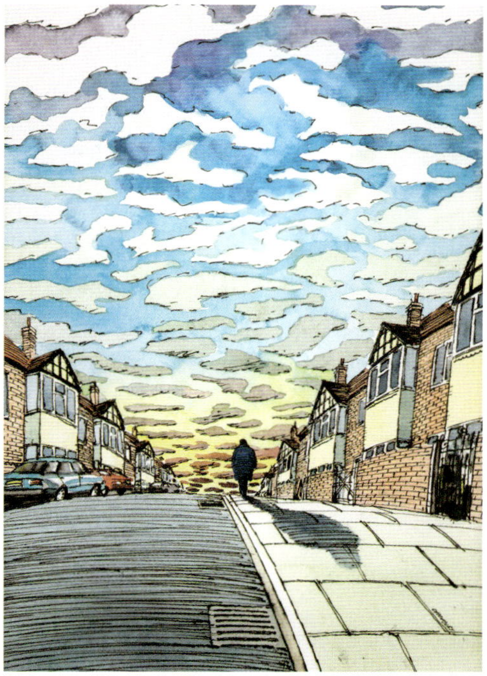

Bookjacket illustration for *The Wimbledon Poisoner* by Nigel Williams

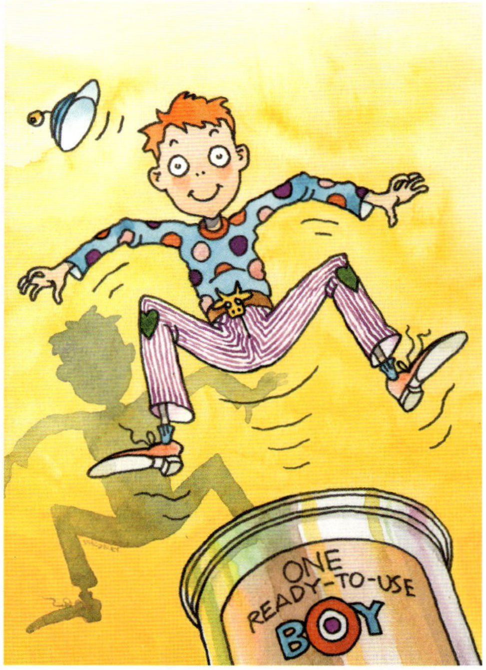

Bookjacket illustration for *Conrad the Factory-Made Boy* by Christine Nostlinger

Unable to find the necessary design or illustration work in this quiet corner of the principality, Cobley moved first to Box near Bath – living in temporary rented accommodation – then the village of Westwood just outside Bradford on Avon, where he found work illustrating book jackets for Redwood Books, Trowbridge. In 1985 he worked alongside his future Bath Society of Artists colleague and fellow portraitist Geoff Shillito at Superior Creative Services (a design and print agency) near Melksham. In 1988 Cobley painted a telling portrait of Shillito – *Geoff* (p. 45) – the first of many frank, relaxed and empathetic portraits of friends, children or artistic colleagues, which was shortlisted for the John Player (now the BP) Portrait Award in 1989.

The Trowbridge job saw Cobley illustrate well over a thousand book jackets, an arduous stint that provided the family with a livelihood to be sure, but ultimately proved creatively uninspiring. As his appetite for commercial design waned, so his desire to pursue painting grew. He also yearned for artistic camaraderie, and while early appearances at Bristol's Royal West of England Academy (RWA) and the Royal Society of Portrait Painters (RP) at the Mall Galleries, London, during the 1990s announced his arrival as an artist, Cobley was in his heart looking to establish an intimate artistic milieu, one in which he could prosper while helping other artists.

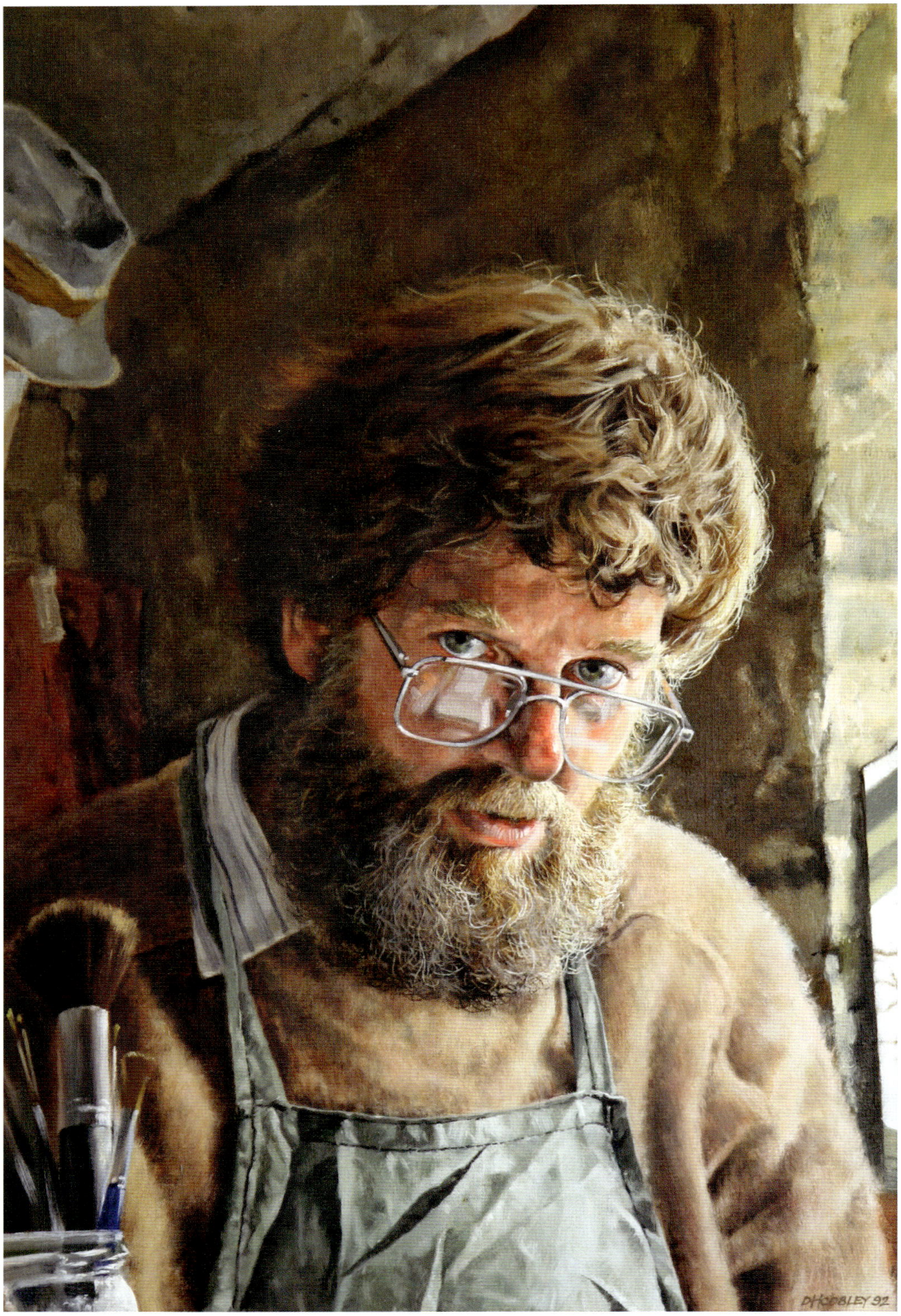

Edward Dowden in His Studio | 1992 | oil on linen | 56 x 40.5 cm private collection

A Bath Bohemia
houseboats and studios

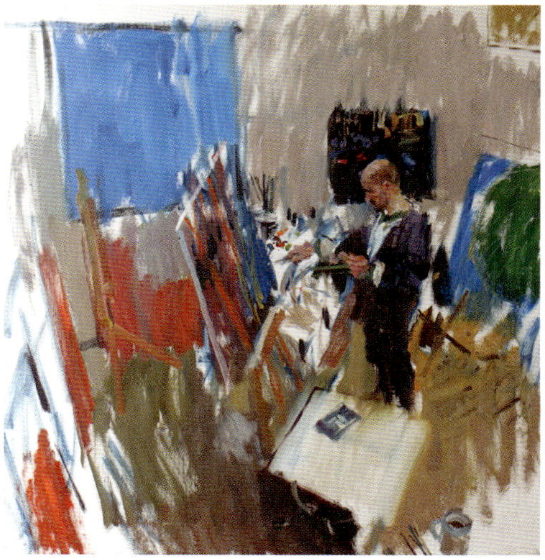

Ben at Work
2001 | oil on panel | 61 x 61 cm
collection of the artist

The big break for Cobley's vision of a supportive environment came with his founding of Widcombe Studios in 1996, renamed Bath Artists' Studios in 2003, when they moved to the Upper Bristol Road. He found the secluded premises, a former infants' school behind Bath Spa railway station, by chance. At the time he was painting a double portrait of solicitor Ralph Haeems and his wife in Reigate, Surrey (p. 47). He had met Haeems at a fundraising event organised by Taylor Woodrow, the CEO of which Cobley had also recently painted (p. 53). At Cobley's prompting, Haeems purchased the building in 1996. He went on to acquire six more Cobley paintings for his private collection.

After purchasing the building, the new landlord allowed David to rent the studios out to local artists, and it was full by 1997. Original studio members included painter-collector Edward Lewis, whose portrait Cobley later painted against a fierce red background, Peter 'The Street' Brown, printer Richard Lawrence, sculptor Sue Larner and painter Brian Elwell. Another early studio holder was Edinburgh-trained Fiona McIntyre, whom Cobley depicted stretched out across the floor in a sari – a wild, expressionistic figure painting reflecting her recent travels to India.

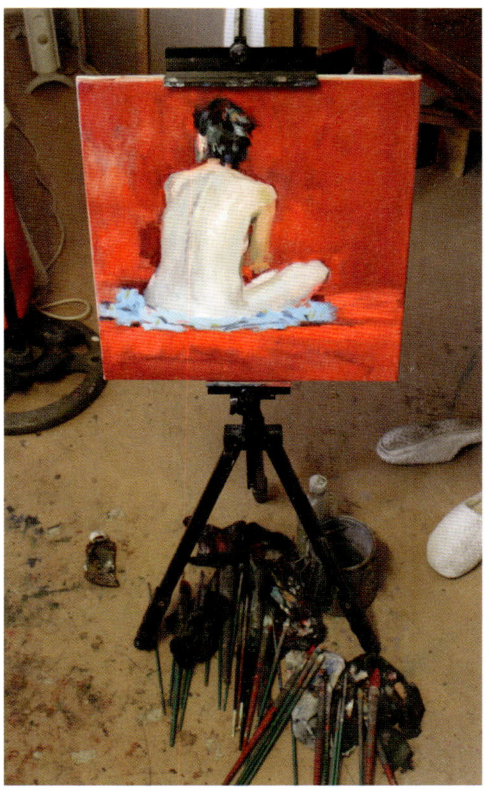

Georgia in progress, Bath Artists' Studios, 2008

Life drawing and other classes began and the Studios soon became the creative hub in Bath that Cobley had envisaged. One regular life-drawing model, Georgia Cox, was later painted by Cobley seated against a distinctive red background (left). Cox, taking a first-floor studio at Comfortable Place, would go on to develop a cogent floral verisimilitude in her depictions of plants and birds. She became a member of Bath Society of Artists. Another BSA member and currently treasurer – long-term studio holder Ben Hughes – was a subject in Cobley's roving portraiture on more than one occasion (above left).

The Studios were set up with the help of Edward Dowden (opposite), painter and exhibition organiser at the Priory Barn, Bradford on Avon, whom Cobley had got to know through living nearby. Dowden recalls the importance of their collaboration in an email correspondence:

> I met David in the late 1980s while organising exhibitions of work by professional artists when I lived in Wiltshire. He was one of the first artists I invited, and when he delivered his work he offered to help hang the exhibition, an offer I gratefully accepted. After that, he and I jointly hung every exhibition I organised, and had a lot of fun doing it. So much easier to do the job together, and enjoy ourselves at the

same time. I have particularly happy memories of our collaboration, lots of laughter whilst doing an interesting job.

Some years later I was able to return the favour by helping David with some of the construction work for the artists' studios he set up in Bath. Now, thirty years after we first met, and despite the fact that I have moved to Yorkshire, I still regard him as my closest friend amongst the artists I know.

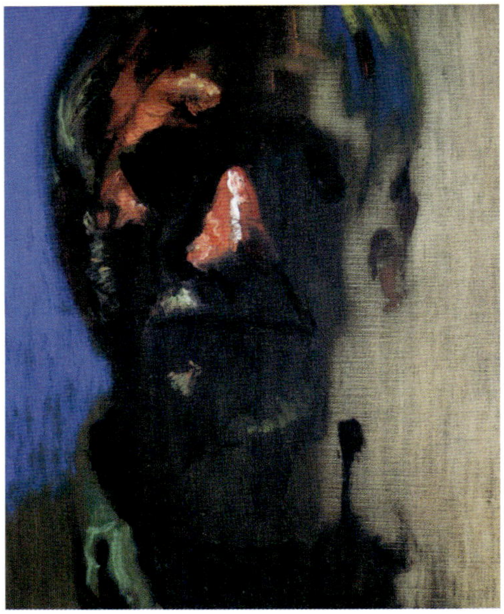

Brian
2000 | oil on linen | 35.5 x 30.5 cm
private collection

The year 1997 was therefore a watershed for Cobley, not only in terms of seeing a creative hub in Bath get off the ground, but of his becoming an RP (membership of the RWA, Bristol, followed soon after in 2001). Membership of the RP certainly paid dividends, with portrait commission opportunities proliferating, significantly from the Inner Temple to paint *HRH The Princess Royal, Princess Anne* at Gatcombe Park, Gloucestershire. Other commissions were thrown up through the crude but effective strategy of sending out a random mail shot to potential sitters such as actor Steven Berkoff (opposite). This modus operandi recalled the celebrated 'Kitchen Sink' artist John Bratby's 'Hall of Fame' series during the 1960s and 1970s when the established, but wayward and eccentric,

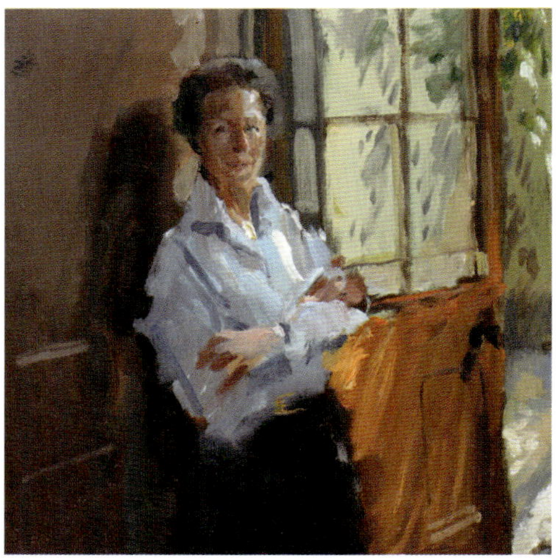

Study for HRH The Princess Royal, Princess Anne
2001 | oil on linen | 40.5 x 40.5 cm
collection of the artist

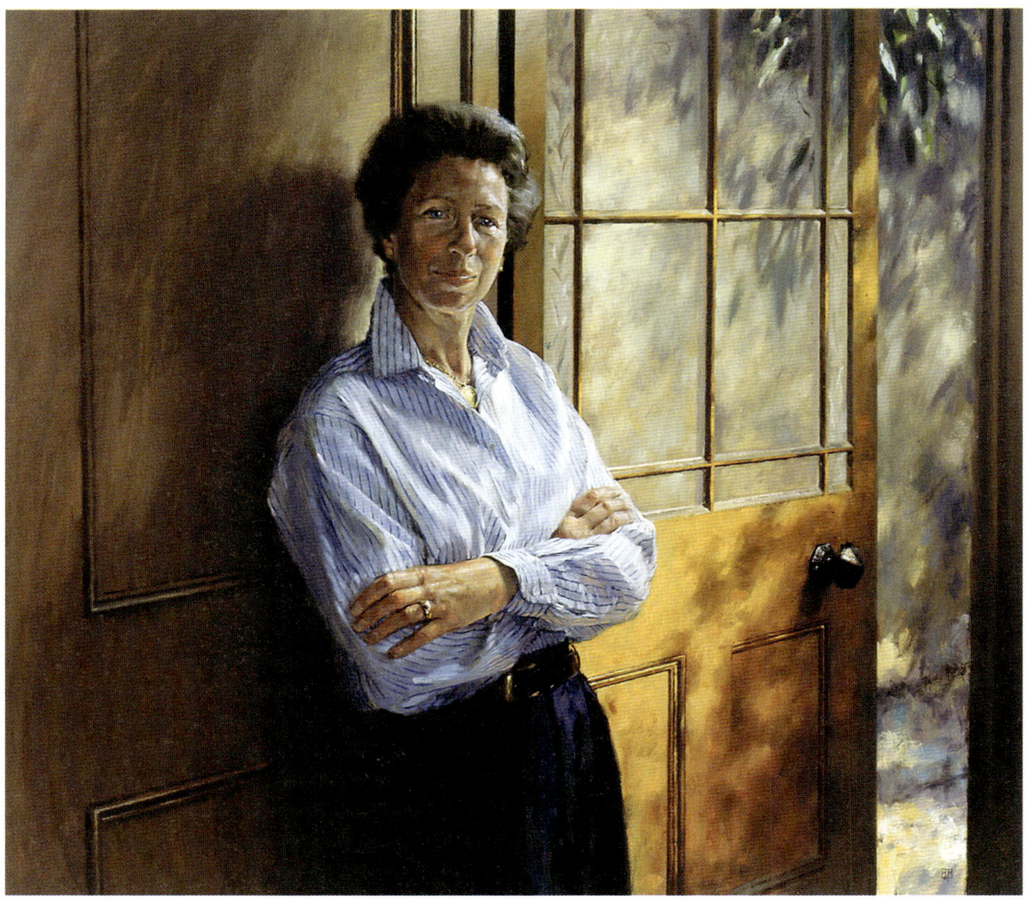

HRH The Princess Royal, Princess Anne | 2001 | oil on linen | 106.5 x 122 cm Inner Temple, London

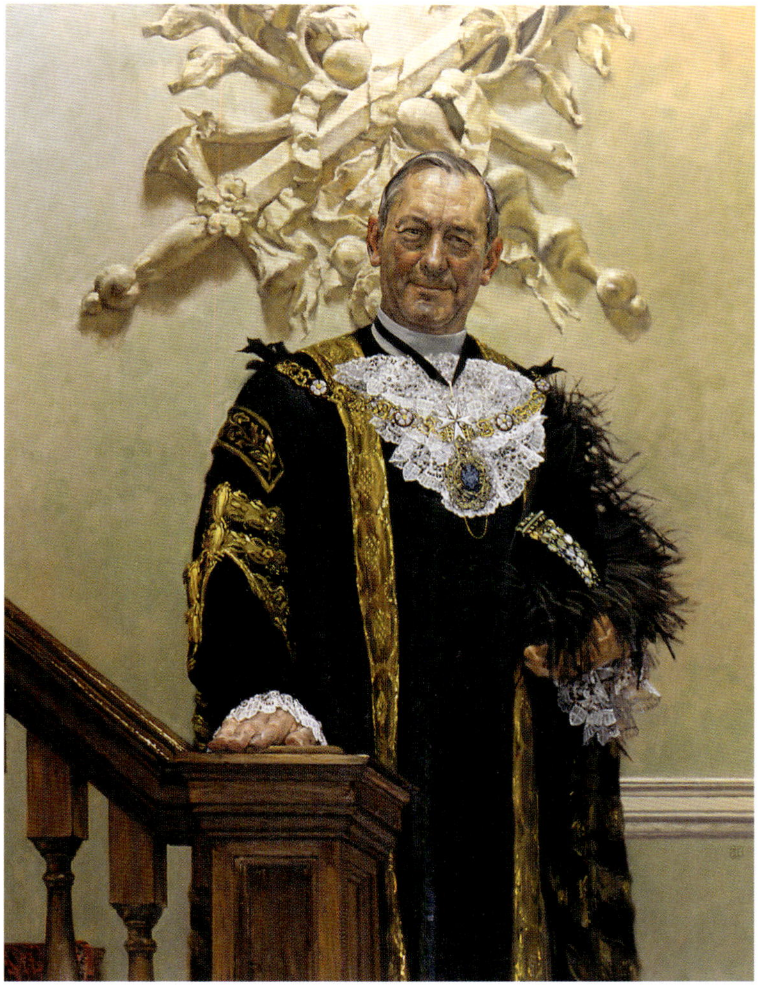

Sir Clive Martin OBE
2000 | oil on linen | 152.5 x 122 cm
Stationers' Hall, London

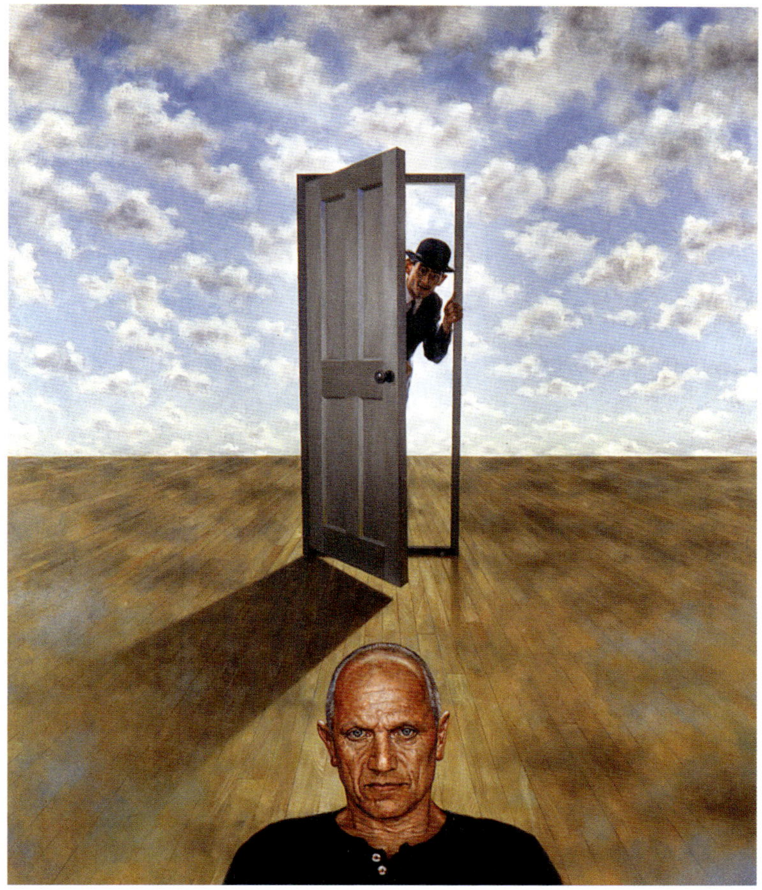

Steven Berkoff
1994 | oil on linen | 122 x 106.5 cm
private collection

Royal Academician approached scores of celebrities and worthies from public life to paint their portraits.

Strident, egocentric and artistically driven in an almost perverse way, Bratby was personally and artistically poles apart from Cobley, an unassuming and introspective character whose motive had none of the elitist agenda of the vainglorious and reactionary kitchen sinker. But, like Bratby, Cobley received positive feedback and with it a clutch of celebrity commissions from the BBC and comedian Ken Dodd. Bath-based actor Stephanie Cole would later commission the artist to paint her on stage (p. 74) after having seen his portrait of Dodd, whom she had met backstage at one of his own epic performances. Chance encounters with these charismatic entertainers contrasted with more formal arrangements like the Gatcombe commission, Sir Timothy Sainsbury at his Berkshire home, politician Norman Fowler, the Lord Mayor of London (above), or the Dean of Westminster (p. 54), dignitaries whose commissioned portraits, far from being fortuitous, in fact came through the agency of the RP.

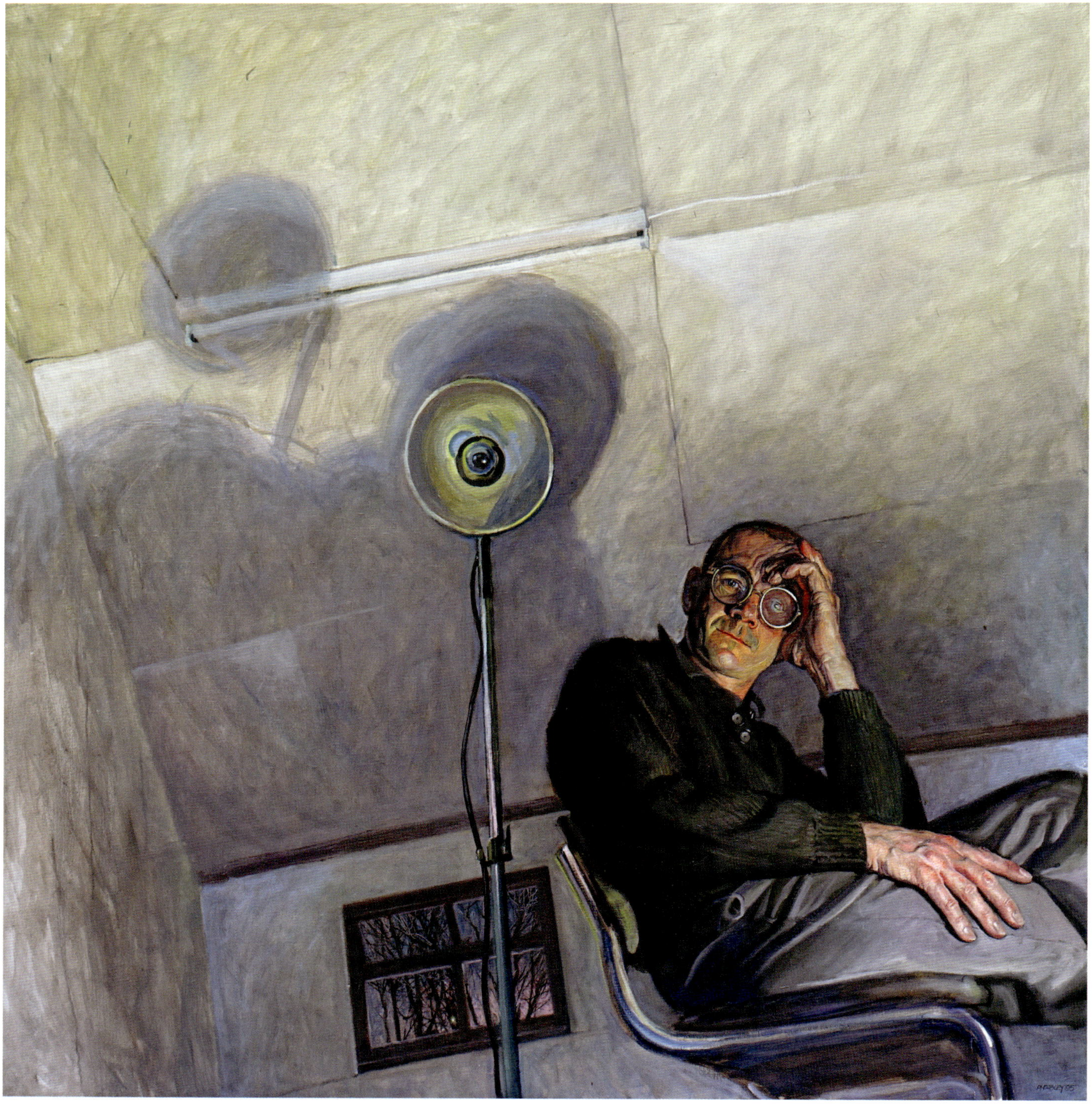

Doubt | 1995 | oil on linen | 142 x 142 cm

collection of the artist

Diddymen and doubts

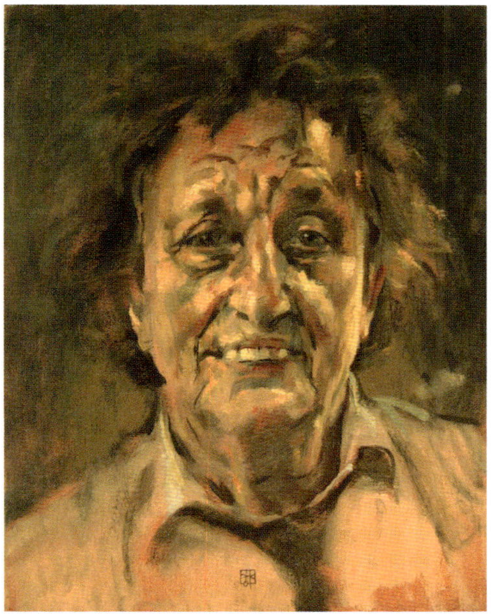

Oil study for the portrait of Ken Dodd
1999 | oil on linen | 51 x 40.5 cm
private collection

Concomitant with the fortuitous portrait was an open-ended and prolonged situation that in the case of Dodd led to several meetings and a long series of studies and preparatory works reflecting as they did the artist's empathy, rapport and admiration for the zany comic of Knotty Ash. They met at Frome's Merlin Theatre, where the prolific and peripatetic performer was appearing, and later at Weston-super-Mare's Playhouse theatre, where the painter went backstage to take candid and informal photos and make preliminary drawings in the dressing room. In the painting arising from this encounter, Dodd is depicted in his vest (p. 73). A gouache study of Dodd's dressing-room clutter (p. 72), later acquired by Bristol artist Vincent Brown, had a disarming informality reflecting the rapport between the pair. The Dodd series engaged Cobley for no less than three years, the final National Portrait Gallery portrait painted from photos at Widcombe Studios and placed in the Holburne Portrait Prize competition in Bath, where it won the Public Prize. NPG Director Sandy Nairne saw it at The Holburne and later purchased it for the Gallery in 2005. The first of two acquisitions (the second being a portrait of Sir Martin Evans) by a national collection was a career watershed, raising the game and giving new impetus and purpose to Cobley's enterprise. This portrait was the choice for the souvenir brochure of the comedian's ninetieth birthday celebration at London's Lansdowne Club. Such was the afterglow of this congenial liaison that the artist made two further visits to the Playhouse to see Dodd perform.

The engagement with a legendary comedian versed in the traditional stand-up acts of the music hall reflected the painter's penchant for humour, satire, social commentary and the bizarre. Evident throughout is a sense of life as a form of theatre, particularly in circus-like crowd or procession scenes. Such latent humour complemented the straight-laced Methodism of his background and the sober, solitary nature of his chosen profession, which it countered in terms of subject.

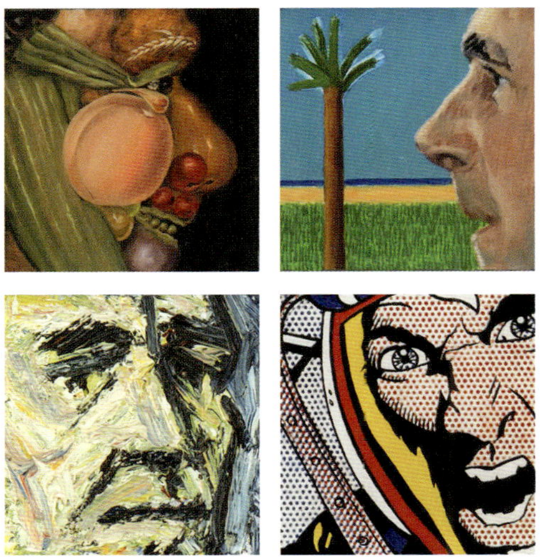

All By Myself (details)
1998 | oil on linen | 122 x 122 cm
collection of the artist

Another work to fashion a major change was the iconic *All By Myself* (left and title page), a therapeutic and cathartic picture of a singular subject, himself, but in a plethora of styles by a multiplicity of celebrated artists. This exercise in technical virtuosity helped Cobley show off his enviable graphic facility while enabling him to unravel and address a deep-rooted confusion concerning his identity both as artist and as person. Describing his illustrational prowess as a two-edged sword, Cobley sought a way to navigate the bewildering gamut of styles to reach a clarity of direction and validity of self-expression. There was something inherently postmodern in this grappling with eclecticism, and a sense that the sequential or dialectical 'isms' of modern art had given way to a new, anything-goes

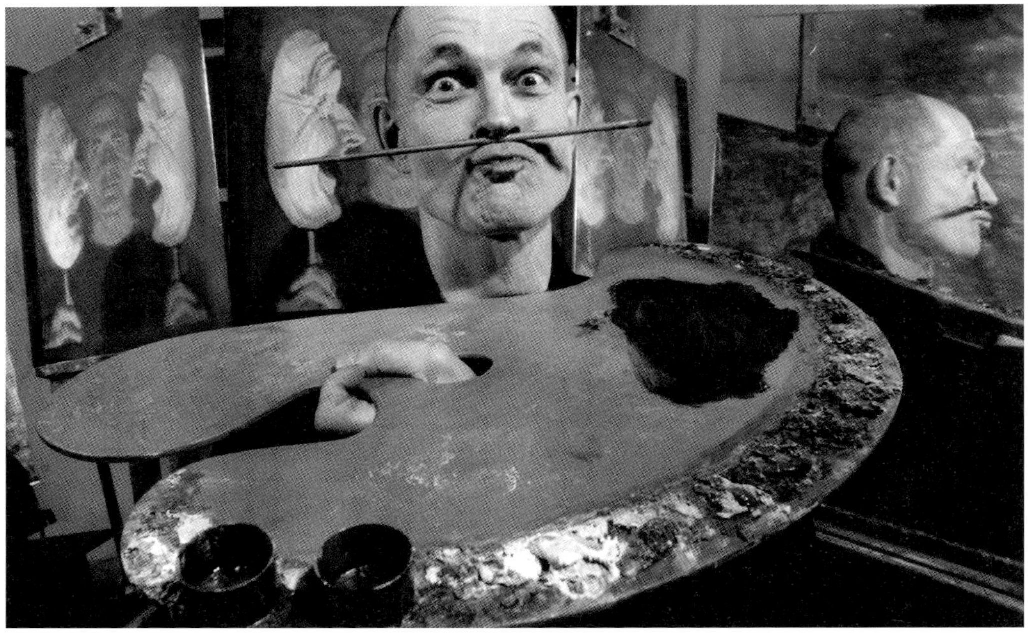

Larking about, 2008 photograph Miranda Kombert

pluralism. This process also addressed a personal restlessness and confusion exacerbated by the break-up of his marriage and family life in the period leading up to the Millennium.

In complete contrast to the Dodd, in 2011 the NPG commissioned the portrait of an eminent scientist – the Cardiff-based stem cell innovator Sir Martin Evans (pp. 60–61) – who is depicted in active scrutiny of a petri dish in his laboratory. Cobley painted it at Bath Artists' Studios from rudimentary sketches and photographs made in the lab and at Sir Martin's home. A lunch and formal unveiling took place at the NPG. Other notable portraits at this time were of Viscount Portman (p. 62), commissioned through the RP and followed later by a portrait of his wife (p. 63), and Festus Mogae, former President of Botswana (p. 64).

These commissions established Cobley's name as a recognised portraitist. But the fecundity of his imagination was such that the artist developed the private, independent and individual side of his work in terms of self-portraiture, studio interiors, still life, nude figures, landscapes or multi-portrait crowd scenes replete with symbolic, cryptic or philosophical associations of a deeply personal kind. Even in individual commissioned portraits like that of Steven Berkoff (p. 19), Cobley let his imagination run wild – happily in accord with the sitter's wishes – to register an enigmatic Magrittean head and shoulders foreground image behind which languished a bowler-hatted figure in the Belgian surrealist's mould. The classic Magritte device of conjuring visual tricks and breaking down Euclidean perspective, questioning the nature of reality and illusory artifice, appeared in this strange picture.

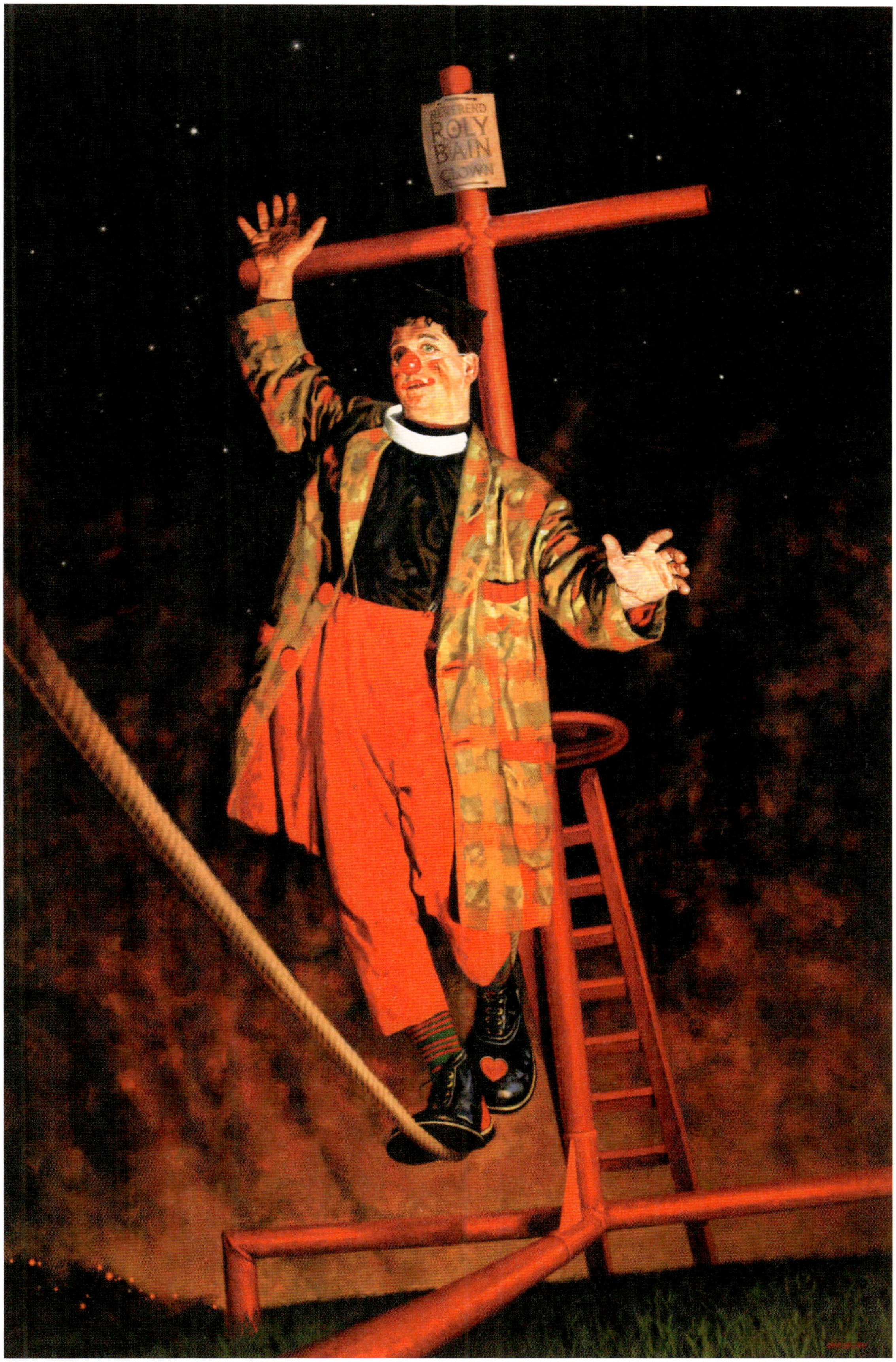

The Reverend Roly Bain | 1992 | oil on linen | 183 x 122 cm private collection

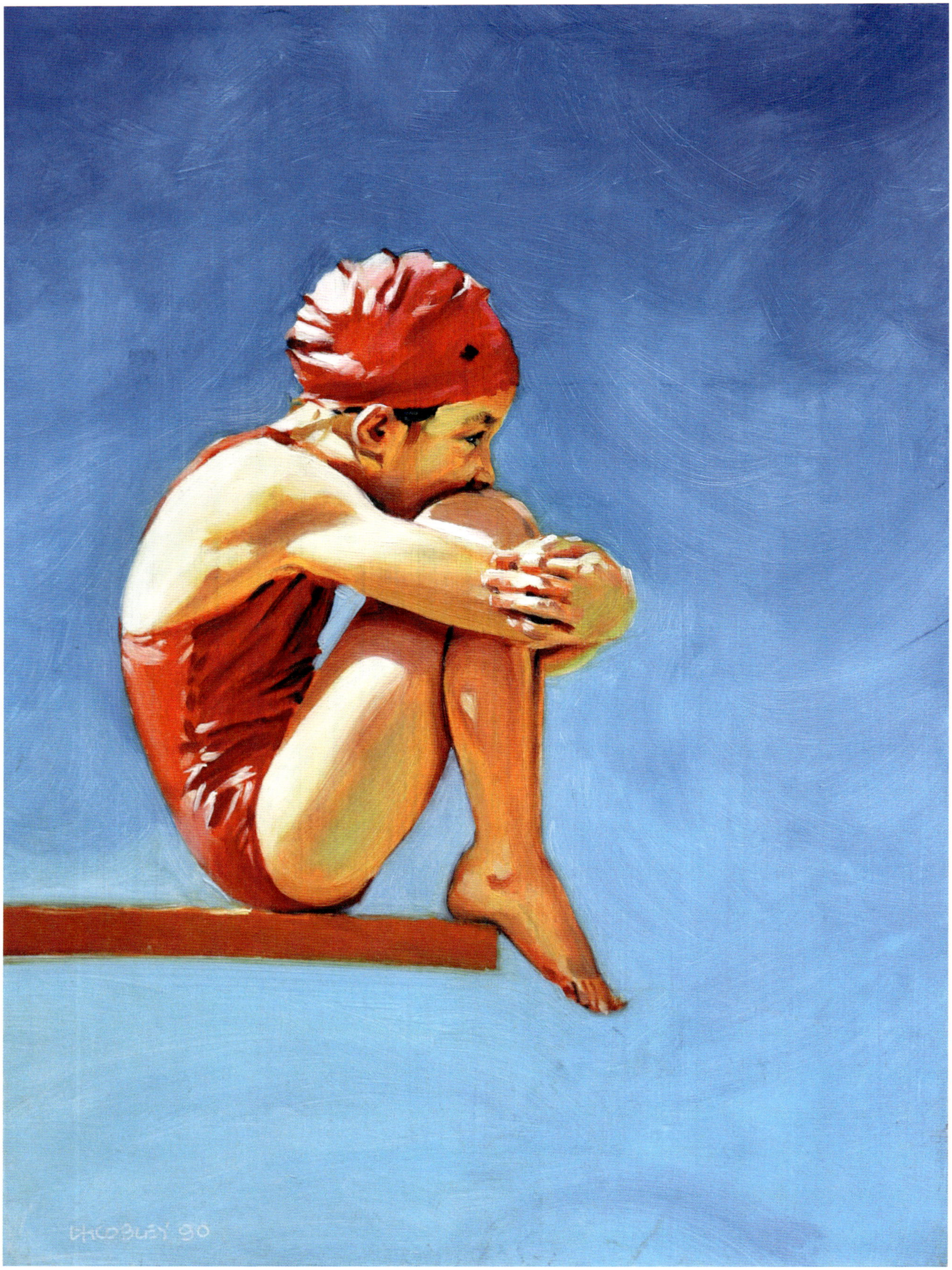

Young Swimmer | 1990 | oil on linen | 43 x 33 cm private collection

A similarly striking image is Cobley's portrait of the Rev. Roly Bain, the renowned eccentric and a Romany parish priest in Bristol, who is depicted on a slack rope in classic fairground gypsy mode (p. 23). This stand-out picture in blacks and reds was exhibited in the RWA's autumn show on Whiteladies Road in 1992, where it sold to musician and Clifton resident Jill White, who later loaned it to the RWA show of circus-related art, 'Sawdust and Sequins', in 2018.

Also in 1992 came the even more bizarre *Bandwagon to Oblivion* (pp. 78–79), a mixed crowd-scene jamboree of assorted characters from the Epilepsy Society's Chalfont Centre in Buckinghamshire, which came about as a result of the artist gaining access to the hospital through Dr Simon Shorvon, who originally commissioned a portrait of the staff there. Among the figures donning headgear – including metal colander, judge's wig, jester's hat, hood, bowler hat, bishop's mitre and paper crown – stood that of his youngest daughter Maya. A year before, his eldest daughter Selima appeared perched on a diving board in *Young Swimmer* (opposite), the warm reds of swimwear and flesh tones offset by a complementary blue-green background. This charming anecdotal composition was an out-take, as it were, or a 'still' from an implied narrative. Accompanying his daughter in *Bandwagon* was the artist himself, cast in the role of cheerleader or court jester and leading the procession from the back. The artist recalled feeling pretty pessimistic about the future of the human race at the time, a downbeat feeling that perhaps translates into the picture's grotesquerie.

Large genre or crowd pictures in this vein continued to appear, reflecting the artist's tragicomic take on human life and existential angst concerning the human condition. *Here We All Are* (pp. 76–77) was a notable case, a magnum opus even, shown at the RWA in 2013 and at the Bath Society of Artists annual a year later in the Victoria Art Gallery. The disconnected and open-ended narrative and random, circus-like figures akin to performers or trapeze artists suggested a Sartrean vision of human life without intrinsic meaning. This fairground make-believe on an epic scale was inspired by the Romantic excesses of Géricault or Velasquez and is at present on loan to the Abbey Hotel in central Bath, having hitherto been displayed at a Bath Abbey exhibition organised by Sue Larner on the theme of the city's street life. In his Bath Abbey talk about the picture in 2016, Cobley explained that

> Life is a circus, full of comedy and tragedy at every turn. Although capable of great acts of kindness we are also capable of great cruelty.

By concentrating as many kinds of human activity as possible into a single picture there is an effort on the artist's part to encourage us to reflect on what it is to be human. The multiplicity of athletic poses, taken from a sporting context as much as from the circus, reflected the fact of the

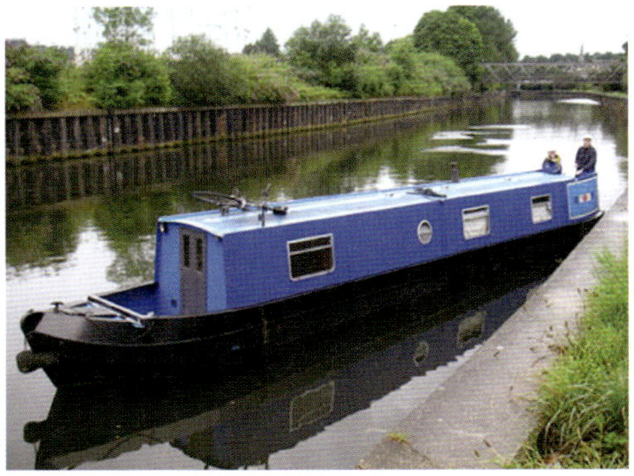

Mooring up outside the studio, 2011

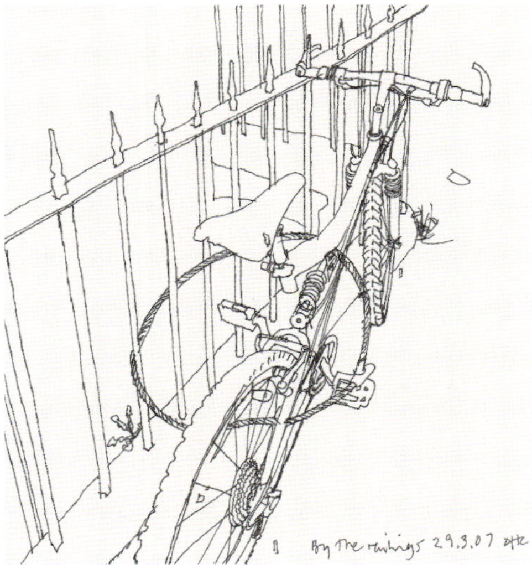

By the Railings
2007 | pen and ink | 25.5 x 25.5 cm
private collection

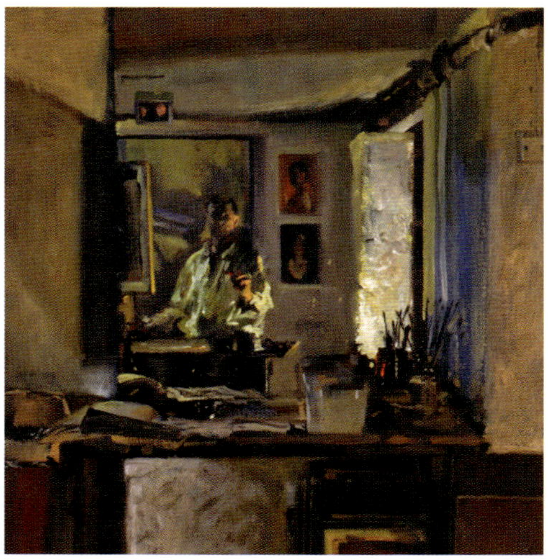

The Widcombe Studio
2000 | oil on linen | 61 x 61 cm
private collection

artist's own athleticism as a fitness fanatic engaged in swimming, single sculling or cycling on an almost daily basis.

The philosophical mindset displayed in these crowd scenes also held true for a series of introspective self-portraits, casting the artist as thinker and wearing his heart on his proverbial sleeve. The BP Portrait Award picture *Doubt* (p. 20), painted at his studio in Westwood, was a harbinger of many introspective self-portraits to come that candidly characterised the artist not as existential hero or disaffected bohemian so much as secular priest or painter-philosopher. Compositions like *The Widcombe Studio* (below left), *What Are You Doing Here?* (p. 95) and the Cartesian *Therefore I Am* (p. 30) cast the artist as shaman or God-like creator, a kind of solitary genius unravelling the Holy Grail in his uniquely visual way. The often dingy, dimly lit studio interior, though an authentic record of the artist's working environment, seemed a suitable metaphor at this juncture for Cobley's sense of a womb-like studio sanctuary.

The post-Millennium years in studios in a former motor mechanic's workshop on Bath's Upper Bristol Road saw an experimental zest and a productive overdrive. In pictures like *Looking at You Looking at Me* (p. 29) there is a literal overdrive, a relaxed painterliness that can only come with experience and confidence. The period marked a personal freedom and release from the responsibilities of family life, though Cobley continued to support his daughters, the youngest of whom opened a café in nearby Kingsmead Square, not far from the Studios and a place where he stored pictures to help with the rent.

Later, alluding to how he loved the freedom of it all, Cobley lived on a houseboat for five years moored at Bath Marina on the westernmost edge of the city and again convenient for his studio. Just before and after the move from Widcombe to Upper Bristol Road Cobley had solo exhibitions at Bath's Beaux Arts on York Street, the first in April 2002, the second and last in July 2004. The 2002 catalogue, written by the present writer, used as its frontispiece the recent iconic picture *Big Alchemy* (opposite), a self-portrait and studio interior whose rough rusticity had the appearance of natural light streaming in like a late-Victorian Newlyn School picture. This contrasted with the artificial light dominating *The Widcombe Studio* (left), setting up an eerie, claustrophobic and sub-terranean feel. Both compositions bore witness to a freedom from the neat finish of the commissioned portraits in terms of painterly bravura, loose, almost gestural, paint handling and a speedy spontaneity. The introductory essay argued that while he paints under either artificial or natural light, Cobley always records from life.

This situation, far from condemning him to the role of tame copyist of that which lies before his eye, confirms the authenticity of a vision tied to the mysterious relationship between form and the surrounding space.

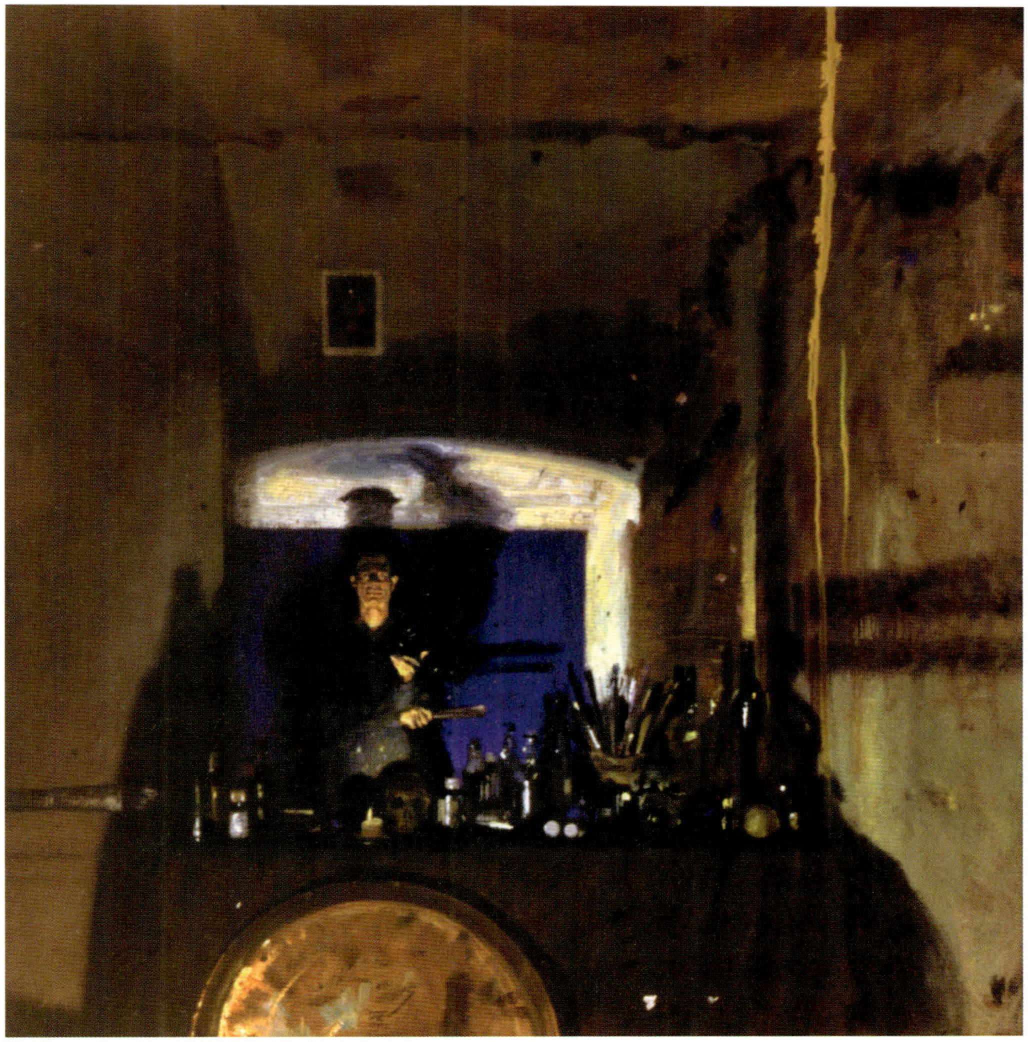

Big Alchemy | 2001 | oil on linen | 91.5 x 91.5 cm private collection

The fall of light is also a deep concern, engaging the artist in subtle and painstaking reconstructions of the atmosphere unique to a room at a given time and place.

This moderately successful 2002 exhibition also announced a recent series of seated or reclining bed compositions, which used sharp, downward views onto the cotton sheets directly below. Though not immersed in an abstract or post-cubist language of disrupted perspectives, Cobley used the conventional language of figurative verisimilitude to challenge or disrupt our normal picture-reading processes. Furthermore, he opted for an unusual sequence of back studies of models on beds. In so doing he reminds us that this anonymous part of the anatomy – without the physiognomic features of the face that normally engage a portraitist – takes on an almost sculptural expressive value, recalling Matisse's bronze series of backs. In like manner Cobley also treated the subject of beds with a tactile interest in the reflective ripples of the surface, with their

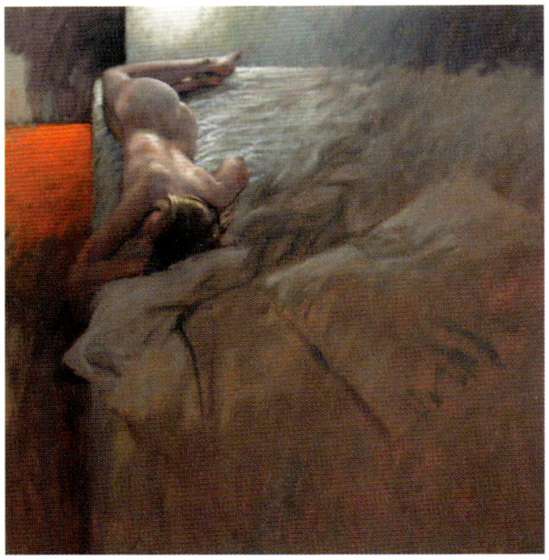

On the Edge
2002 | oil on linen | 183 x 183 cm
private collection

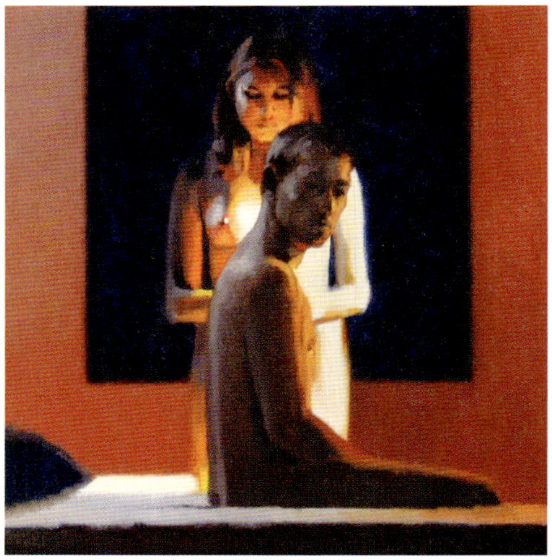

Man and Woman XI
2008 | oil on linen | 45.5 x 45.5 cm
private collection

textural patterns created by previous human occupancy. Such devices also anticipated the artist's growing interest in themes of human absence. Human presence came to be implied rather than directly stated, prompting the well-known *Times* critic John Russell Taylor to title his catalogue essay for Cobley's 2005 Messum's solo in London's Cork Street 'Absent Presence'.

The artist's second and final Beaux Arts solo in July 2004 included a picture on the theme of absent presence *par excellence* called *Empty Bed* (p. 103). *On the Edge* (left) also featured a single reclining female figure perched precariously on a bed. A change was afoot during the mid-noughties, which soon saw the introduction of double-figure formats, often that of male and female. *A Kind of Equilibrium* (p. 121) on the 2004 Beaux Arts catalogue cover comprised a male and female almost conjoined, or at least sitting back-to-back on the bed. Paintings from the axiomatically titled *Man and Woman* series (left) and *Two Figures* also featured in the show. While set in dark and gloomy interiors at Bath Artists' Studios, these figure groupings elicited a human presence. In these Beaux Arts pictures the bed is a constant feature, functioning not only formally as a dais, plinth or stage onto which the passive and posed human protagonists are positioned, but as a symbolic or thematic subject replete with social or psychological associations to do with birth, illness, death or a place of rest where we spend as much as a third of our lives.

The 2004 catalogue frontispiece, *A Sense of Drama I* (p. 31), again reverted to the other, more introspective self-portrait strand of his current work. The artist is placed peripherally at bottom left and casts a large blue shadow across the roughly brushed ochre wall. A symbol of the id, this amorphous shadow proves once again the artist's uncanny ability to say more with less and to suggest presence through the use of oblique or blurred imagery.

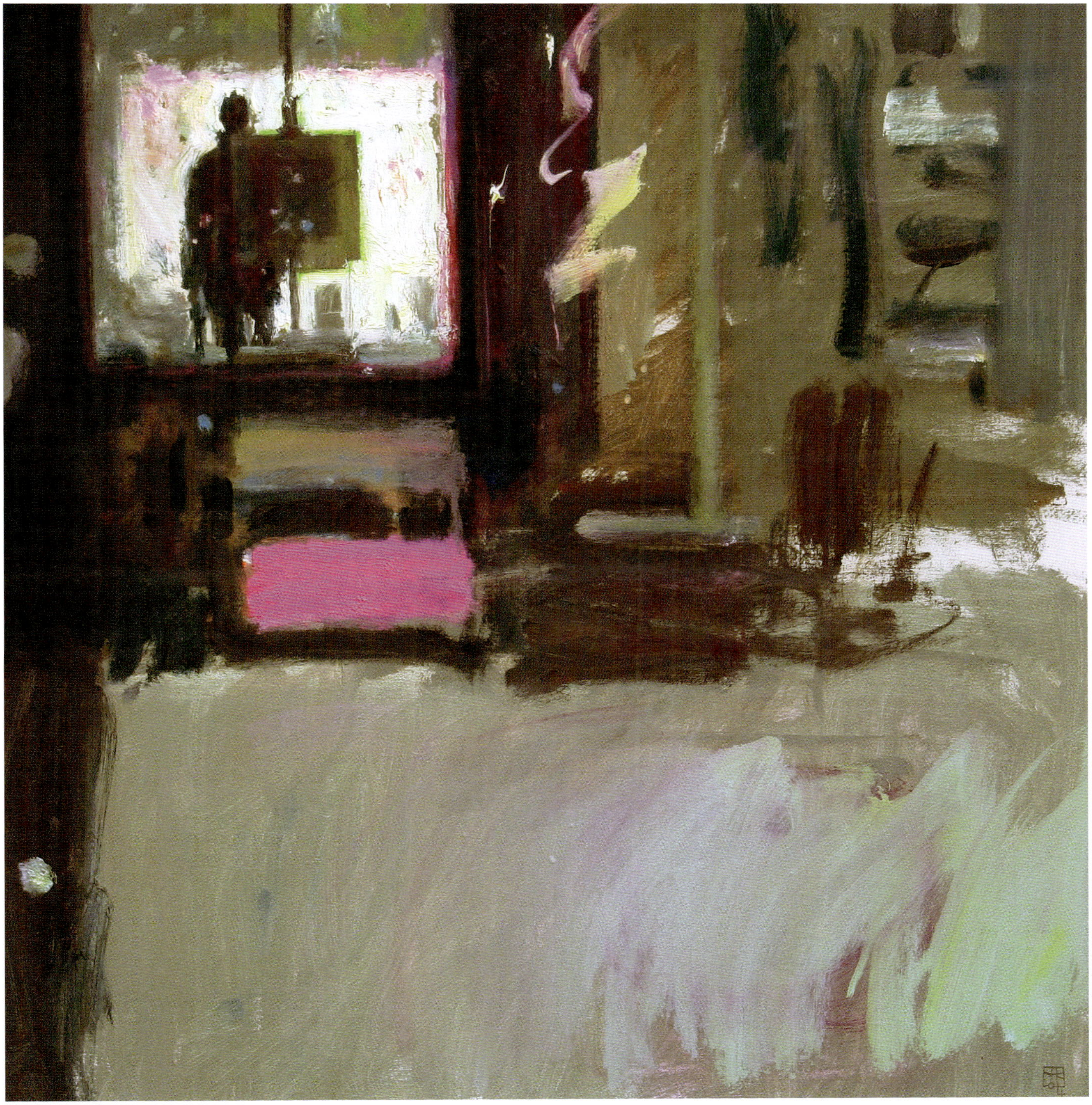

Looking at You Looking at Me | 2004 | oil on linen | 61 x 61 cm private collection

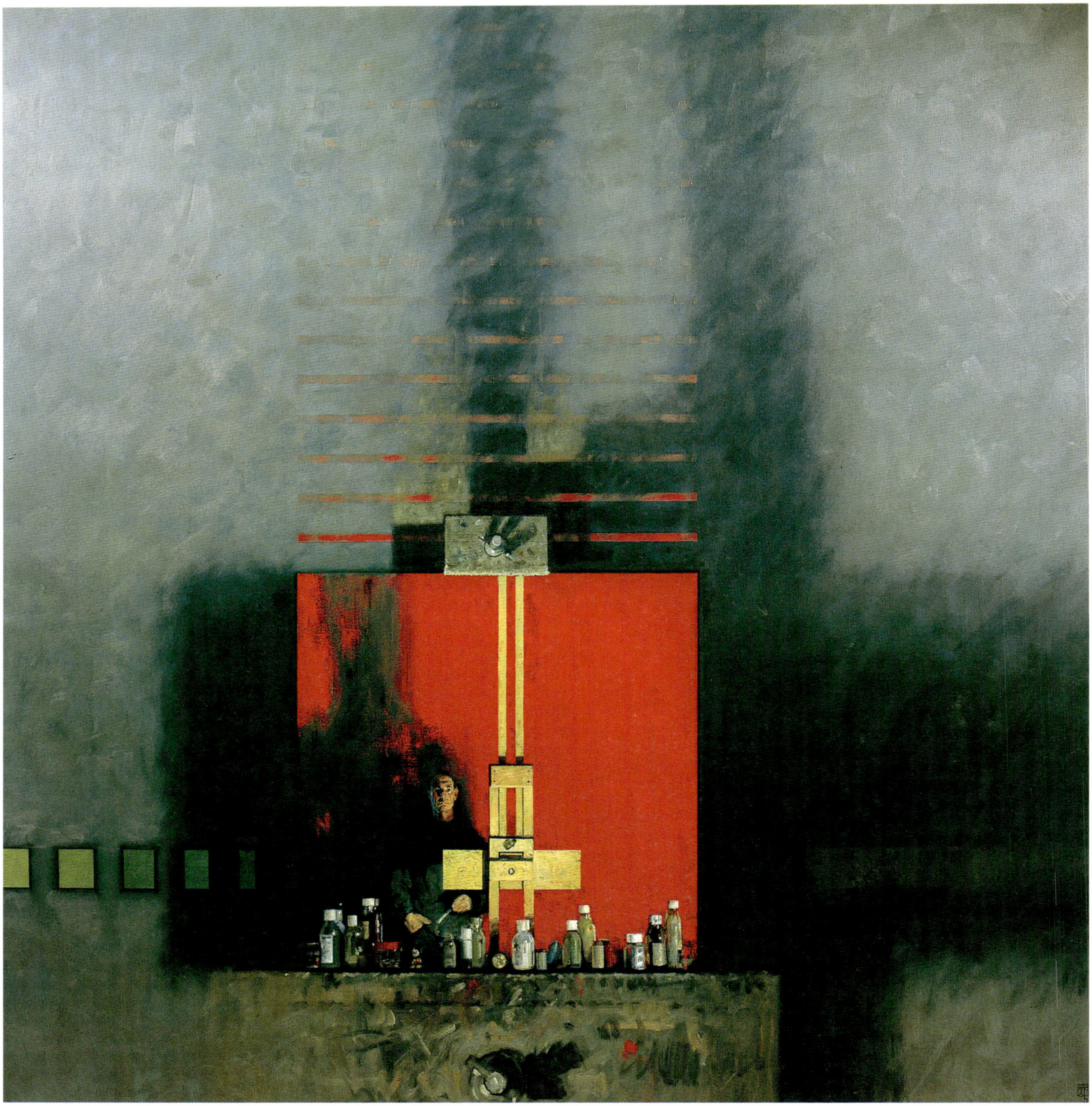

Therefore I Am | 2005 | oil on linen | 183 x 183 cm collection of the artist

Absent presences

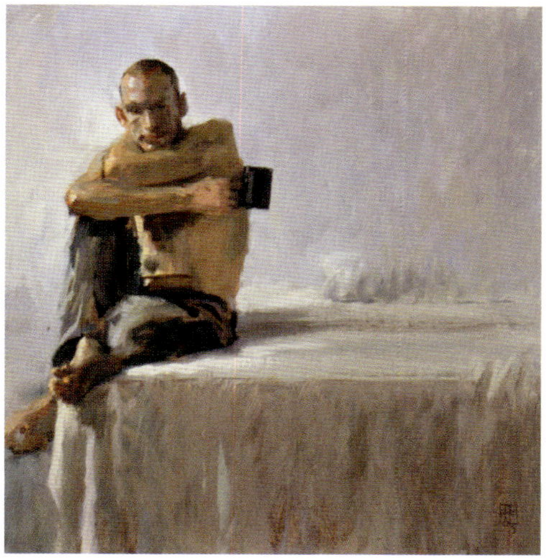

Pause I
2003 | oil on linen | 30.5 x 30.5 cm
private collection

The Beaux Arts exhibitions of the early noughties proved popular enough, at least as far as his nude and figure subjects were concerned. Among these was a series of male nude or semi-nude pictures depicting model Tristram, with whom the artist struck up an accord and who also sat for *A Kind of Equilibrium*. *Pause I* (left) again featured Tristram in jeans relaxing on a bed with coffee cup in hand. It was later exhibited at Brian Sinfield's gallery in the Cotswolds. Beaux Arts sold two from this series and requested more works in the same vein, but Cobley feared a commercial treadmill and felt not a little under pressure, the artist later explaining that the series had 'started to become a commercial enterprise and I had lost interest in it'. Nevertheless, Cobley's next major solo after the 2004 Beaux Arts show – the 2005 Messum's exhibition – included several Beaux Arts pictures, presumably unsold in Bath. *A Sense of Drama I* (below left), *Empty Bed* and *On the Edge* were old friends that were complemented at Messum's by a spate of new pictures from the 'Mirror' series. Furthermore, this curatorially clever mix and match gave the exhibition the semblance of a retrospective, particularly in the way that the catalogue frontispiece was a full-page image of his iconic self-portrait *Doubt* (p. 20), a candid and almost confessional image transcribing his innermost uncertainties. The searing subjectivity of this memorable self-portrait has the probing honesty of Van Gogh, Gauguin or Spencer, the downward glance of the artist accompanied by a large studio spotlight, a symbol with perhaps as much medical or therapeutic associations as purely artistic ones.

Cobley's recent 'Mirror' series featured partially clothed female figures seated on beds against background mirrors. Several, like *Lipstick* (overleaf), imparted anecdotal or narrative qualities, emphasising that these functional models were living women, countering the clinical, posed and impersonal. They were also harbingers of 'message' paintings in Cobley's later work where the artist turned small narrative compositions into satirical or social skits on the humour, absurdity or injustices of contemporary life. These are morally probing works playing out the artist's undoubted social conscience and bemusement about the modern world.

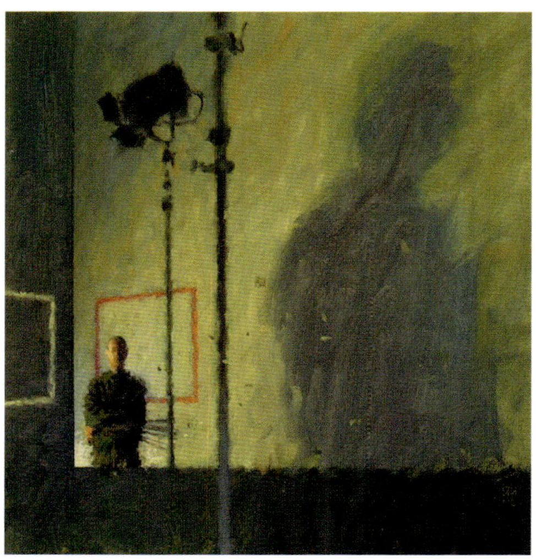

A Sense of Drama I
2004 | oil on linen | 45.5 x 45.5 cm
private collection

The other notable feature at Messum's was the large square composition *Therefore I Am* (opposite), which integrated self-portrait, studio interior and still-life elements into a compelling composite. The picture-within-a-picture format added another plastic and psychological layer to the subjectivity of the self-portrait theme. This 'copying' of a previous self-portrait certainly added an irony or self-consciousness to proceedings, but also apparent in this complex work were latent, oblique or implicit references to artists of a very different ilk. The monochromatic red with

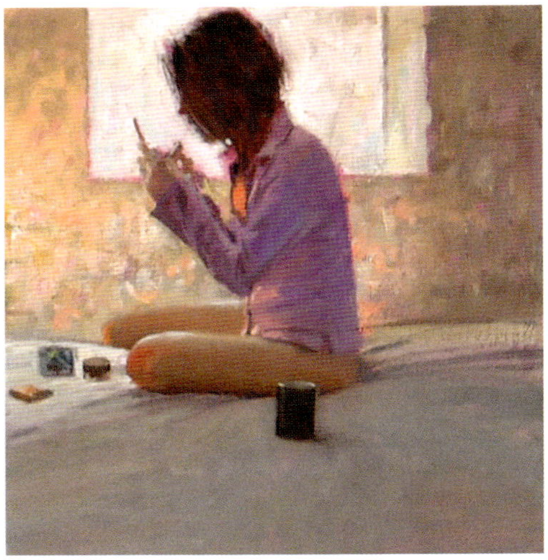

Lipstick
2005 | oil on linen | 30.5 x 30.5 cm
private collection

vertical, ochre wooden wedge – provided by a large easel in front – recalled American abstract expressionist Barnett Newman's so-called 'zip' paintings, while a collection of turps or linseed bottles on the horizontal ledge of the adjacent easel made fortuitous or incidental reference to Jasper Johns' pictures incorporating 'found' concrete objects into illusionistic abstract paintings. The studio interior background, though hazily and darkly atmospheric and impressionistic, carried an 'afterglow' of red stripes recalling the sequential minimalism of American Donald Judd, though this was essentially a fortuitous visual effect within the gloomy light of the studio setting.

Another prominent feature of mid-noughties works, and seen at Messum's, was that of directly aerial downward perspectives on a range of still-life objects that, while authentic to his everyday life as a jobbing artist, were unconventional, indeed innovatory, additions to the traditional parameters of post-sixteenth-century Dutch still-life painting. For the first time frying pans, oranges and lemons, paint tubes, staple guns, paint-spattered palette boards and other tools of his trade entered the iconography at hand. Equally, several works, like *Pub Grub* (p. 140) and *Dark Tan Two Lumps* (left), suggested an absent human presence, with a full pint of beer, half-drunk cup of coffee or cheese and bacon sandwich whetting the lips and just asking to be consumed. Such works prompted the catalogue author John Russell Taylor to declare that in Cobley's unmistakeable work

> The life may be lent, even in absence, by the spectre of human use; the mug of coffee is half drunk, and it must have been drunk by somebody.

Like Caulfield, human presence is implied rather than directly stated. There is also a pantheism at play, Taylor going on to speculate that

> A still life would not fulfil the still life part of its brief unless the artist made us aware of that secret life humming within all things.

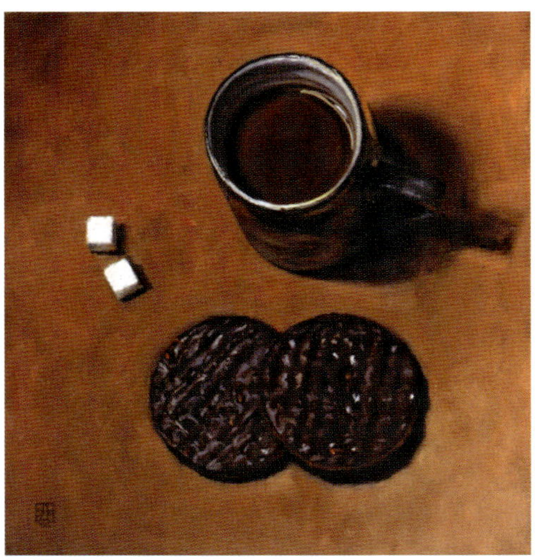

Dark Tan Two Lumps
2002 | oil on linen | 30.5 x 30.5 cm
private collection

Cobley's habit of staying within the bounds of an art predicated on the inert and academic disciplines of the life room with its analytical formal scrutiny made his compositions akin once again to 'stills' from an implied narrative. This aspect of his art was not lost on the *Times* art critic and reviewer, whose roots were as a film critic rather than as a seasoned commentator on the plastic arts per se.

During the noughties, an active decade when he entered mid-career with a creative flourish, Cobley enjoyed notable solo exhibitions roughly every two years to complement and augment myriad group shows at the Mall Galleries, London, the RWA, Bristol and Bath Society of Artists. This ideal time gap allowed a body of new work to emerge, confirming

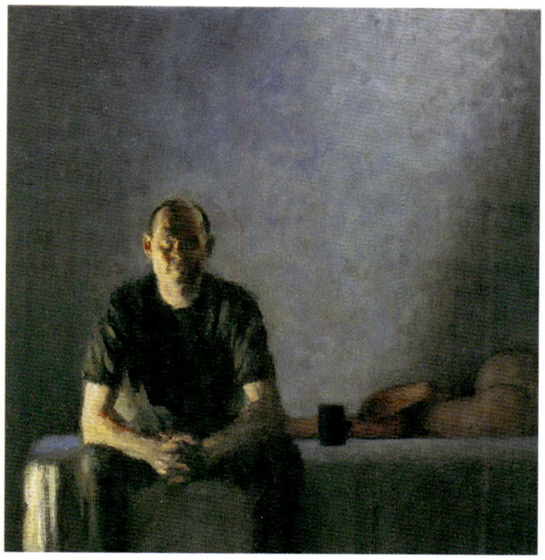

Artist and Model
2007 | oil on linen | 30.5 x 30.5 cm
private collection

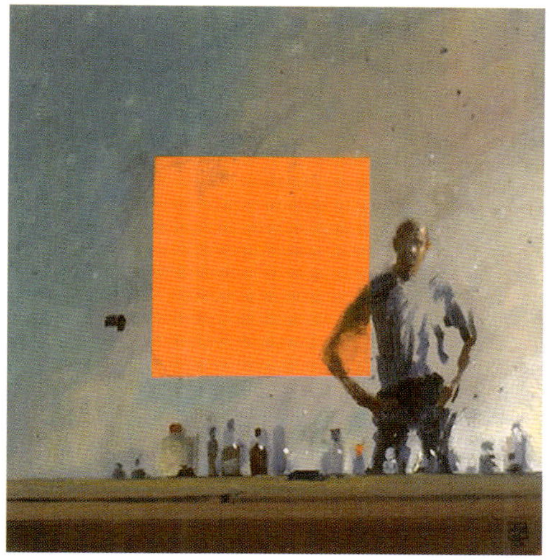

The Future's Bright
2003 | oil on linen | 30.5 x 30.5 cm
private collection

Tea Break
2004 | oil on linen | 30.5 x 30.5 cm
private collection

an inventive artist on the creative move in terms of extending old themes or experimenting with novel ones.

The mid-decade Beaux Arts and Messum's shows were followed, during autumn 2007, by an aptly titled solo – 'Inside and Out' at Victoria Art Gallery (VAG), Bath – with a catalogue foreword by VAG manager, the Courtauld-trained curator-historian Jonathan Benington. Though his commentary began by making music rather than film analogies, Benington echoed Taylor's description of an implied human presence, an understated narrative, by stating that

> the vital spark that informs all Cobley's work is the human presence, the human psychology, whether overtly implied, whether that of his models, himself, or reflected back at him by objects that mean something to him.

The critical consensus spun by Taylor and Benington created a useful framework for a fruitful discussion of Cobley's evolving art, but in his essay Benington went even further by identifying a putative pantheism at play. For Benington, the artist's recurring nudes

> go much further than being mere anatomy lessons. There is a sense of dramas and relationships being played out, of things said and unsaid, of the protagonists' thoughts and feelings towards each other and towards the painter, and vice versa.

The catalogue frontispiece, the modestly sized but memorable *Artist and Model* (above left), particularly bore out Benington's observation, although the professional and psychological bond between the two

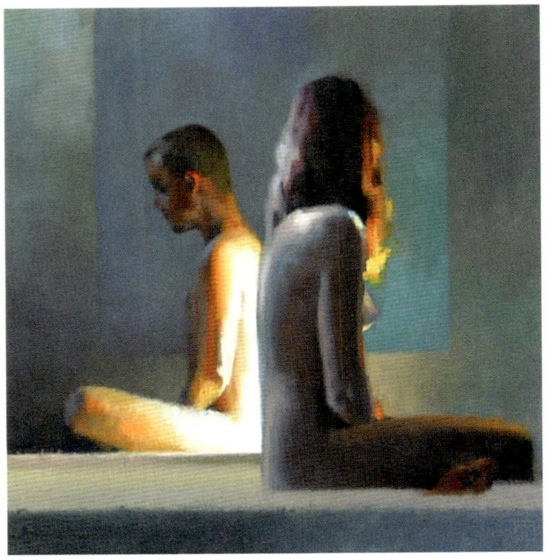

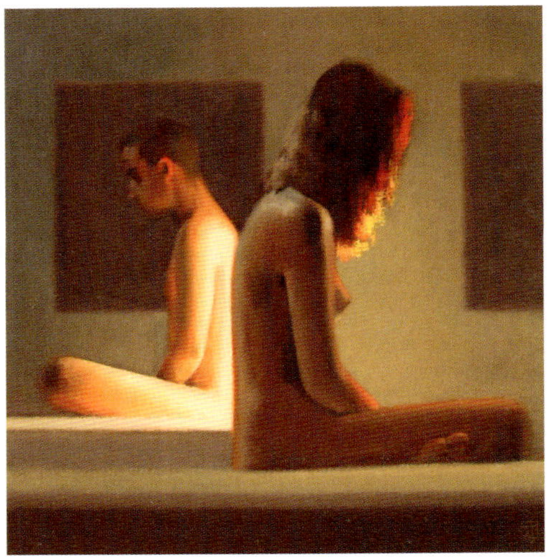

Between Themselves III and **VI**
2002 | oil on linen | 45.5 x 45.5 cm
private collection

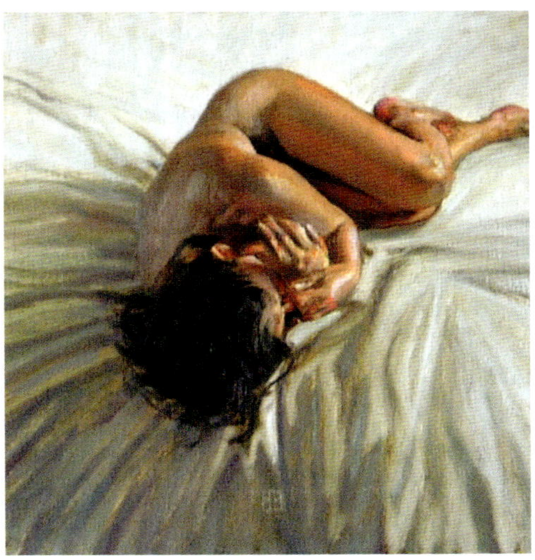

Curl
2001 | oil on linen | 30.5 x 30.5 cm
private collection

seems disconnected, broken down almost, as the artist seated on the edge of the bed gazes back at us, the spectators, in a satisfied way. Is the sanctity of the studio upheld or is it impregnated with possible brothel-like undercurrents?

Though a well-mined and timeless art-historical theme, the 'artist and model' subject gained enhanced significance in the art of Picasso, who explored it in the interwar *Vollard Suite* etchings and returned to it in old age in order to register diminishing sexual potency and the beauty-and-beast scenario. As with all good art, Cobley avoids rhetoric and keeps a degree of mystery or open-endedness in proceedings, Benington continuing by explaining how

> the undercurrents are never explicit, however; they remain sufficiently open-ended for us to be kept guessing, allowing us to bring our own imagination to play or perhaps interweave threads of our own personal histories.

This key work belongs to the ongoing series of double figures in inscrutable, dimly lit studio interiors. A long, dozen-plus series of *Between Themselves* pictures (left), for instance, possessed psychological ambiguity, mystery and thematic innuendo. The protagonists become agents of formal and thematic contrast: the former in terms of golden highlight and illumination versus deep shadowy dark purple grey; the latter in terms of gender contrast with all the wider social and psychological ramifications that this brings. The artist has explained how

> The centrality of the male/female relationship to our existence as human beings means that it has been the subject of art for thousands of years, and it is still fertile ground.

As well as gender and tonal contrast, Cobley also explores the nature of artifice and reality or the gap between art and life – both concerns with Magrittean and Rauschenbergian overtones. These probings are apparent in pictures exhibited in the VAG show such as *Among Friends* (opposite) – another enigmatic self-portrait set against a wall of completed portraits of friends and colleagues like Bath artist Brian Elwell and life drawing tutor Charlotte Edge – and *The Klimt Conspiracy* (p. 110), taken from a jigsaw puzzle given him by friend and Bath Artists' Studios sculptor Caroline Waterlow. This painting contains an image by the Viennese painter Gustav Klimt and provides the English painter with the perfect metaphor for his sense of life's fragmentary chaos, which certainly held true at the time of the Viennese Secession. In *Among Friends* the artist's head is positioned against a monochrome canvas, a device taking Cobley out of the 'real' space of the room and placing him in the artificial, plastic world of art. For an artist of few abstract credentials – or pretentions – this is clever stuff. Here the colour red's original

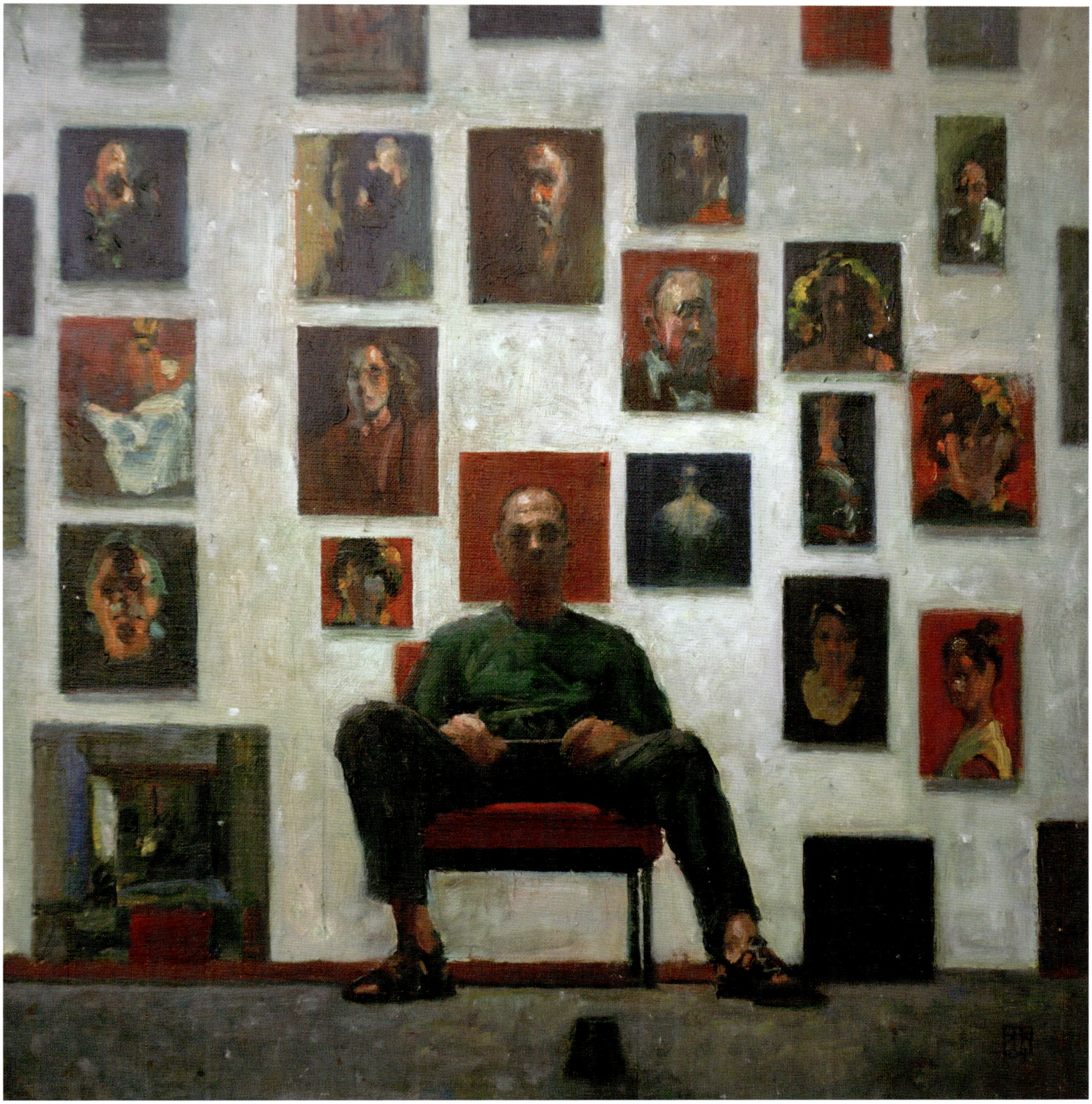

Among Friends | 2004 | oil on linen | 40.5 x 40.5 cm private collection

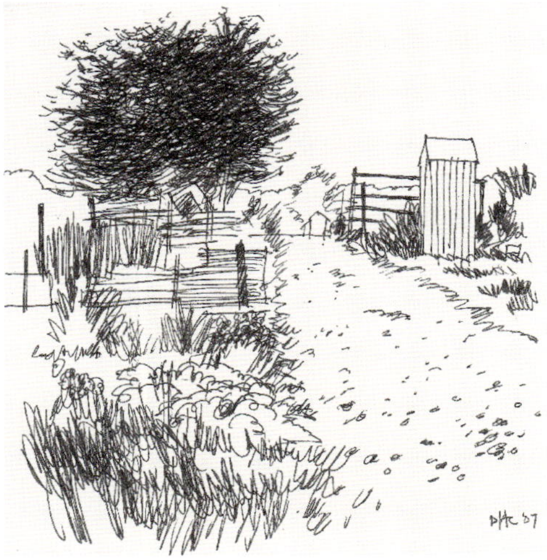

Allotment
2007 | pen and ink | 19 x 19 cm
private collection

function as an accent was elevated to one where, as the artist has explained, 'it vies with the figure as the subject.' Once again Benington has something more to say concerning Cobley's work at this point, explaining that *The Klimt Conspiracy*

> is only a fragment, and one piece stands apart from the hole into which it is obviously waiting to be inserted. The fragmentation suggests that, notwithstanding the intimacy of the preceding moment, something remains unresolved. And the fact we are looking at a fragmented image of another fragmented image, in other words with three levels of reality, only serves to add to the mystery.

The Bath exhibition also reflected a new playfulness in Cobley's still-life repertoire, which introduced paint tubes, palette knifes and brushes. There were also outdoor records of the surrounding Bath landscape, particularly that stretch on the Upper Bristol Road between the studios and the moorings where he kept his houseboat. A series of 'Allotment' pictures shared Bath *plein-air* artist Peter Brown's interest in a suburban horticultural haven within the city. But there were other pictures, such as *On the Towpath* (left), that were more specific and autobiographical takes on his life on the houseboat.

The localism evident in 'Inside and Out' did not extend to the group show 'Self-Portrait' at the Bulldog Trust, London, which saw Cobley exhibit alongside fellow RP and NEAC (New English Art Club) members like Daphne Todd, Tom Coates, Jane Bond, John Wonnacott, Alastair Adams and Bath's Saied Dai. Following a short few months after 'Inside and Out' in October 2007, this exposure of Cobley's prominent self-portraiture within his overall *oeuvre* served to distinguish his own work in this vein from that of many contemporary colleagues.

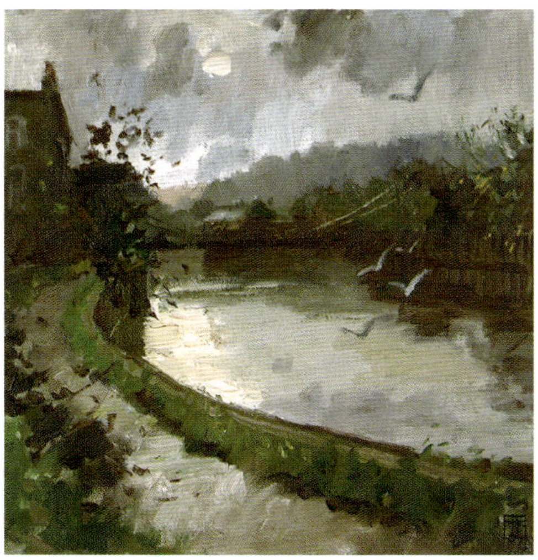

On the Towpath
2007 | oil on linen | 30.5 x 30.5 cm
private collection

In the Bulldog Trust catalogue, essayist Philip Vann, author of *Face to Face* (2004) about contemporary British portraiture, described 'accentuated accounts of core individuality' among the participants. Apart from the distinction of being chosen for the catalogue cover with his work *Clutter I*, a trademark self-portrait within a tellingly chaotic studio interior, Cobley stood out by virtue of describing himself not through an amplified physiognomy but rather through identifying his 'core individuality' in terms of the hermetic microcosm of his working environment as a jobbing artist with its symbolic extensions of his inner self, namely the paraphernalia of the studio. He resisted the Warhol-inspired blown-up poster-like self-portrait used by some of the others whose images were close to the picture plane. In place of brash, narcissistic self-confidence the artist offered an image of doubt, introspection and pensiveness. Later, he took the short step towards depicting fellow artists at work, an instance perhaps of Cobley making self-consciously arty statements.

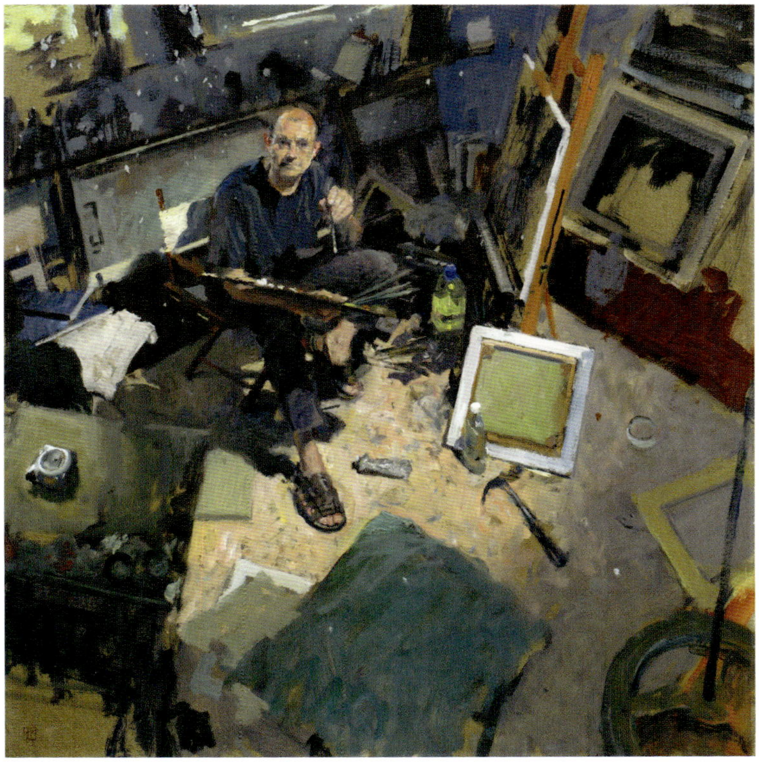

Clutter I
2003 | oil on linen | 61 x 61 cm
private collection

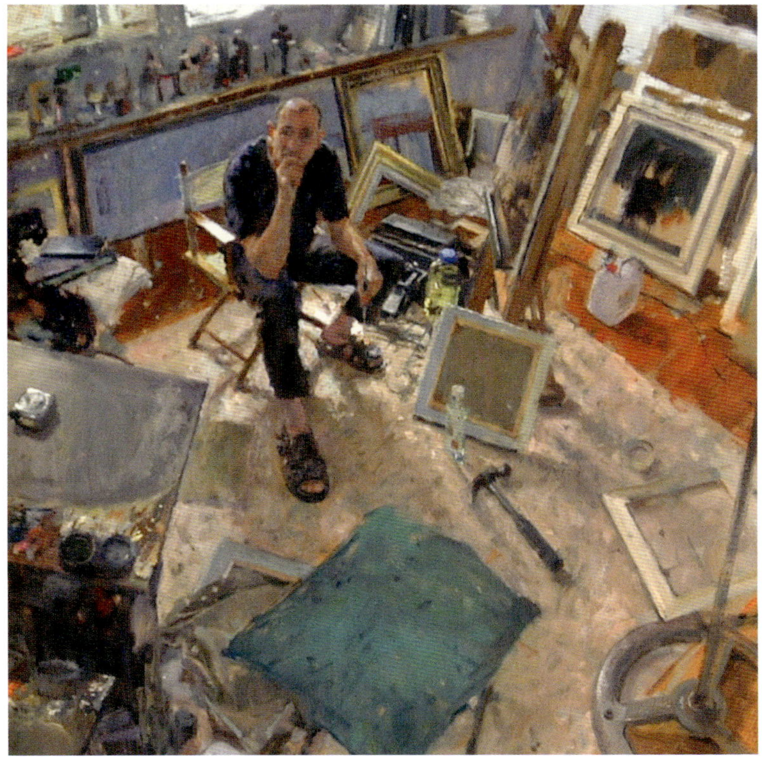

Clutter II
2003 | oil on linen | 61 x 61 cm
private collection

To celebrate his term of office as RWA President, Cobley painted a huge triptych of the Bristol-based painter Derek Balmer and his RWA Council members in 2004 (pp. 58–59). The striking red and gold background reflected colourist Balmer's own hot, eye-catching palette. It also became a bonding exercise between the respective Bristol and Bath artists, Cobley later remarking, in some notes he made about the work, how it became valuable

> to be asked to paint someone who also spends a large part of his life grappling with paint. I knew Derek as President, but wanted to know him better as a painter, and this commission gave me the opportunity not only of visiting the studio but working with him there.

Several visits to Balmer's Sneyd Park studio and home in west Bristol ensued, though an ever-restless Cobley later resigned from the RWA in order to concentrate on his RP and NEAC priorities.

It was indeed at the NEAC that the artist later showed his next intimate depiction of a fellow artist, that of the famous golden boy of sixties Pop in both Britain and America and the favourite son of Bradford: David Hockney. Though an intimate and candid take on a celebrity artist at work in his native Yorkshire *Marvellous Mr Hockney* (p. 39) was not

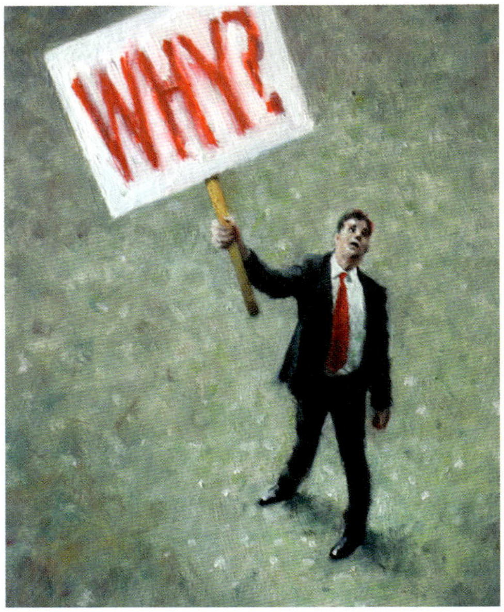

Placard
2019 | oil on panel | 24 x 20 cm
collection of the artist

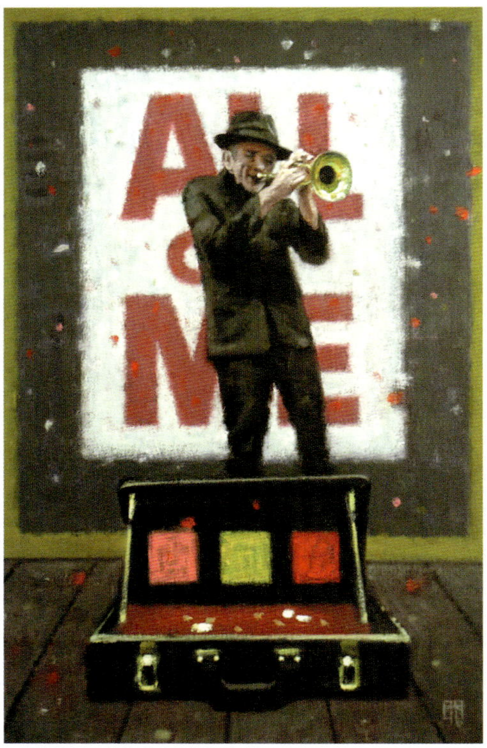

All of Me
2016 | oil on linen | 45.5 x 30.5 cm
collection of the artist

produced working alongside Hockney as had been the case with Balmer, but was rather taken from a TV documentary that Cobley saw and was fascinated by. He was clearly drawn to the mystique of Hockney's celebrity. With his disarmingly down-to-earth Yorkshire brogue, Hockney provided a suitable subject – one, moreover, that perfectly chimed with a New English ethos with its plein-airism and observational naturalism. Like Sargent's *Claude Monet Painting by the Edge of a Wood* (?1885, Tate), *Marvellous Mr Hockney* is an artistic homage, eulogy almost, where the younger painter highlights the dapper artist as dandy, dressed for a performance to the largest possible audience. An explosive and amorphous green shrub recalls *A Bigger Splash* from Hockney's seminal early Californian swimming pool *oeuvre*. Personal experience allows Cobley to associate with the act of painting to an audience, and in his notes about the painting he explained how

> it is a performance as much as a serious effort to make art. There is a heightened sense of immediacy to the act of painting in front of an audience, and this can be an exciting and rewarding experience.

Marvellous Mr Hockney was acquired from the 2016 NEAC exhibition by former President Tom Coates, plein-airist *par excellence* who epitomised more than most the central tenets of the New English. Founded during the mid-1880s as a radical breakaway from the stultifying academic and neo-classical orthodoxies of the Royal Academy with its late Victorian grandees Leighton, Alma Tadema et al., the New English became a clarion call for a return to realism and to nature with its observational *plein-air* naturalism. Cobley captures Hockney in animated paint-handling mode in front of the canvas. The younger artist's sensitivity to bodily posture not only reveals his skills as a draughtsman but also contains the physical expressiveness of working figures – a tradition in art handed down from Millet to the expressionists Permeke, Herman (Josef) and Van Gogh. There are also psychological ramifications tied up with bodily gesture as espoused by the body armour concepts of the psychoanalyst Wilhelm Reich.

In the coming years Cobley produced small, deftly articulated narrative pictures depicting a multitude of human activities laden with emotive social symbolism, satire or humour. A jazz trumpeter in *All of Me* (left), placard-weilding office worker (above left), builders (p. 142) or houseboat men negotiating lock gates (p. 156) are just some of the many genre works in this vein. Cobley has something of the preacher in him too, and his sense of injustice at the gross inequalities in the modern world and the often-ridiculous rituals of modern materialism are sometimes alluded to in his pictures.

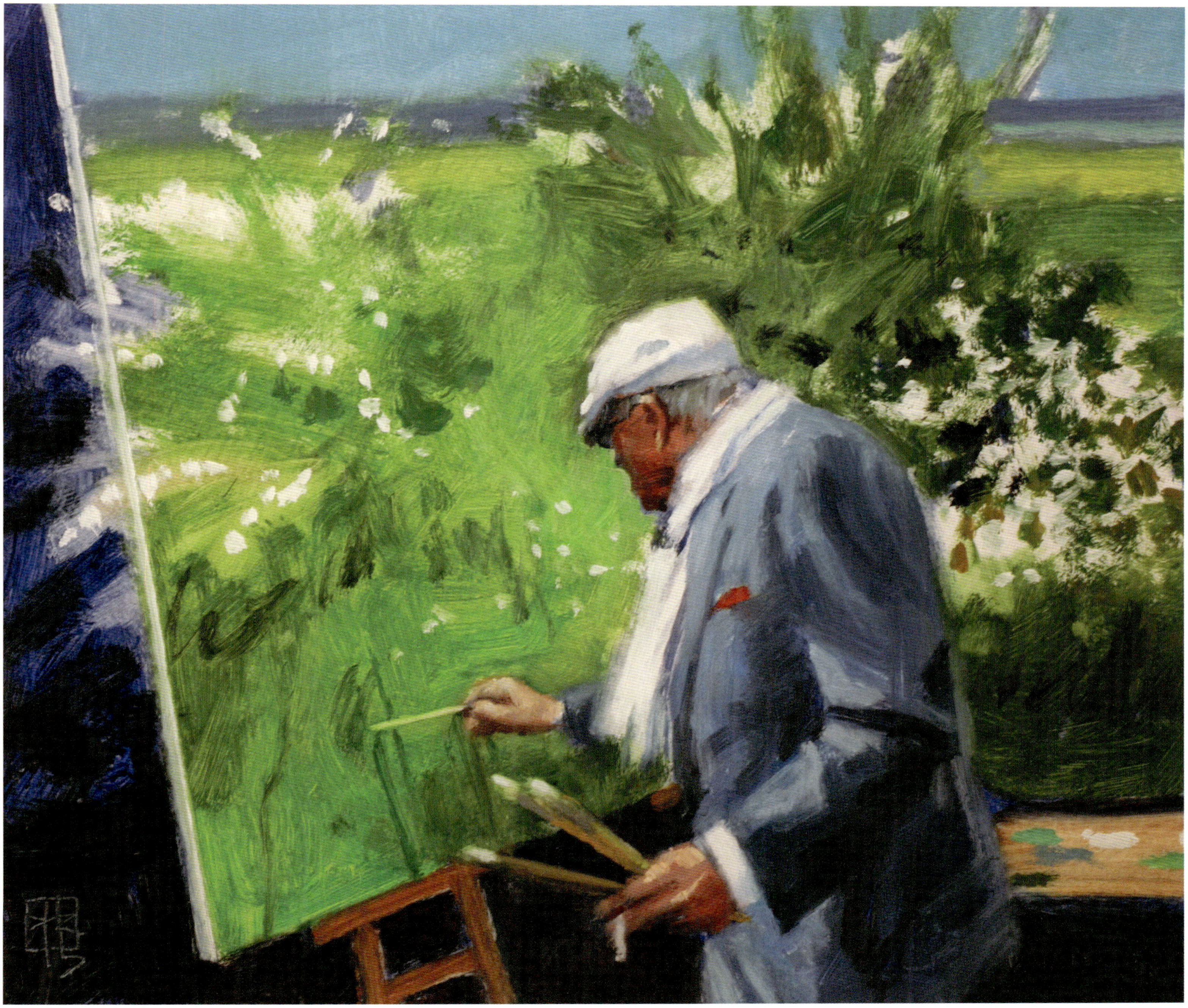

Marvellous Mr Hockney | 2015 | oil on linen | 20 x 24 cm private collection

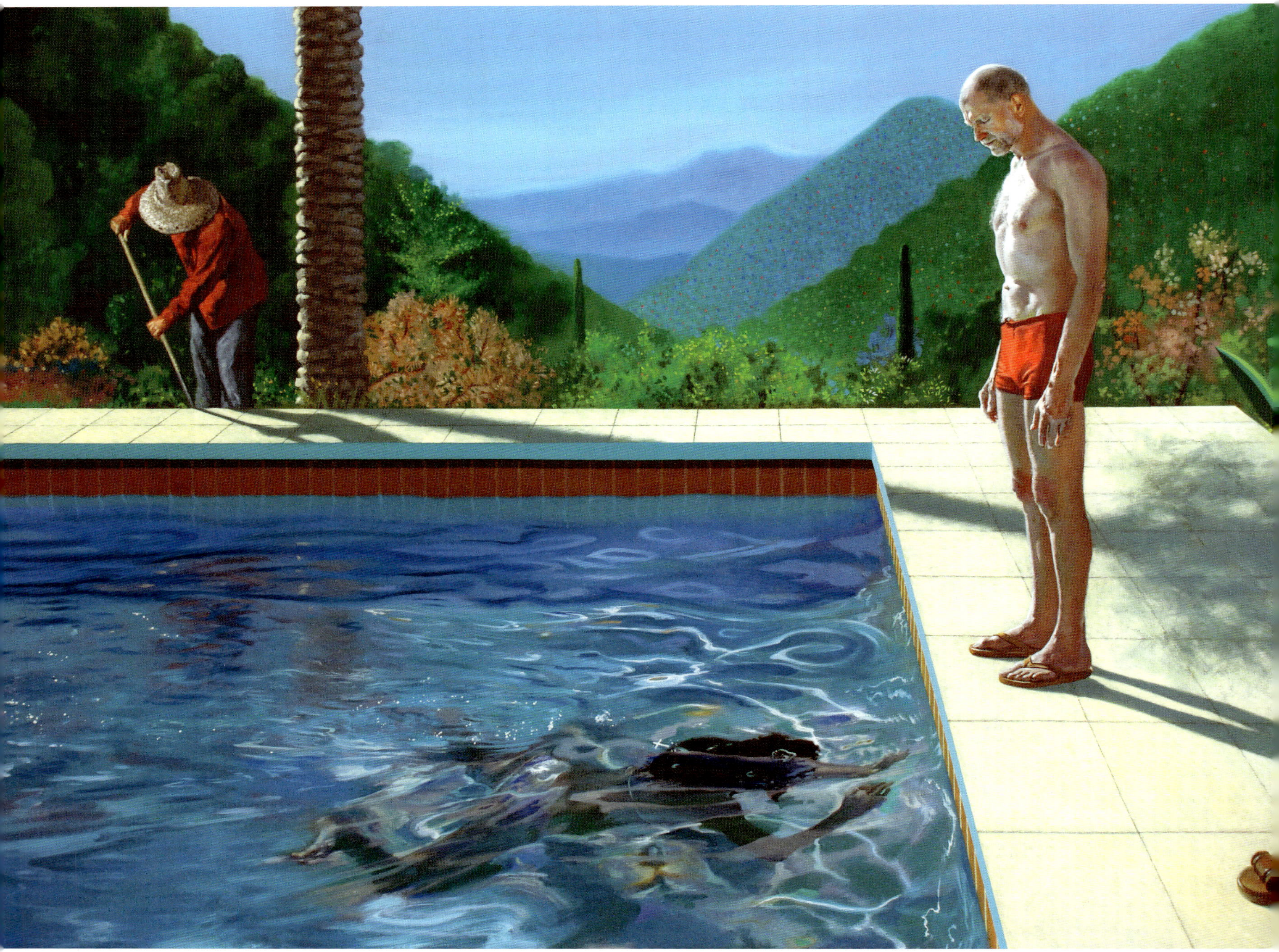

Portrait of an Artist (Pool with Three Figures) | 2019 (work in progress) | oil on linen | 122 x 172.5 cm

collection of the artist

Branching out and standing alone
the Devizes years

Concomitant with his technically accomplished role as portraitist is a sense of the 'soul', or inner being, in all things, or that hidden identity that animates the subjects of his pictures. In 2013 Cobley branched out on his own, relinquishing his houseboat and space at the communal Bath Artists' Studios and purchasing the first of two flats in the pleasant Wiltshire market town of Devizes, where he now works. Within striking distance of Bath, where he remains a founder trustee of the Studios and intermittently shows with Bath Society of Artists, Cobley is also within easy reach of London, where he continues his membership of the NEAC and the RP. He also makes trips to southern California to visit two of his daughters and inevitably perhaps elements of the West Coast scene might influence his future work. Given his perennial interest in the theatre of modern life the exposure to Tinseltown would surely have an influence.

There is also, perhaps, a Hollywood factor in the showbiz razzmatazz of Cobley's 2015 portrait of Philip Jones, Vice-Principal of Sheffield Hallam University (p. 66), Jones exuding the gaiety of a stage performer against a carnival-like red background. At the time of writing, the artist is painting an adaptation of Hockney's auction-record-breaking picture *Portrait of an Artist (Pool with Two Figures)* (opposite) in which the younger of the two Davids substitutes the personnel in the 1972 picture for his own very different heterosexual cast, including his ex-wife Masami as the submerged figure and himself as the standing poolside figure in place of Hockney's boyfriend Peter Schlesinger. In the original the setting is a South of France (rather than Californian) location belonging to Tony Richardson. A further example of his interest in richly symbolic decor comes with a portrait painted two years prior to the Jones picture, *Dieu et Mon Droit*, an unofficial image of the Queen against the regalia of an ornate backdrop. He enjoyed 'giving myself the freedom to paint her however I chose', as he puts it in some painting notes made at the time, and the result is an essay in the artist's feeling of admiration for her long reign dedicated to 'a life of service to her people'. A more recent use of background regalia appears in the portrait of Baroness Hale of Richmond, first female President of the Supreme Court, a commission for Gray's Inn (p. 56).

The relative informality of the uncommissioned and improvised Queen portrait (p. 57) also holds true in the 2008 painting *Blues, Beer and Rock 'n' Roll* (p. 69), a candid and relaxed portrait of Trevor Dighton, a friend of David's brother Andy, relaxing at home. This genre picture epitomises the composite nature of Cobley's art, in this case embodying the downward view, the iconographic combination of interior, unposed portrait and still life in one compellingly candid composition. There is an evident narrative richness too, abundant music references pertinent to a party in terms of an old vinyl record player, Little Richard and legendary sixties Marquee Club posters and an adjacent bookcase of books and record sleeves. Cobley is a master of reflected light, throwing up those localised, often contradictory, colours created by the effect of natural or artificial light sources.

Reflecting his personal restlessness, Cobley is an artist constantly on the move, forever testing himself with new creative challenges and an imaginatively fertile range of new ideas. Never resting on his artistic laurels, by the same token he parodies and backtracks, recycling or revamping old ideas even to the extent of referencing previous works in recurring picture-within-picture scenarios. As with the Bloomsbury interior, Cobley invests ordinary domestic bric-a-brac with cultural, social and auto-biographical significance, another key sign that his essential life as portrait painter carries him beyond the superficialities of outward appearance to capture an inner character for which the surrounding domestic environment becomes a telling analogue, or extension of 'personality'. And that personality is an unmistakably contemporary one, replacing the Bloomsbury Group's hand-made Omega range with the mod cons of a contemporary hi-tech or mass-produced consumer age.

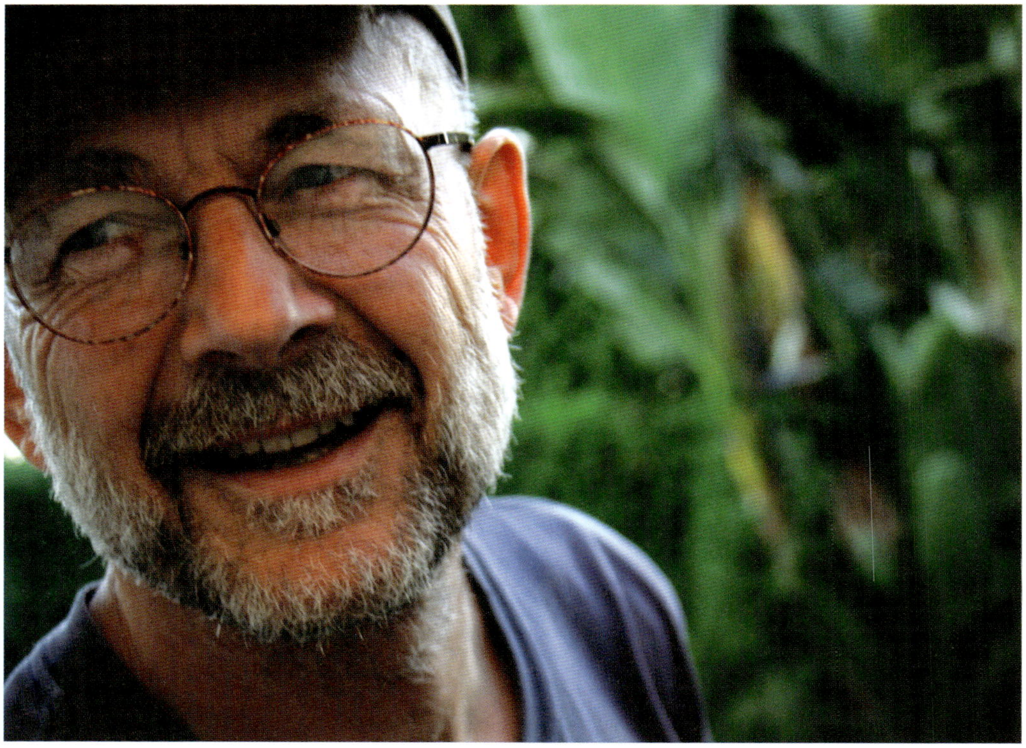

In Orange County, California, 2017 photograph Selima Thomson

PLATES

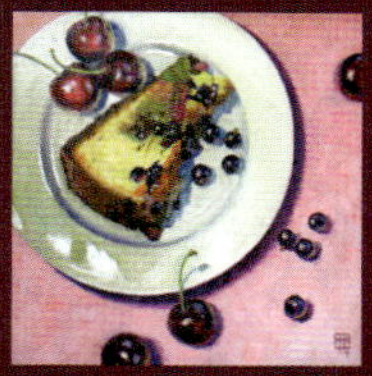

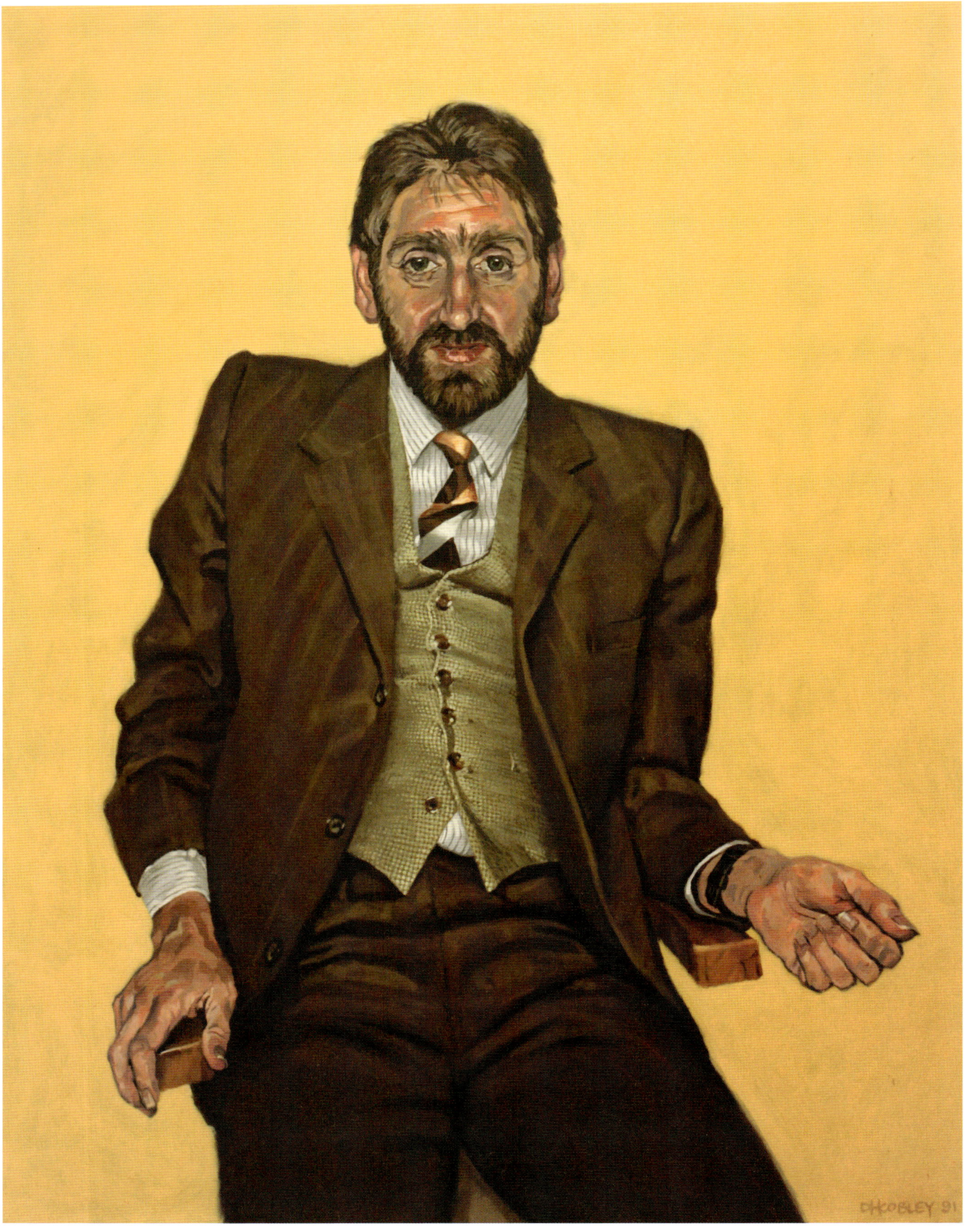

Bernie Hobbs | 1991 | oil on linen | 152.5 x 122 cm private collection

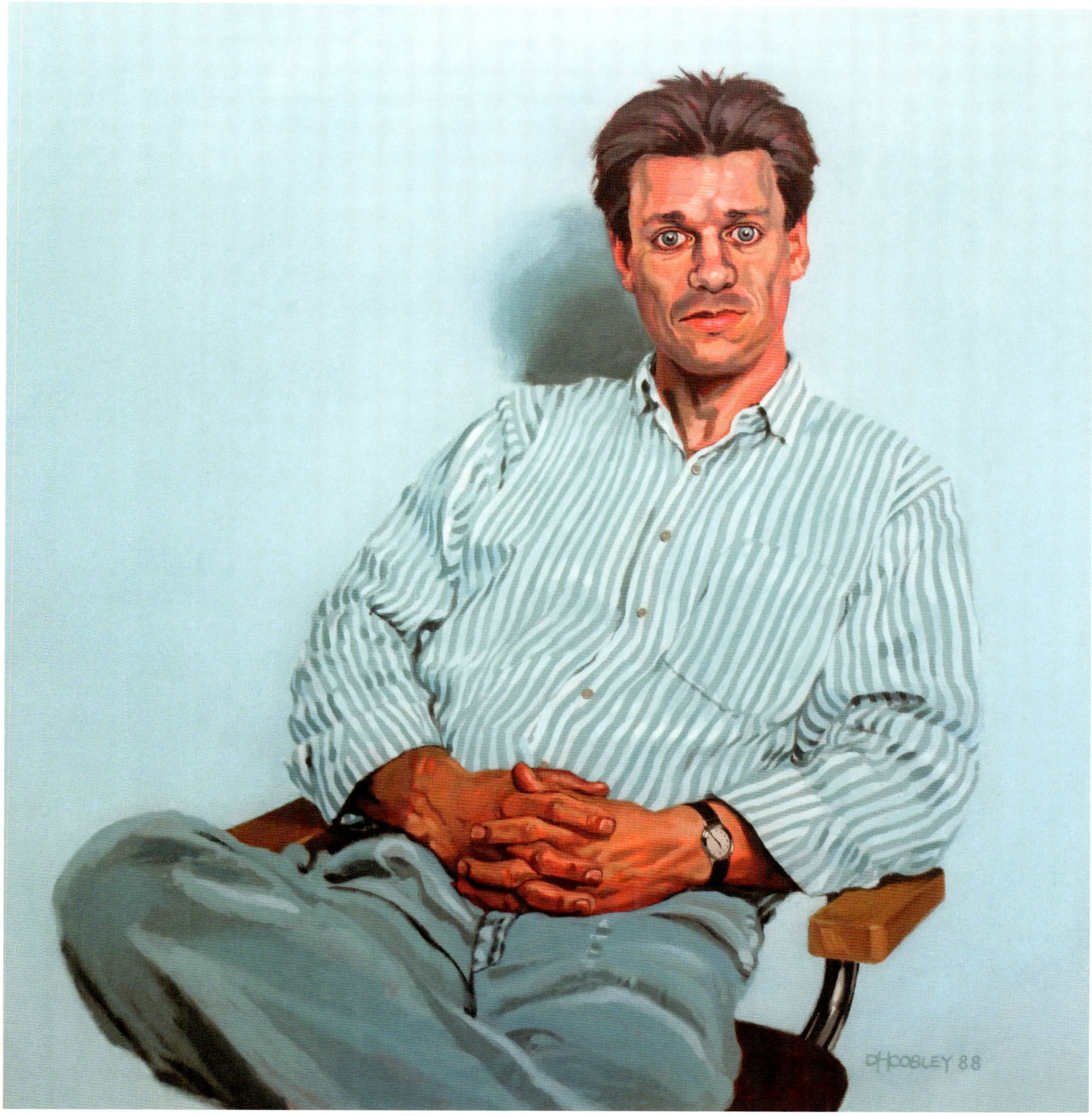

Geoff | 1988 | oil on linen | 122 x 122 cm

private collection

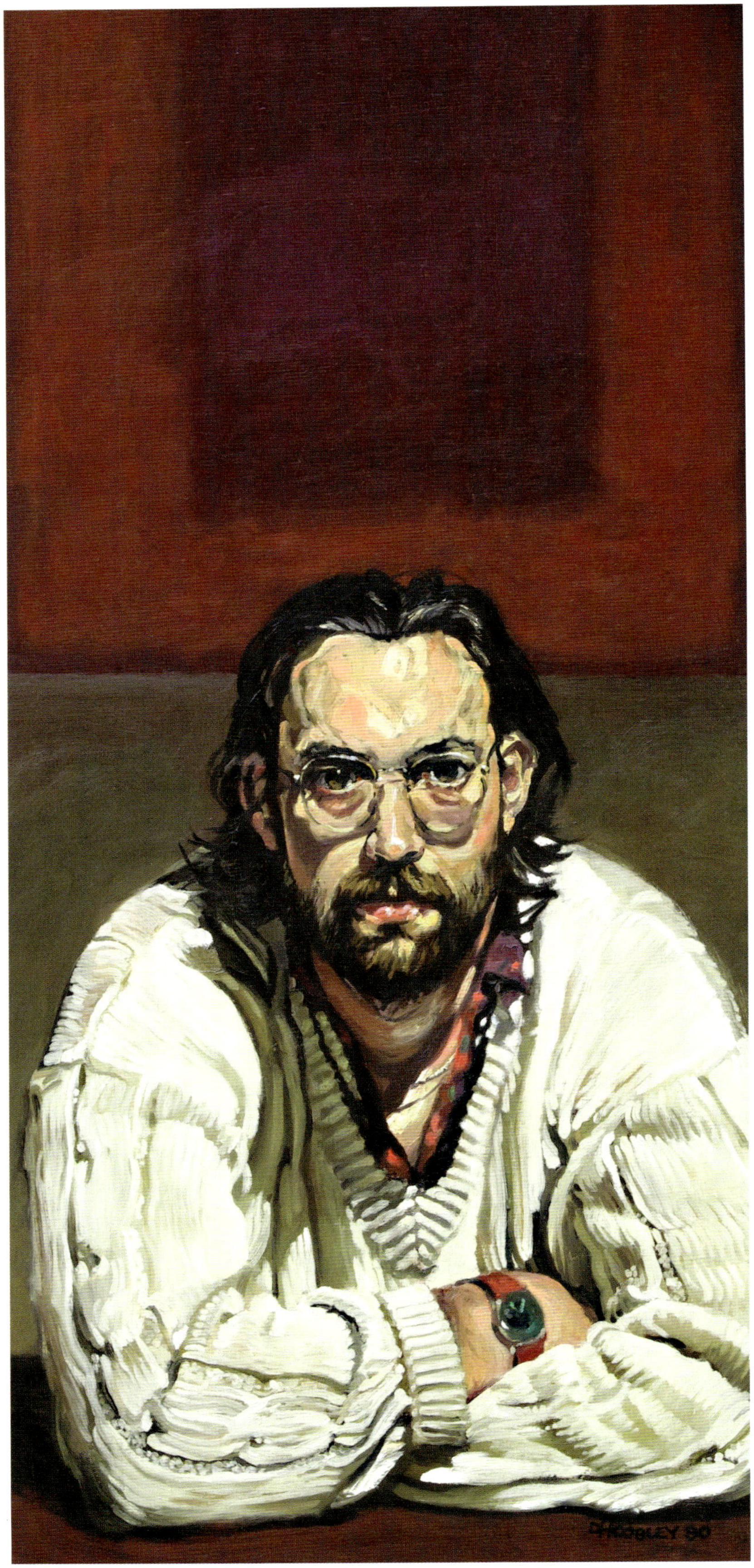

Andy | 1990 | oil on board | 122 x 61 cm private collection

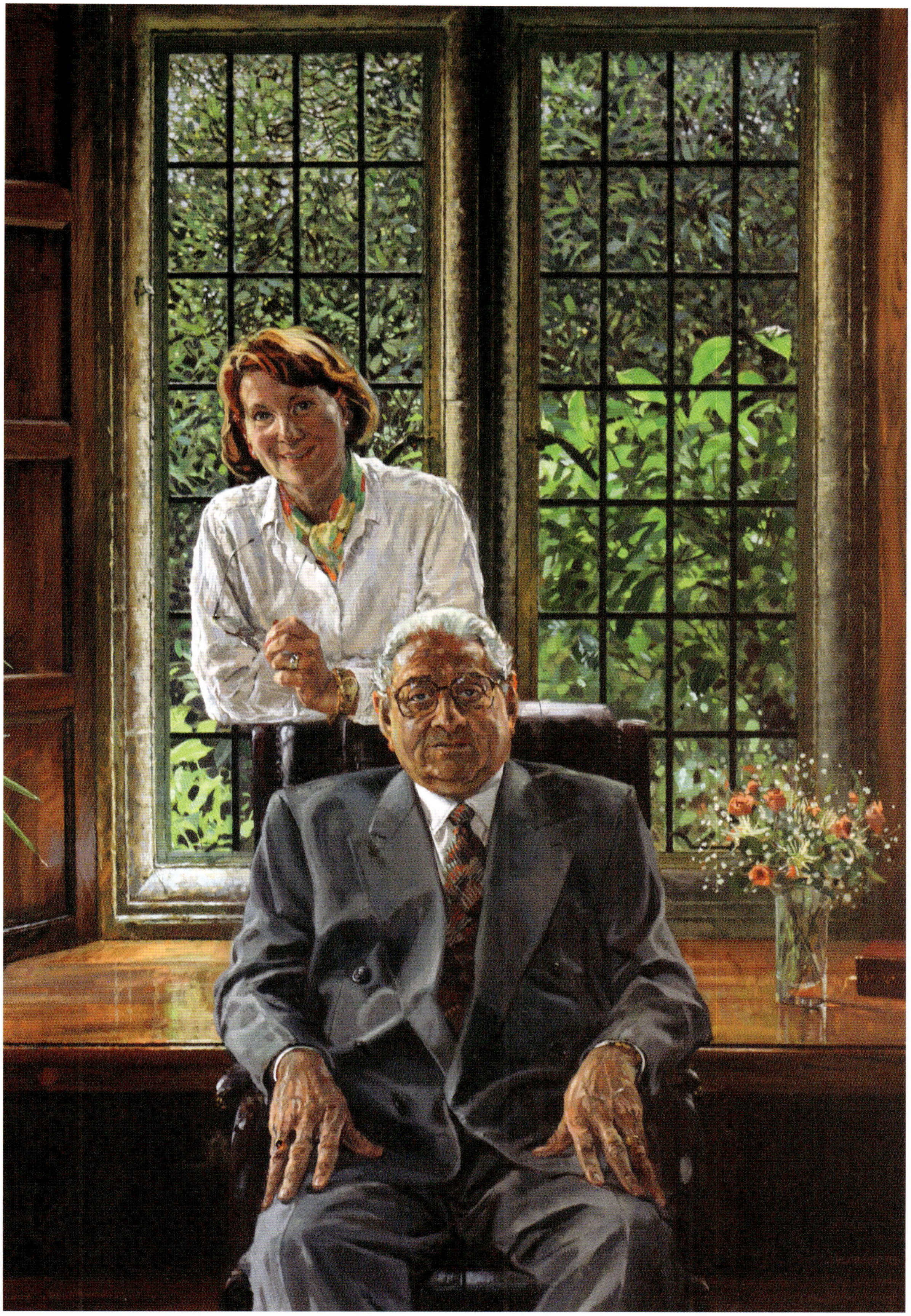

Ralph and Angela Haeems | 1996 | oil on linen | 122 x 101.5 cm private collection

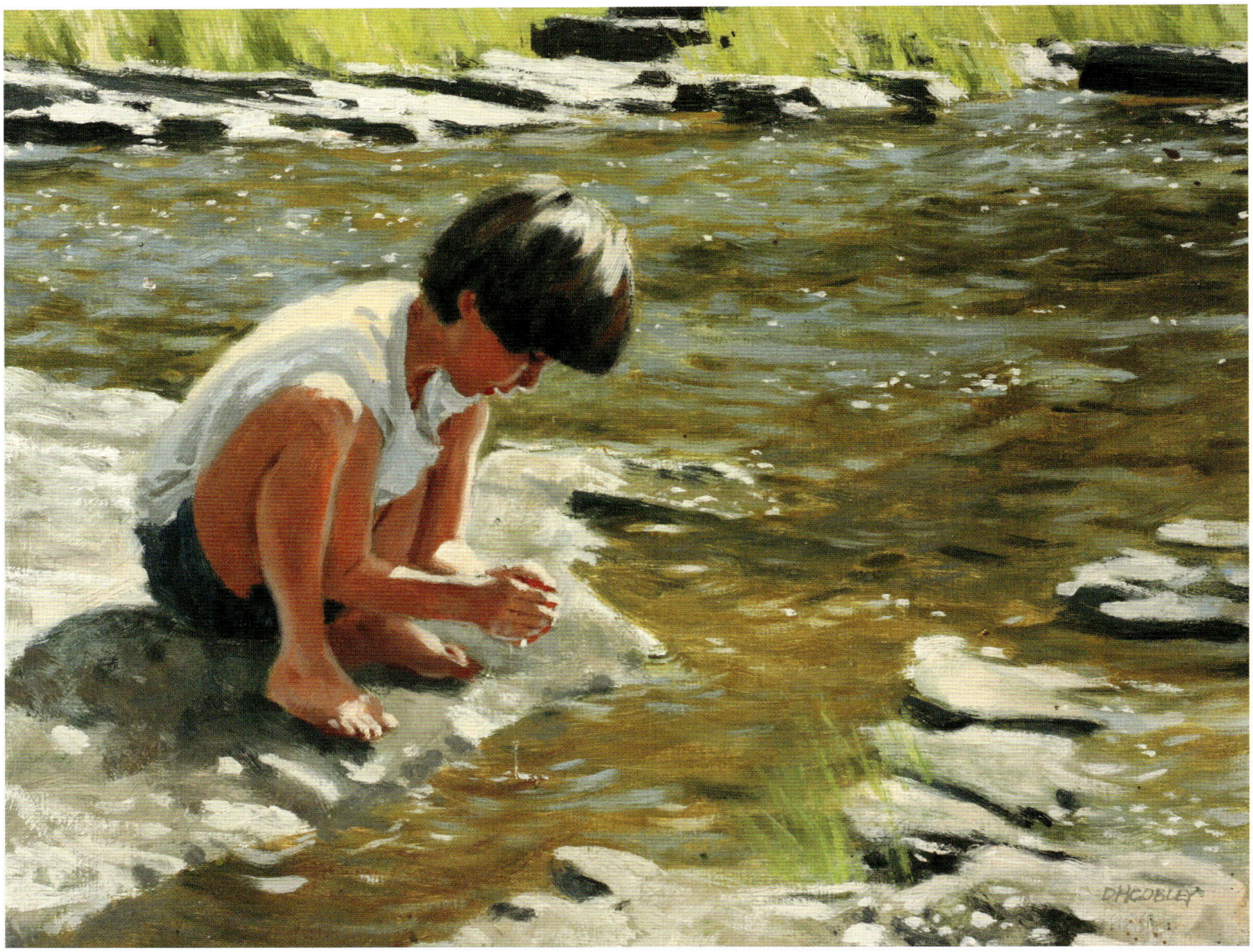

Catching Minnows (Melanie) | 1992 | oil on linen | 30.5 x 40.5 cm private collection

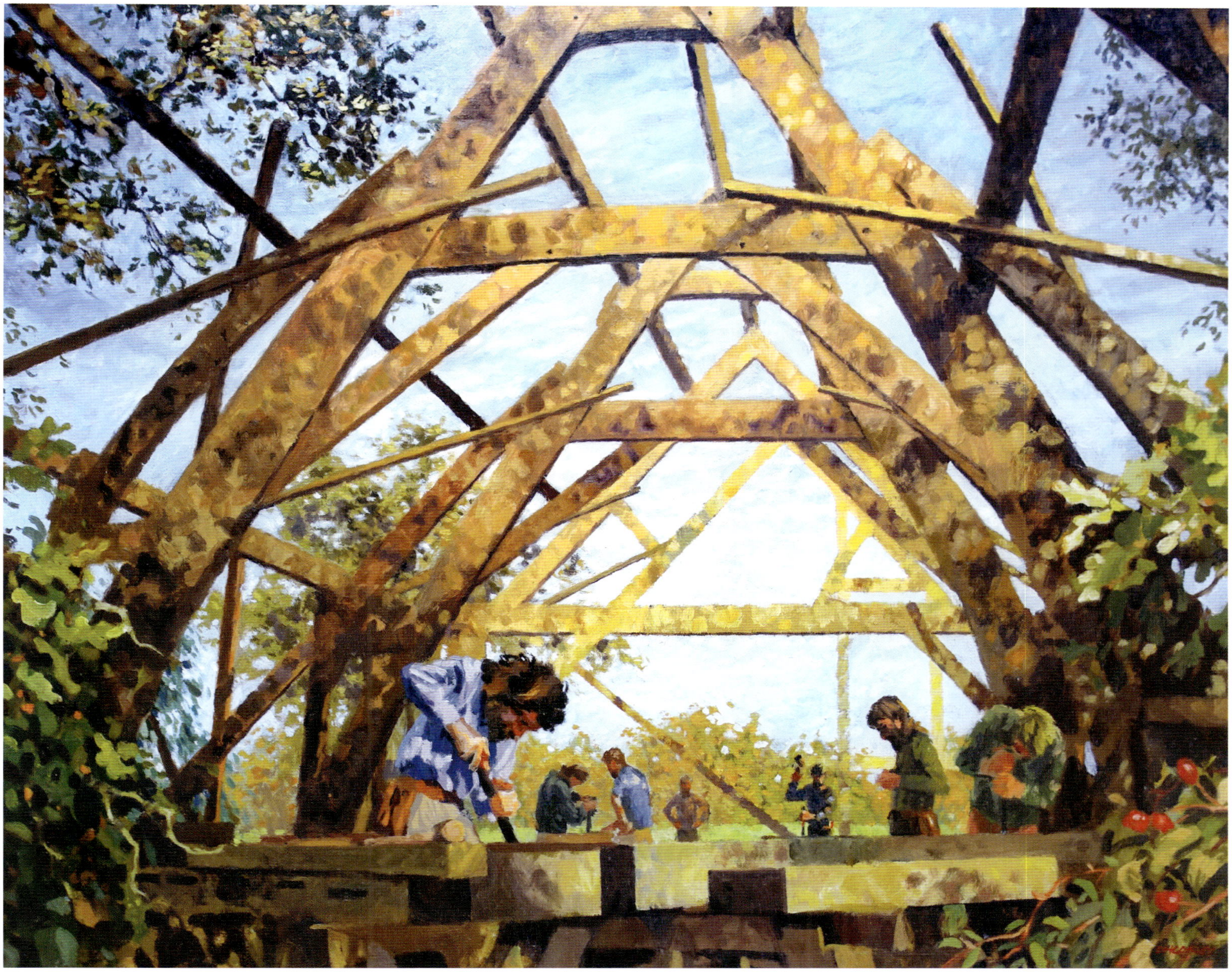

Carpenters in Oak | 1996 | oil on panel | 56 x 71 cm collection of the artist

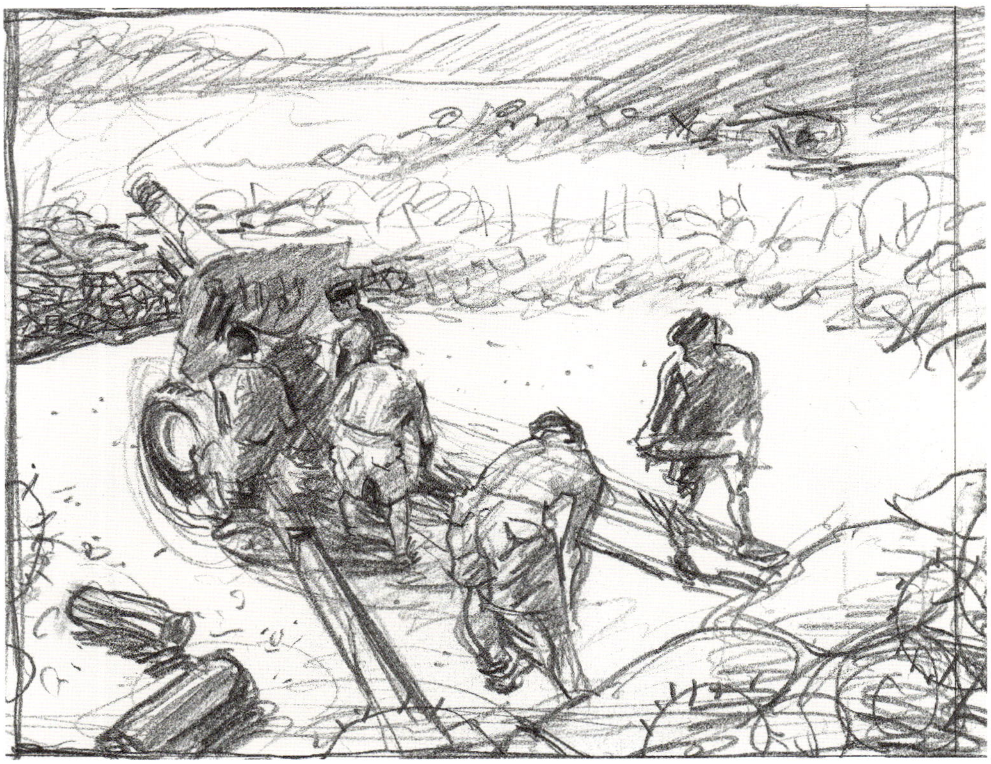

Study for Action in South Arabia
1998 | pencil | 20.5 x 25.5 cm
collection of the artist

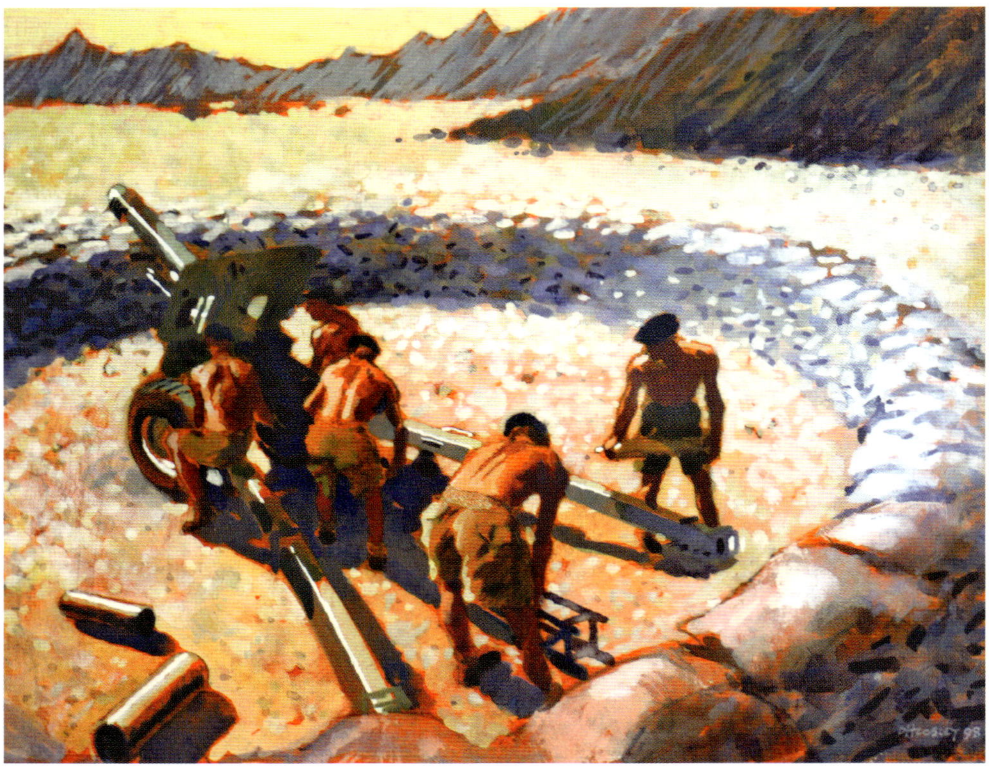

Study for Action in South Arabia
1998 | gouache | 20.5 x 25.5 cm
private collection

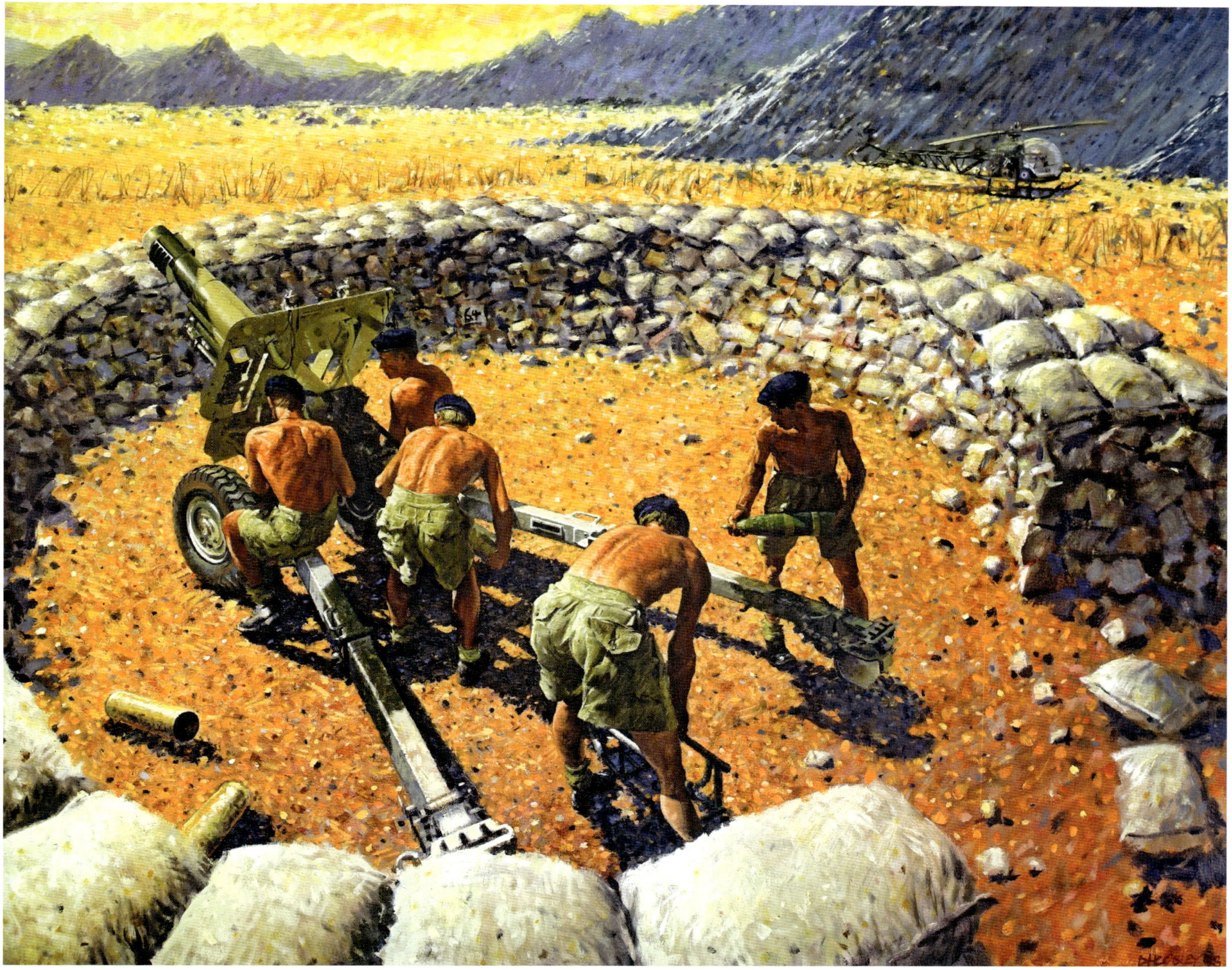

Action in South Arabia | 1998 | oil on linen | 81.5 x 100 cm 1st Regiment Royal Horse Artillery

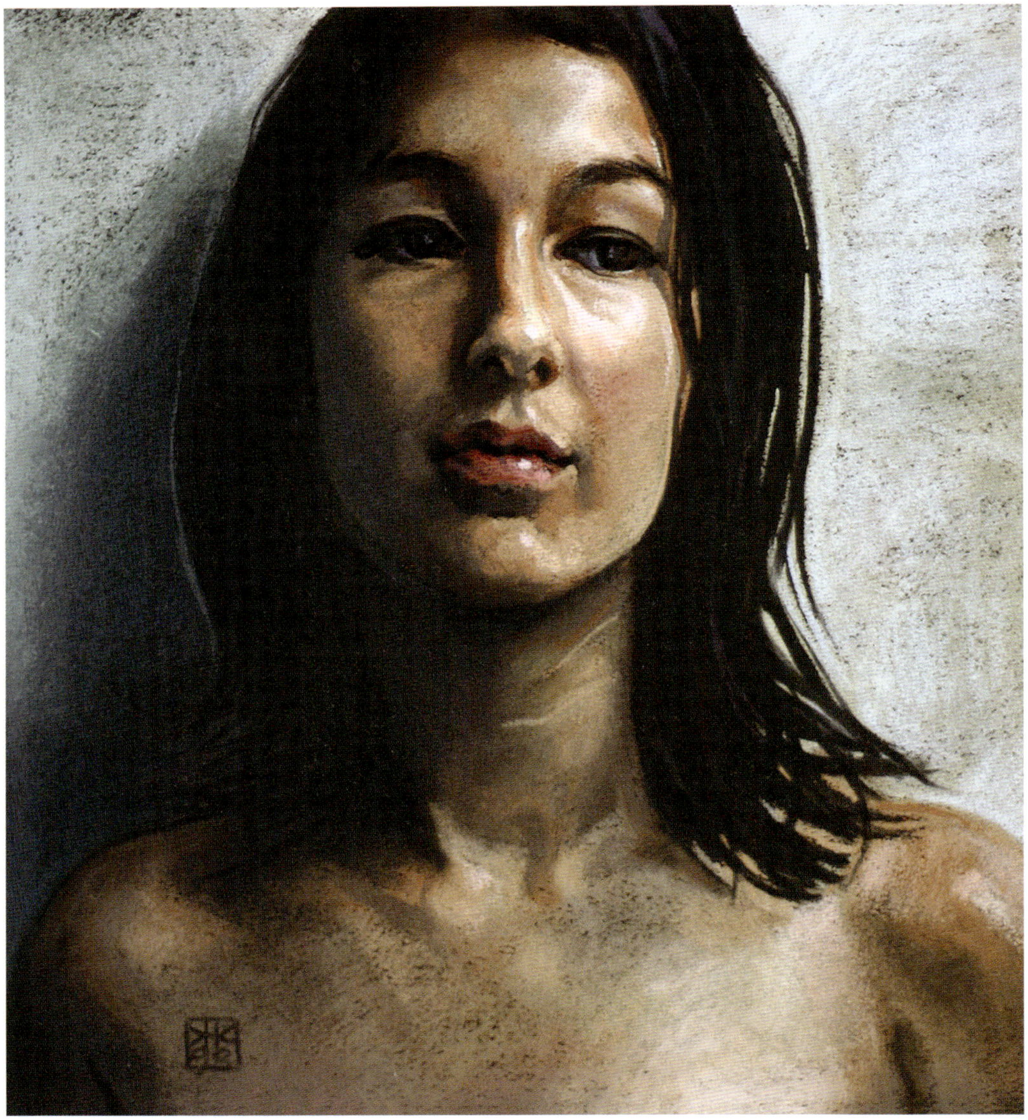

Girl with Wet Hair (Selima) | 1998 | pastel | 30.5 x 28 cm private collection

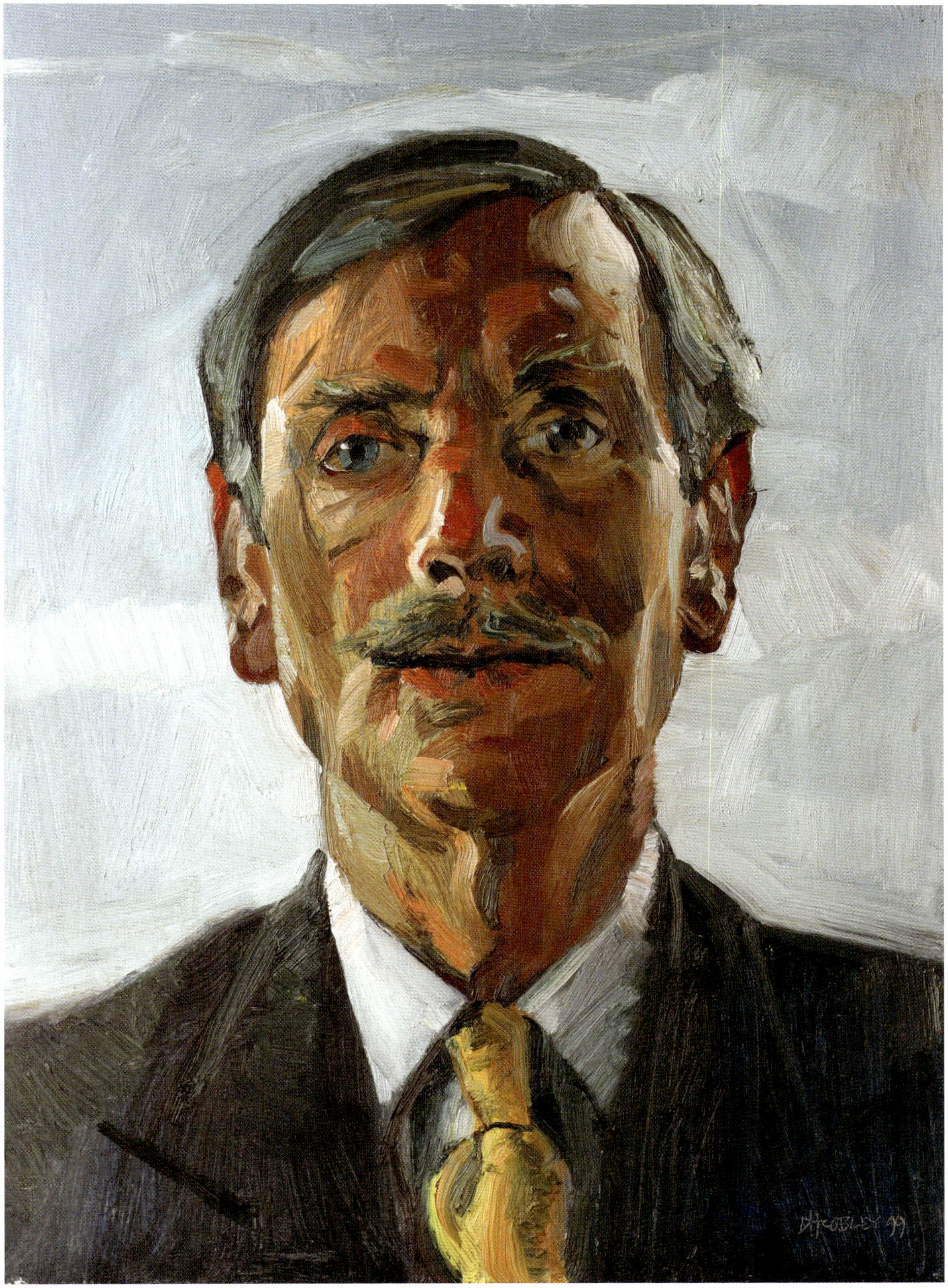

Oil study of Colin Parsons (of Taylor Woodrow)
1999 | oil on board | 40.5 x 30.5 cm
collection of the artist

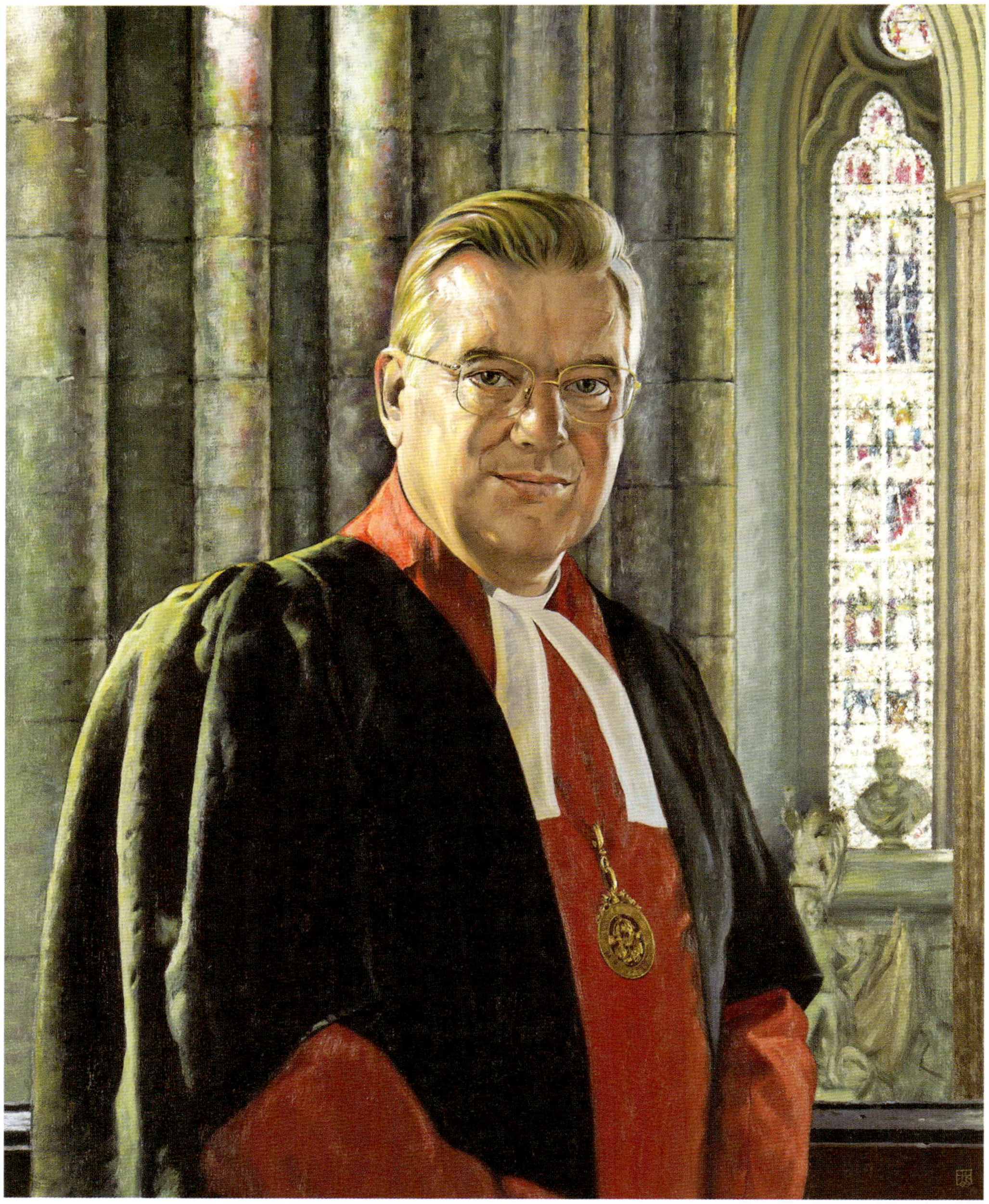

The Very Reverend Wesley Carr, Dean of Westminster
2001 | oil on linen | 76 x 63 cm
Dean and Chapter of Westminster Abbey

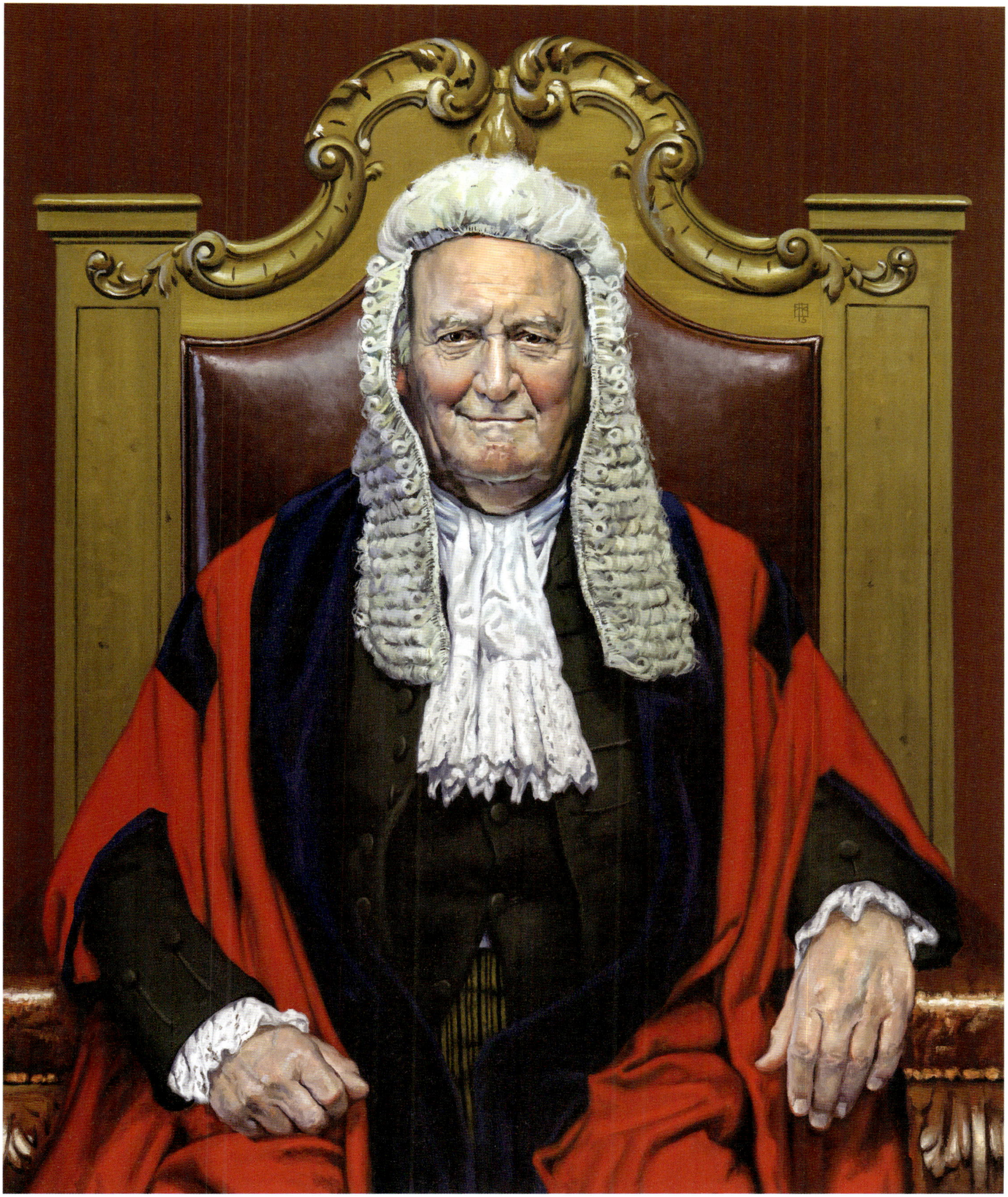

Judge Peter Beaumont | 2013 | oil on linen | 101.5 x 86.5 cm The Old Bailey

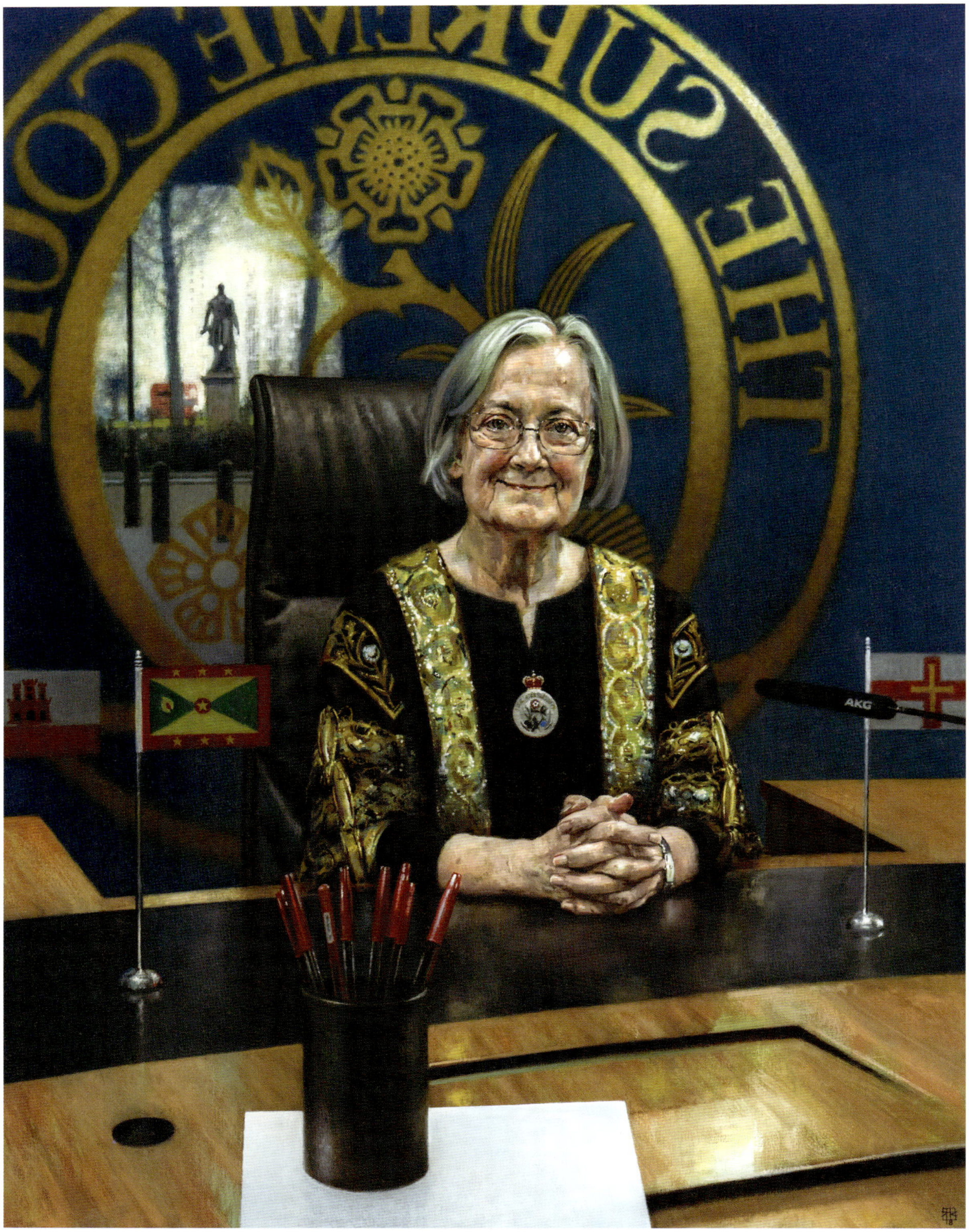

Baroness Brenda Hale | 2018 | oil on linen | 127 x 101.5 cm Gray's Inn

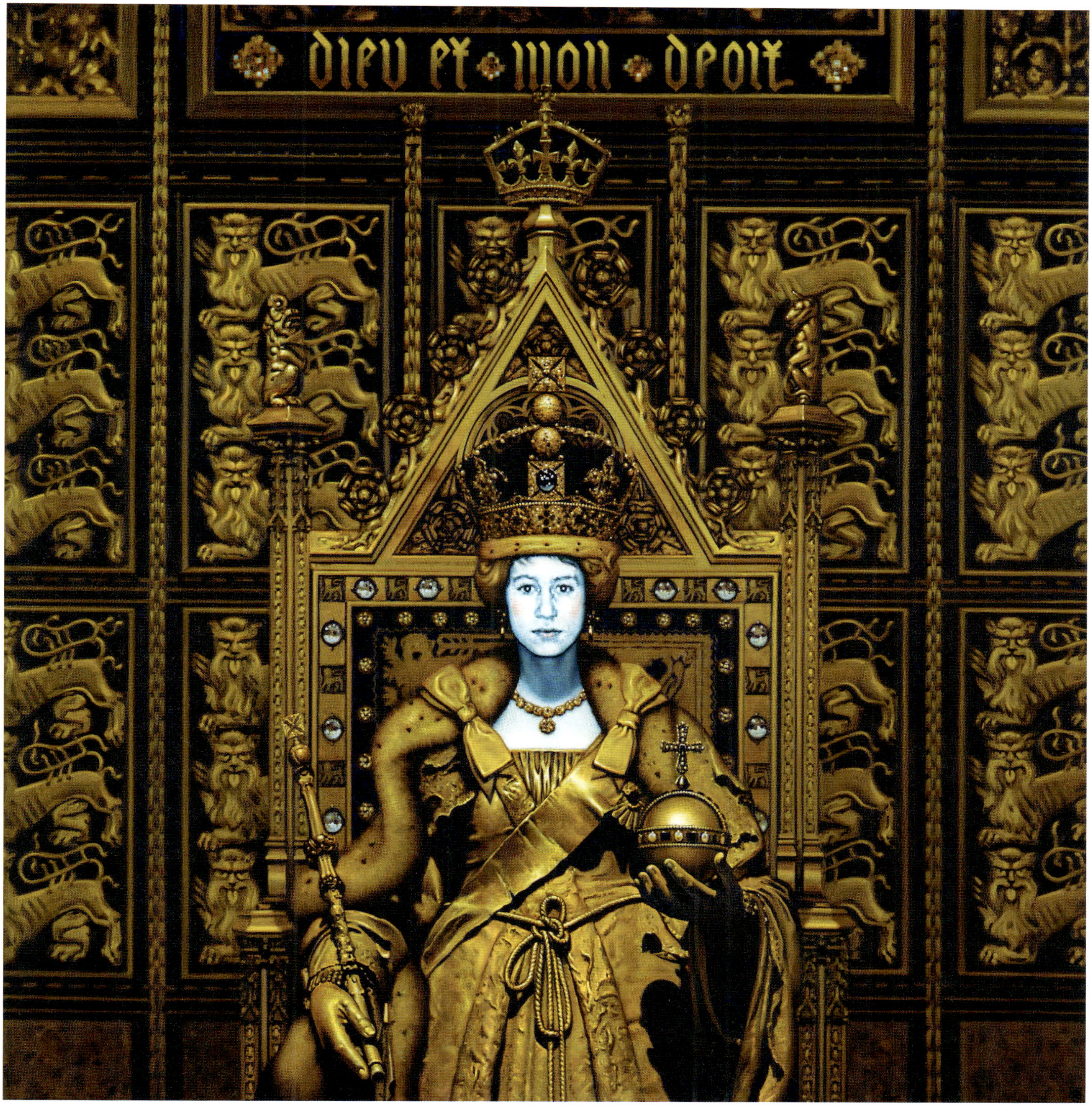

Dieu et Mon Droit | 2013 | oil on linen | 183 x 183 cm

collection of the artist

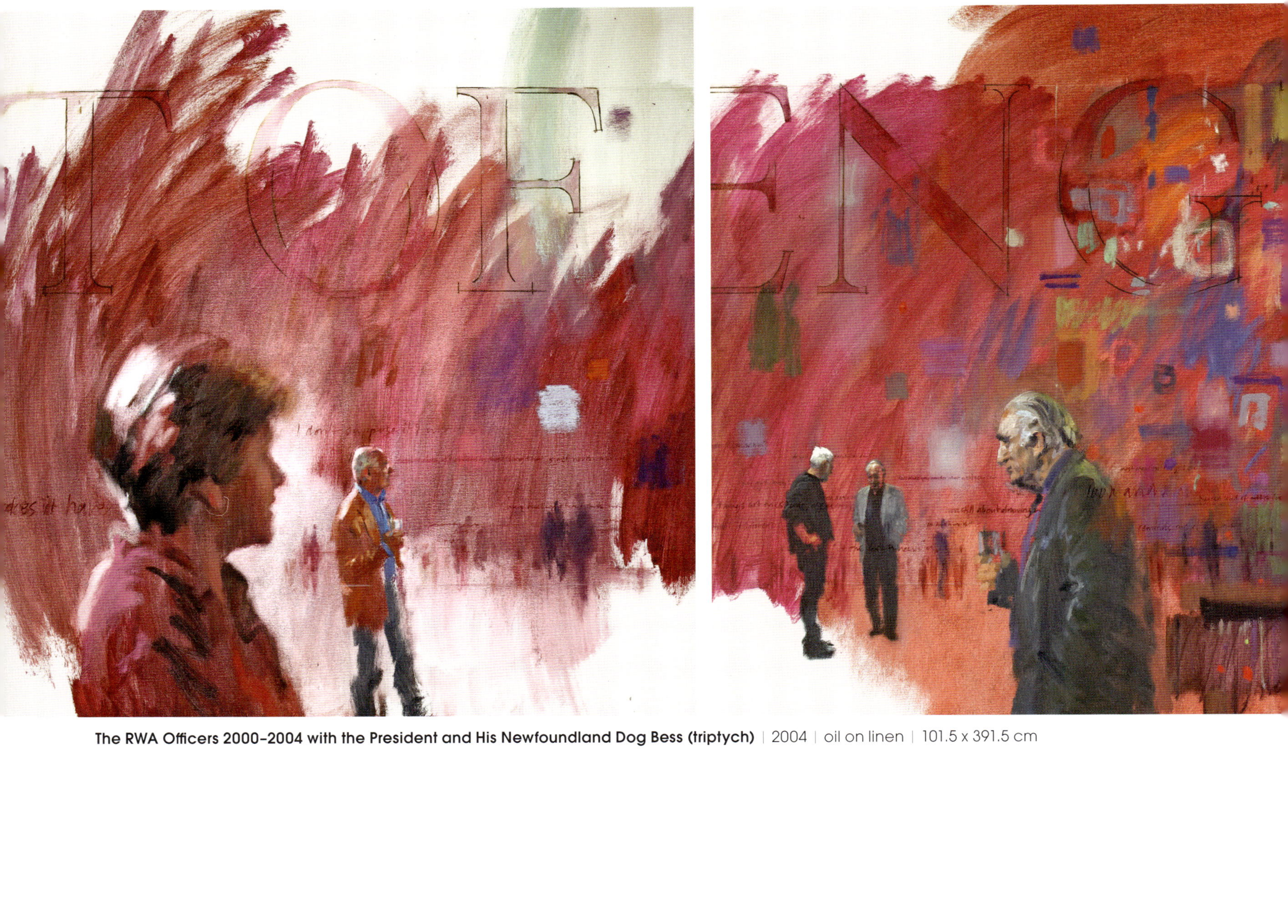

The RWA Officers 2000–2004 with the President and His Newfoundland Dog Bess (triptych) | 2004 | oil on linen | 101.5 x 391.5 cm

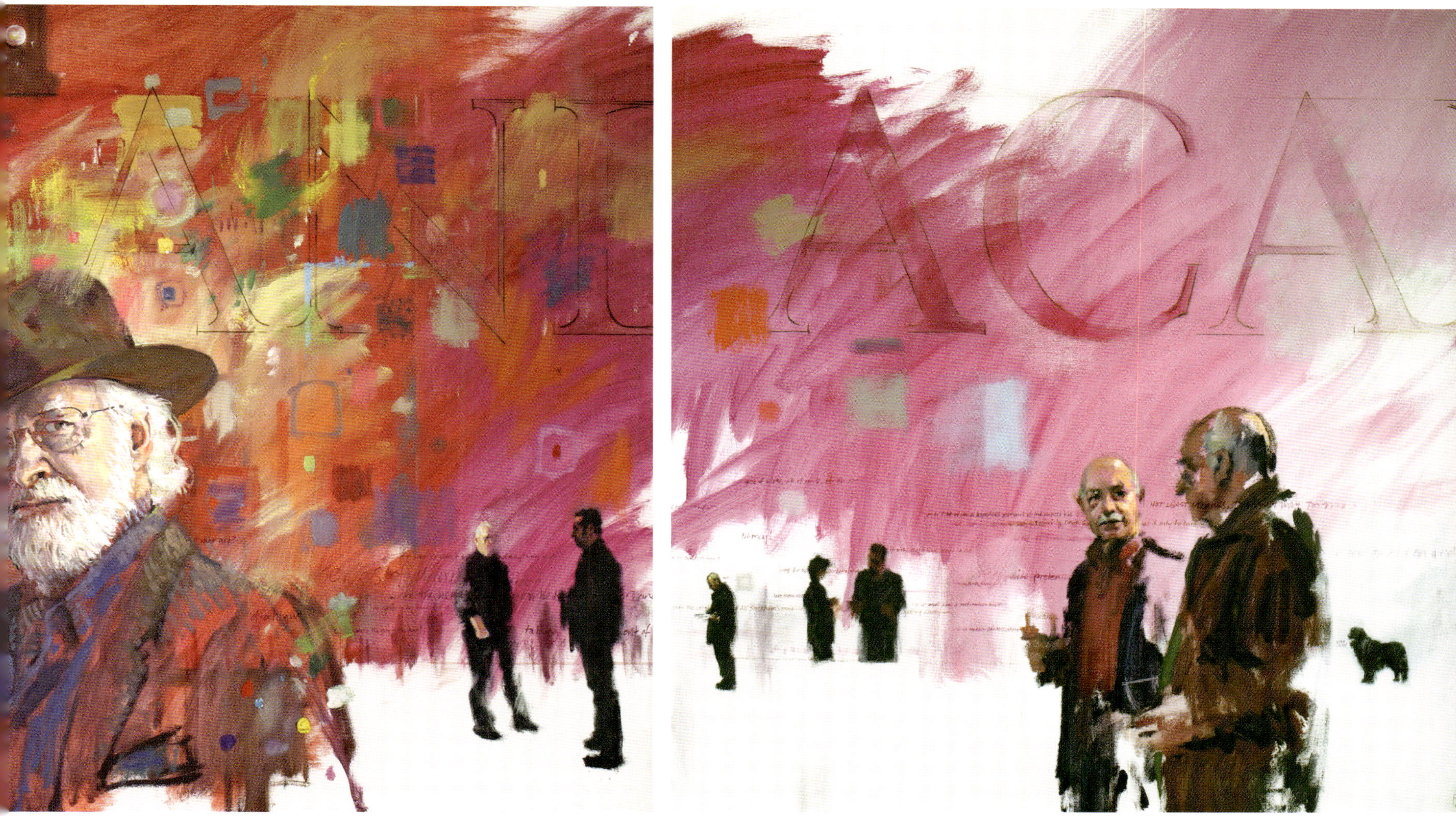

RWA Bristol

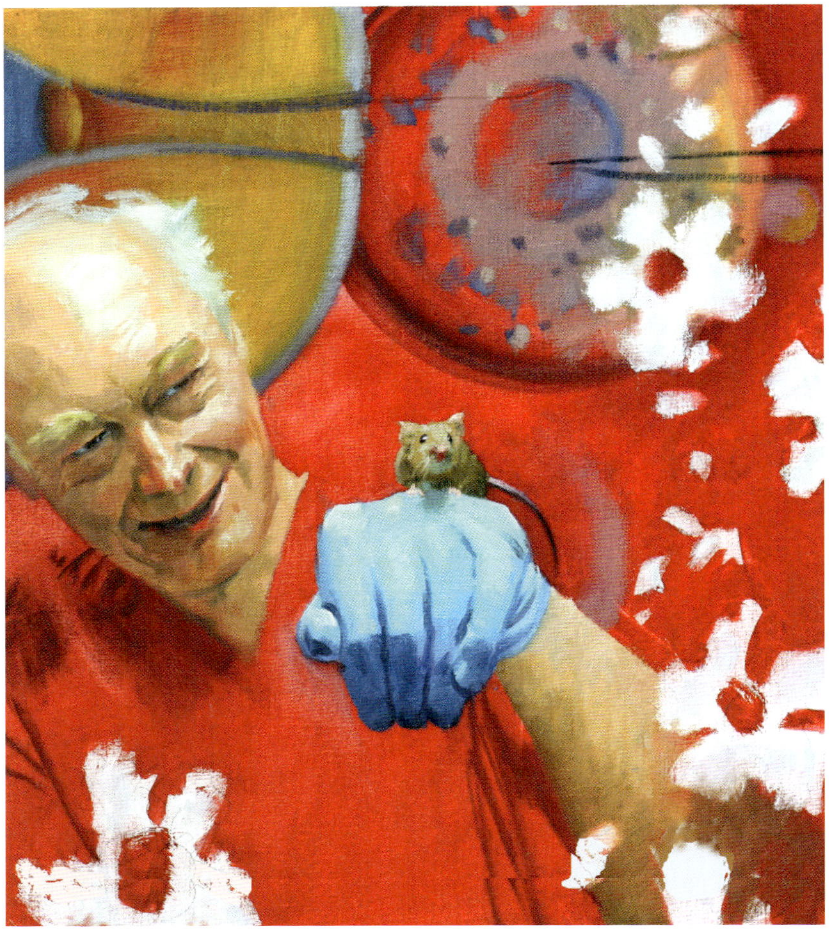

51 x 45.5 cm

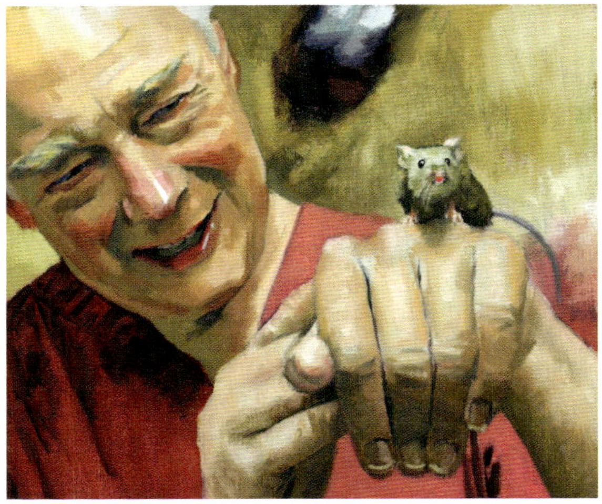

25.5 x 30.5 cm

Studies for Sir Martin Evans
2010 | oil on linen
private collection

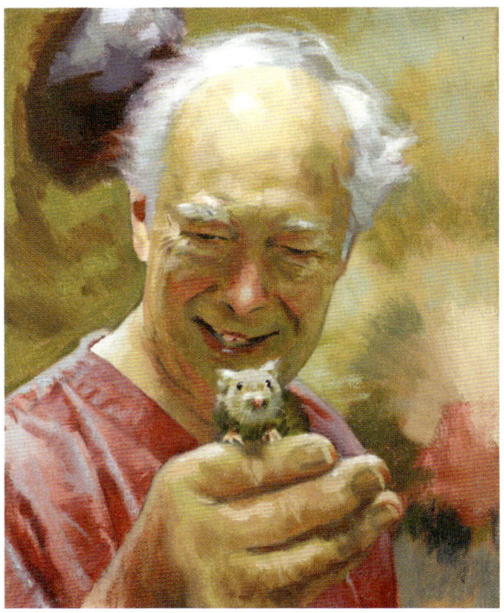

30.5 x 25.5 cm

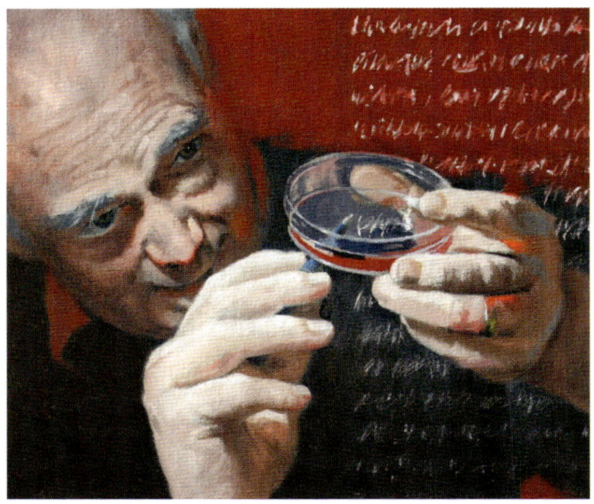

25.5 x 30.5 cm

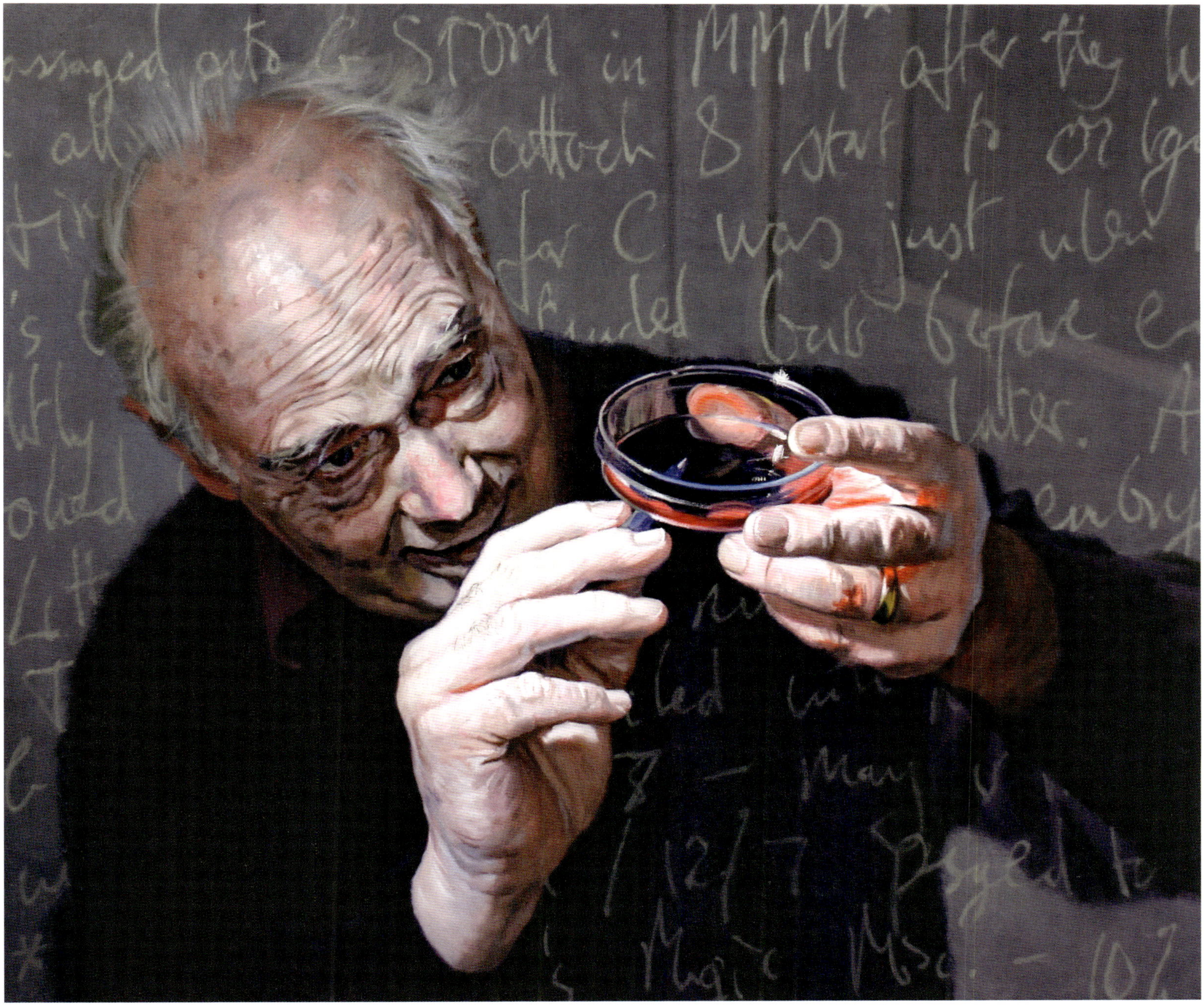

Sir Martin John Evans | 2011 | oil on linen | 58.5 x 71 cm

National Portrait Gallery

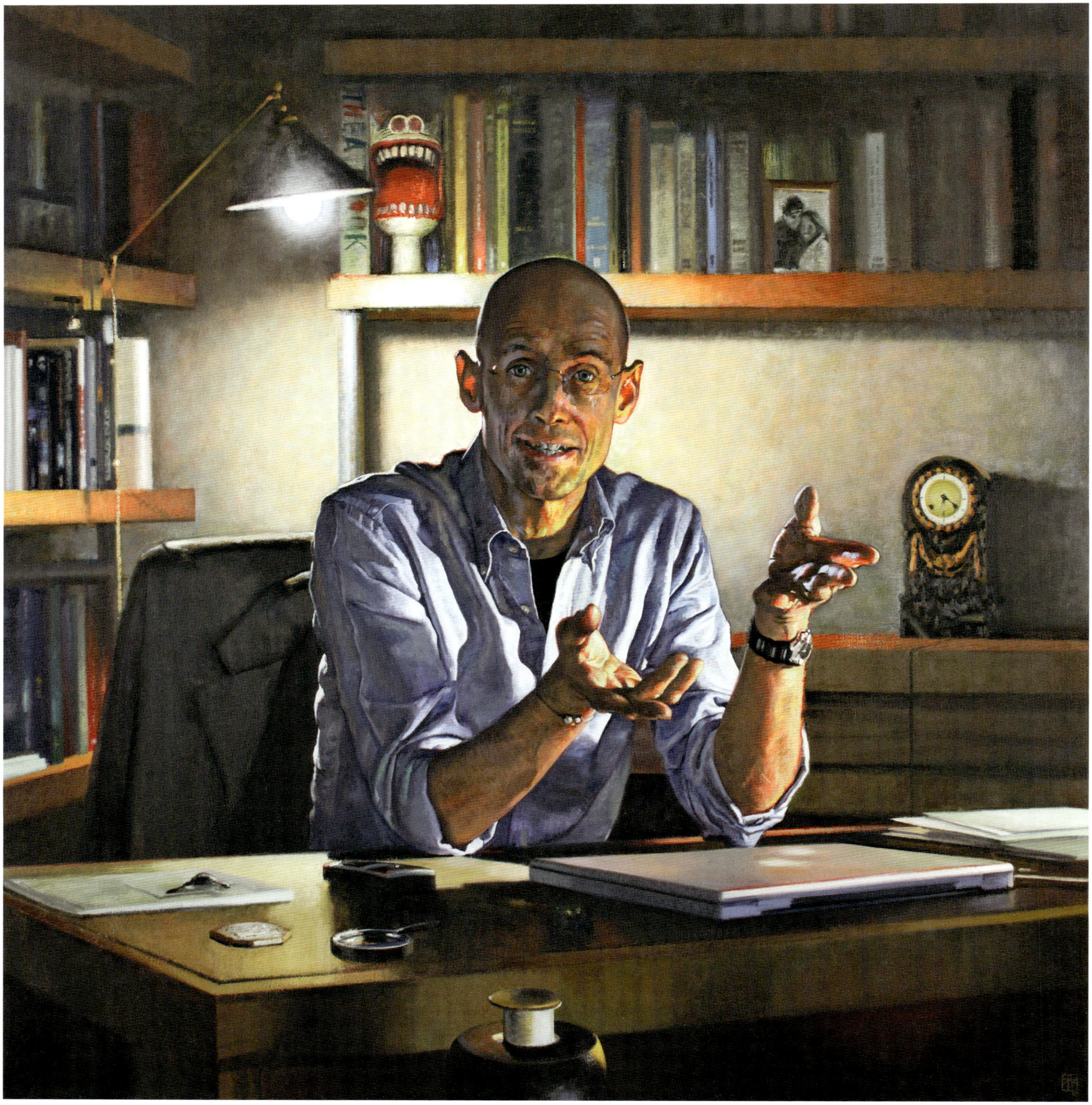

Viscount Portman | 2010 | oil on linen | 122 x 122 cm

Portman Estate

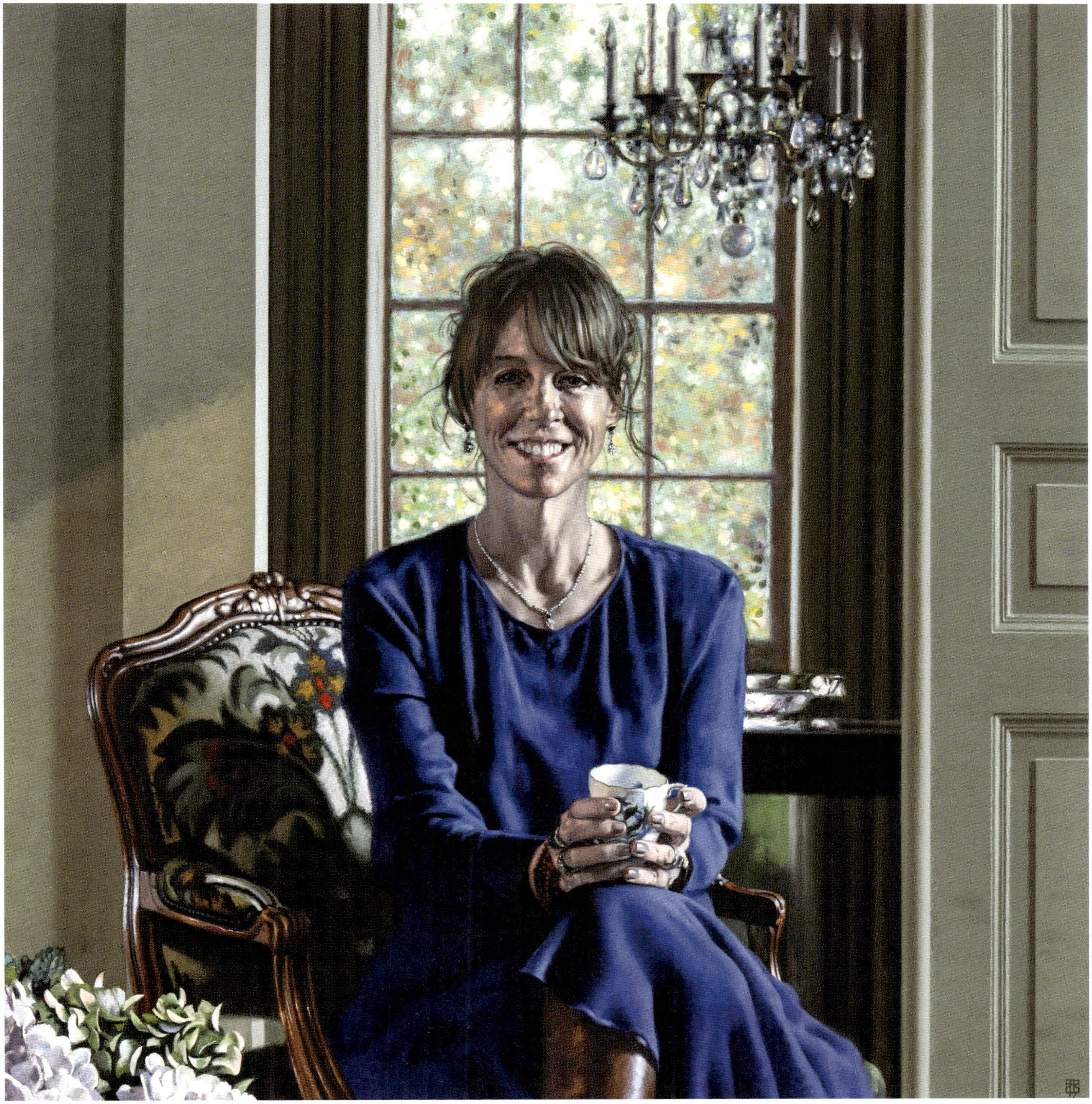

The Blue Dress | 2017 | oil on linen | 122 x 122 cm

Portman Estate

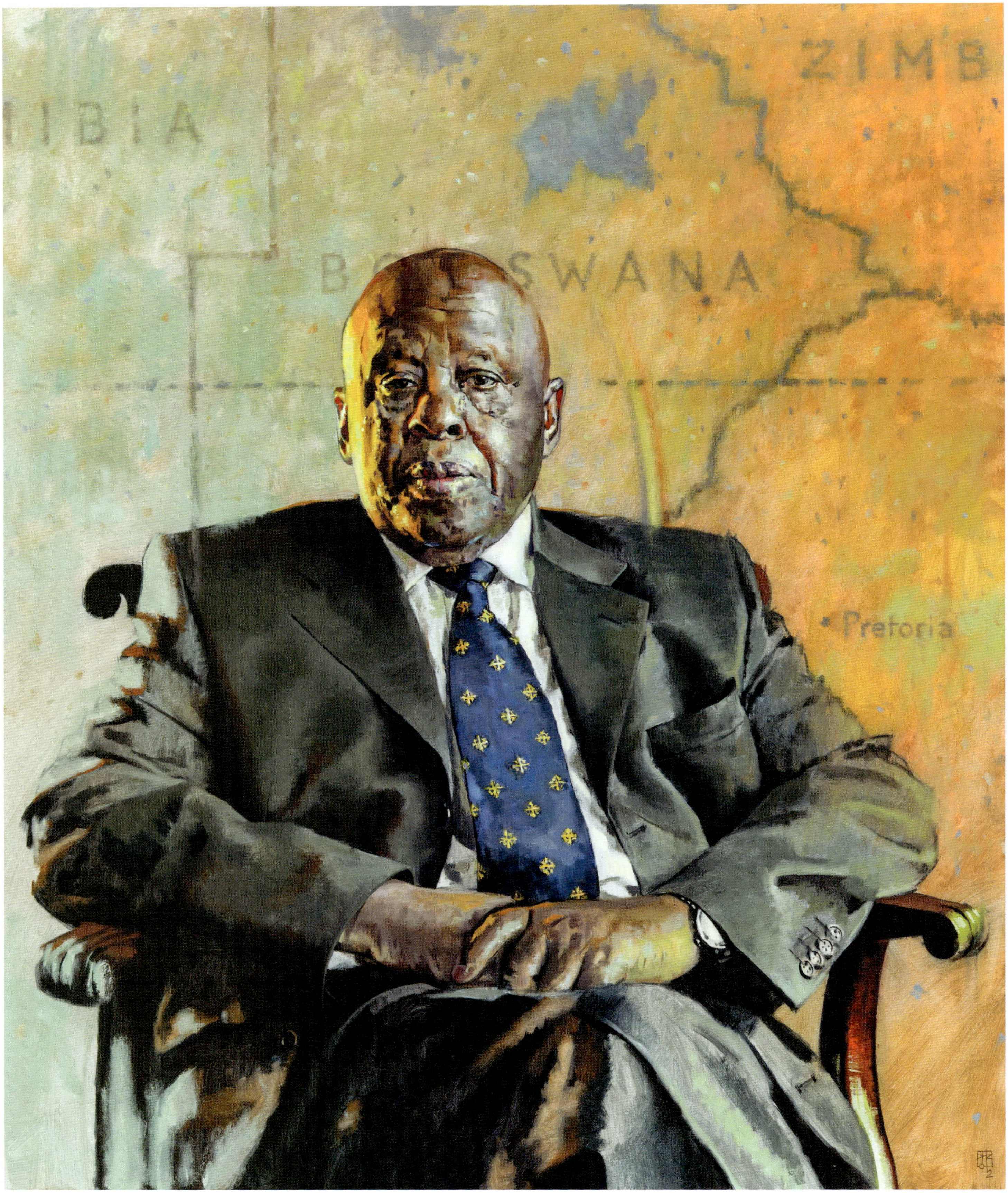

Festus Mogae | 2016 | oil on linen | 125 x 101.5 cm University College Oxford

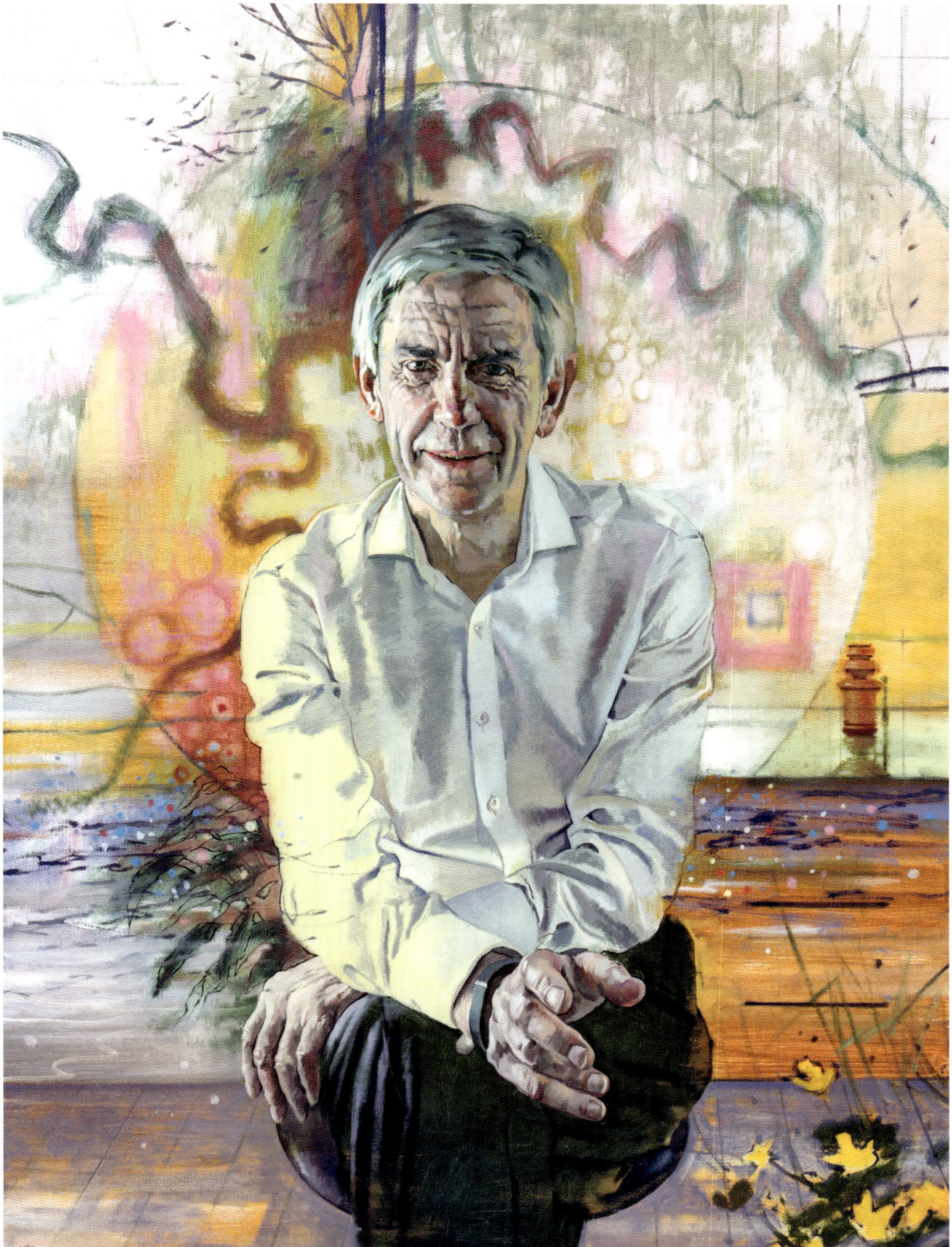

Sir John Tooke | 2015 | oil on linen | 122 x 91.5 cm The Academy of Medical Sciences

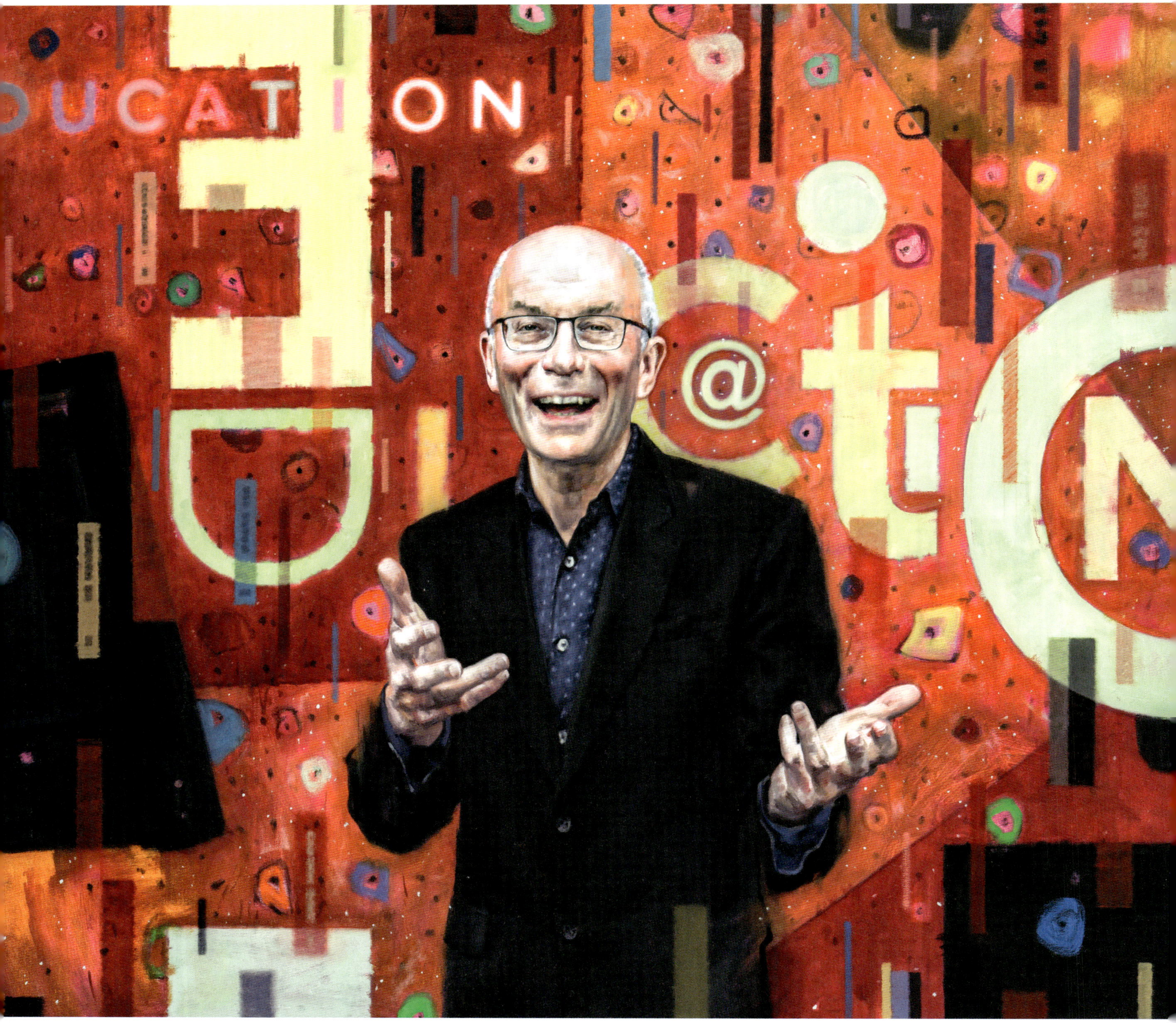

Philip Jones, Vice-Principal, Sheffield Hallam University | 2015 | oil on linen | 111.5 x 137 cm

Sheffield Hallam University

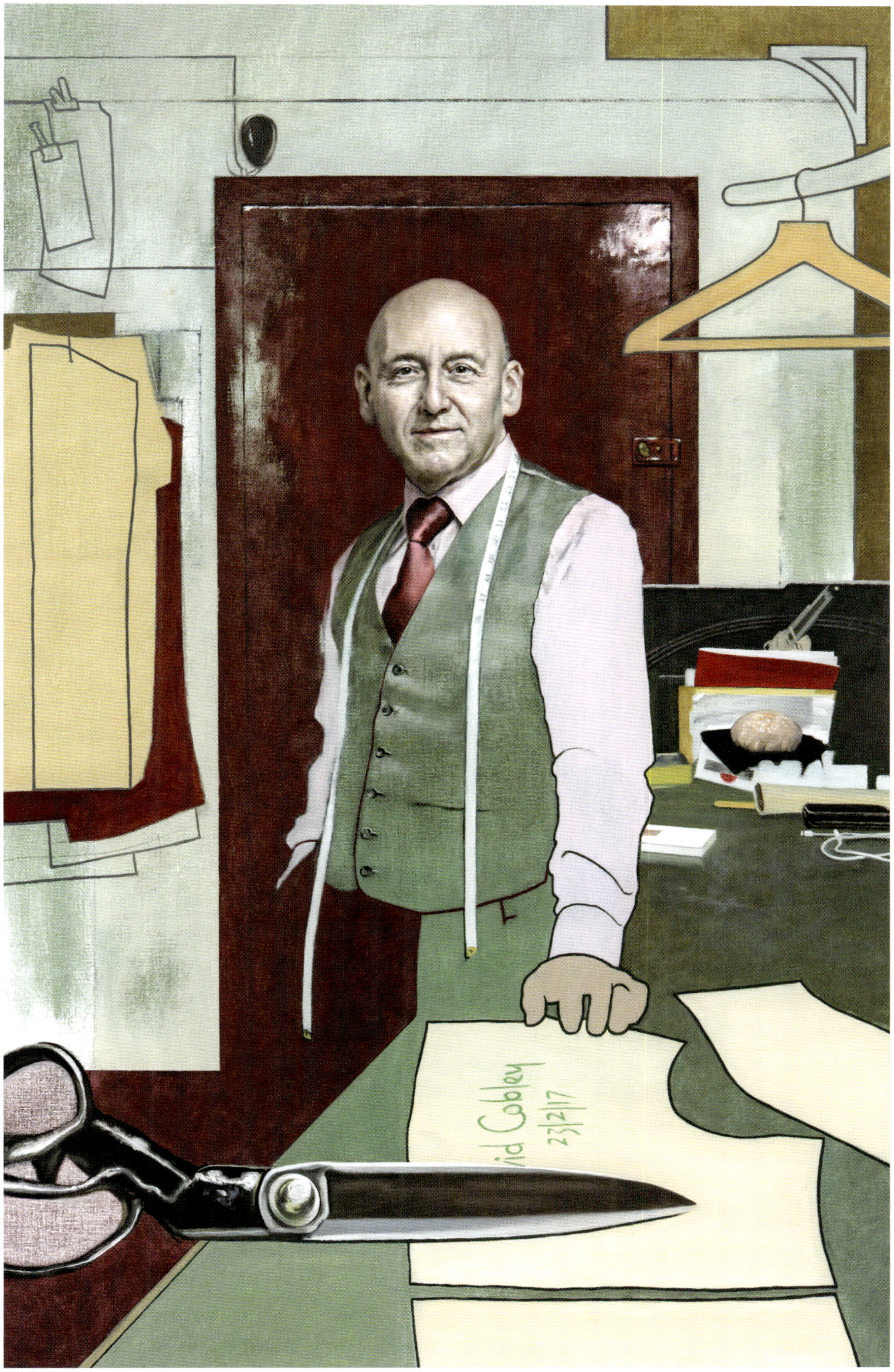

Made to Measure | 2017 | oil on linen | 89 x 64 cm Smallwood Architects

Blues, Beer and Rock 'n' Roll
2008 | oil on linen | 122 x 122 cm
private collection

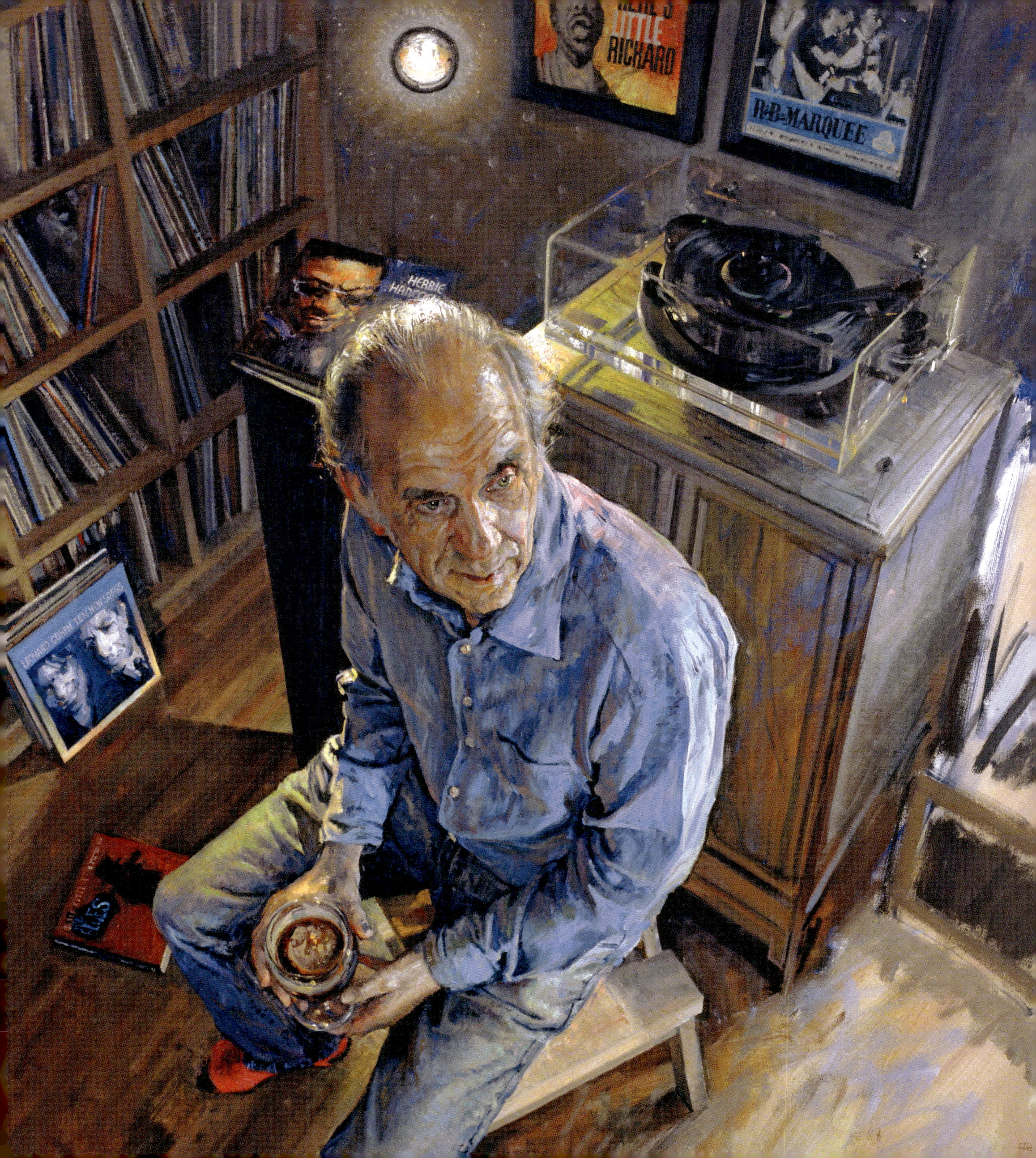
LITTLE
RICHARD
R&B MARQUEE
HERBIE
LEONARD COHEN TEN NEW SONGS
BLUES

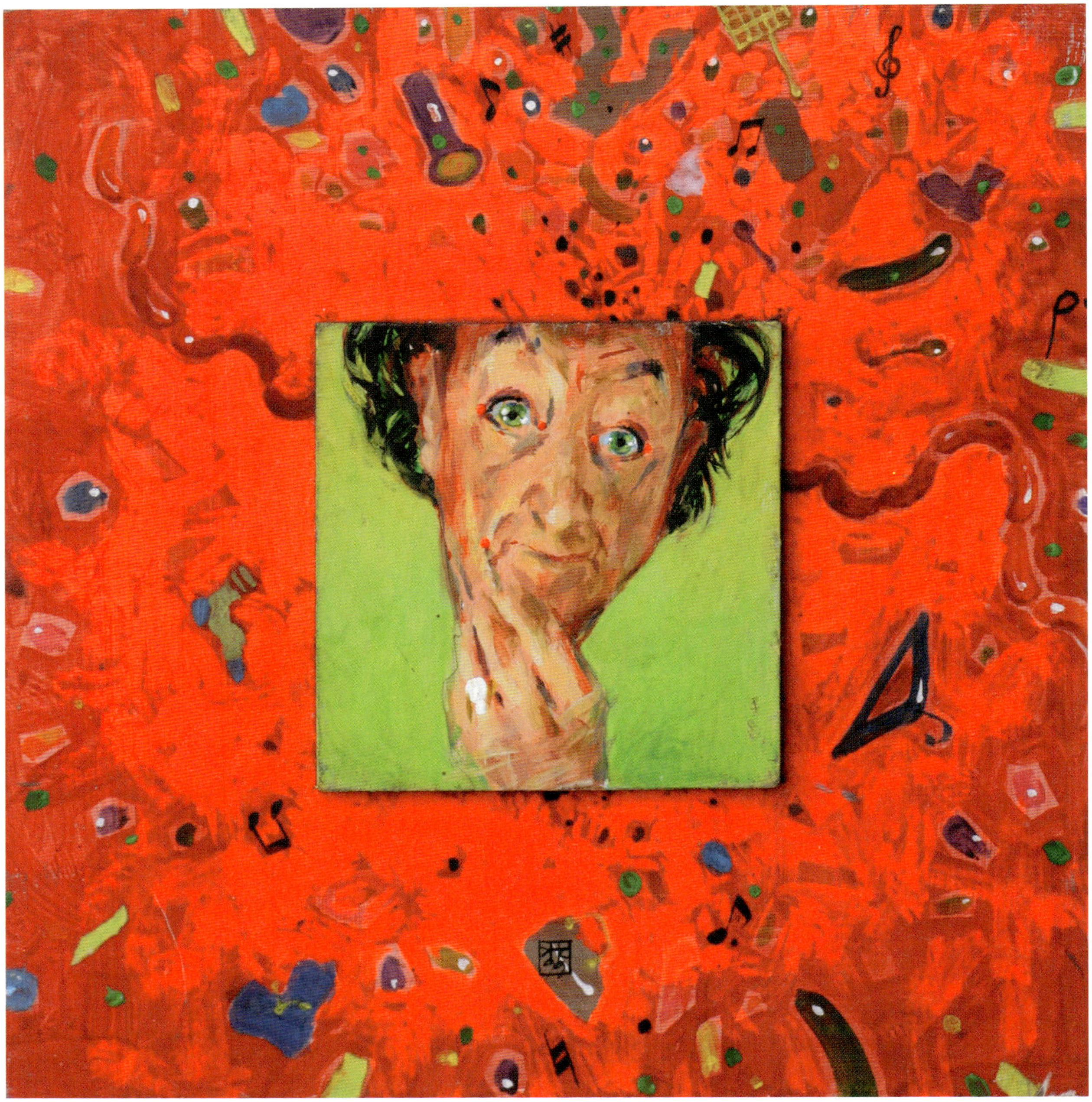

Study for the portrait of Ken Dodd | 1999 | acrylic | 30.5 x 30.5 cm collection of the artist

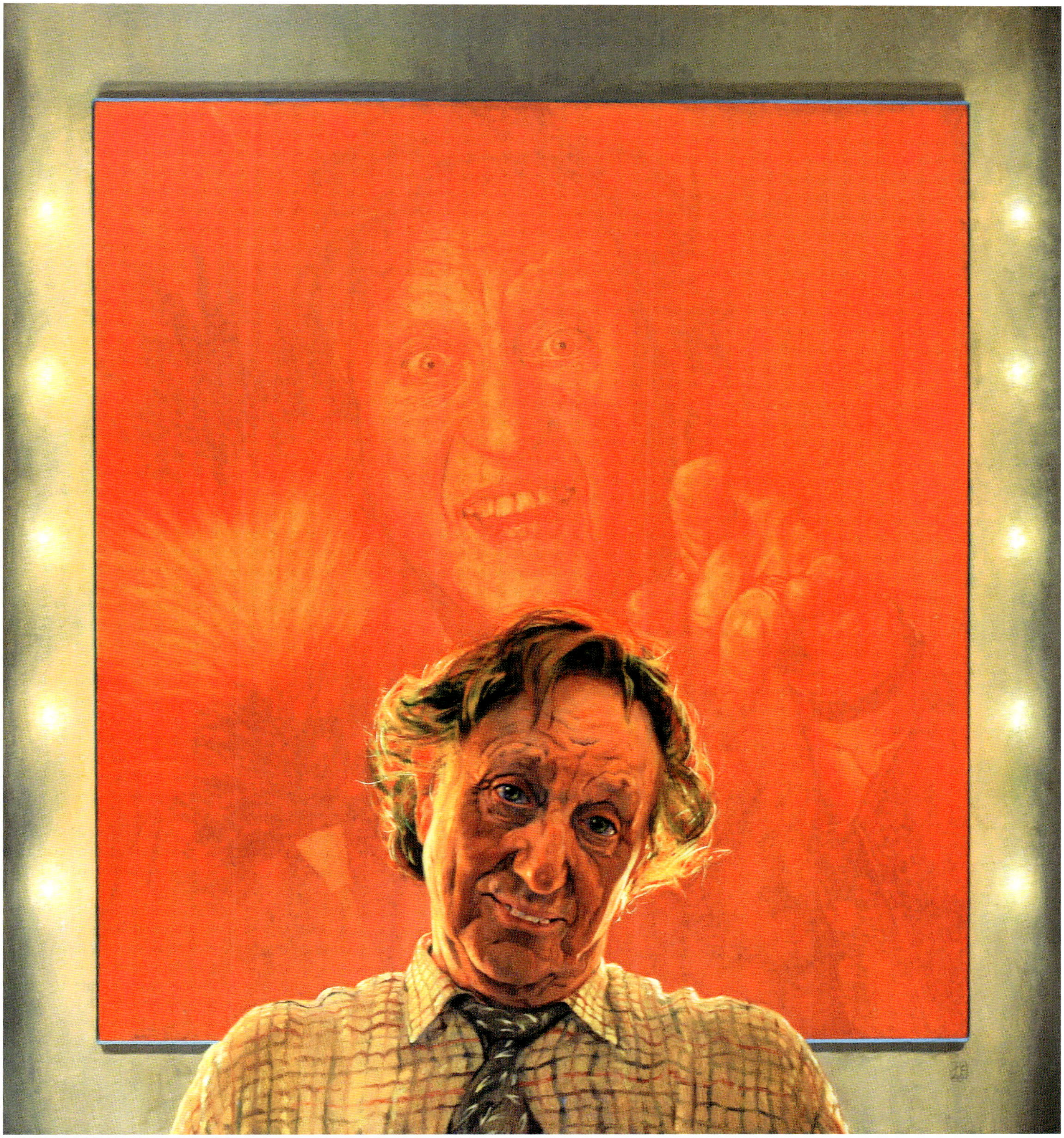

Sir Ken Dodd OBE | 2000 | oil on linen | 91.5 x 86.5 cm private collection

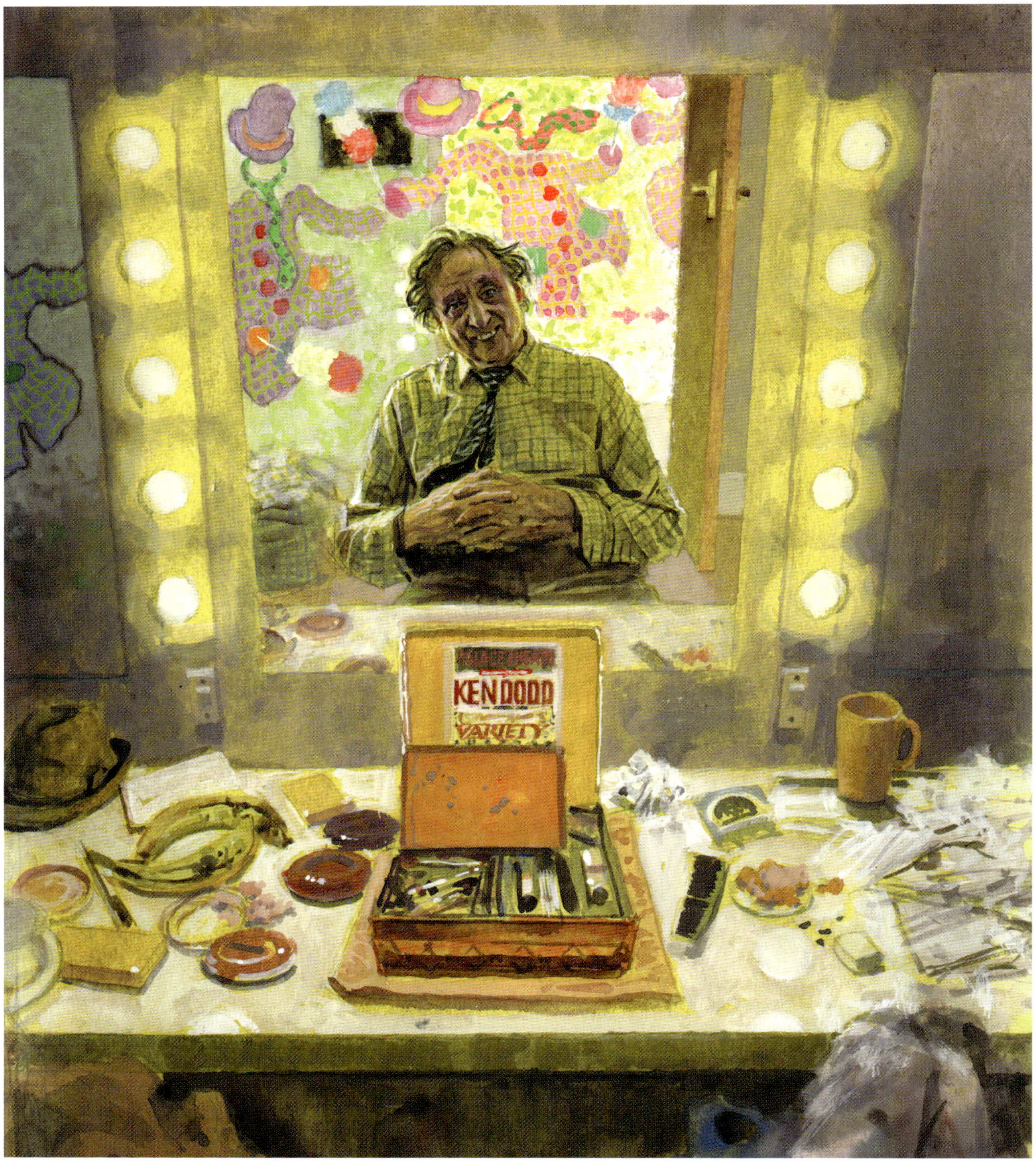

Study for the portrait of Ken Dodd | 2001 | gouache | 30.5 x 25.5 cm private collection

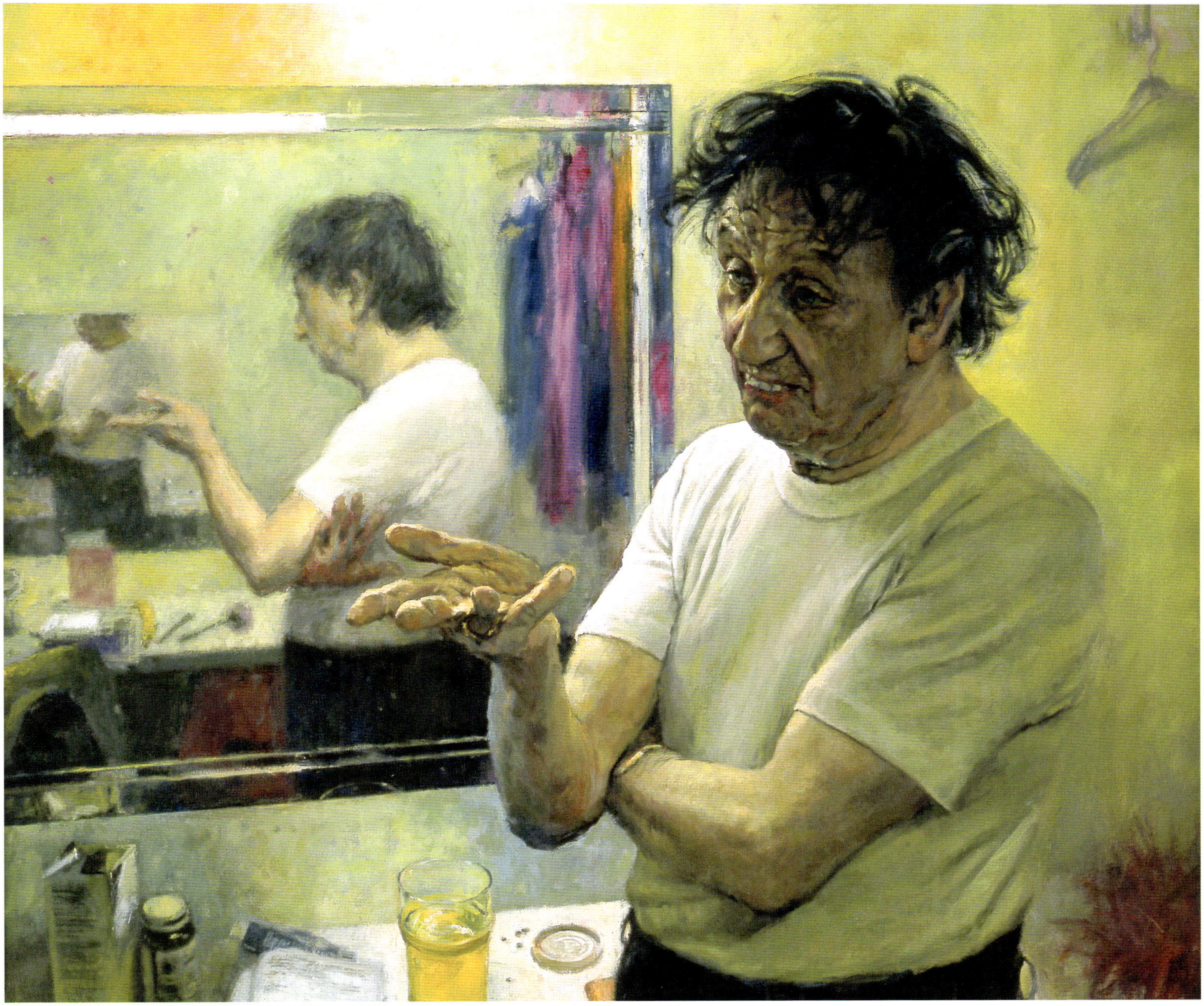

Sir Ken Dodd OBE | 2004 | oil on linen | 76 x 91.5 cm

National Portrait Gallery

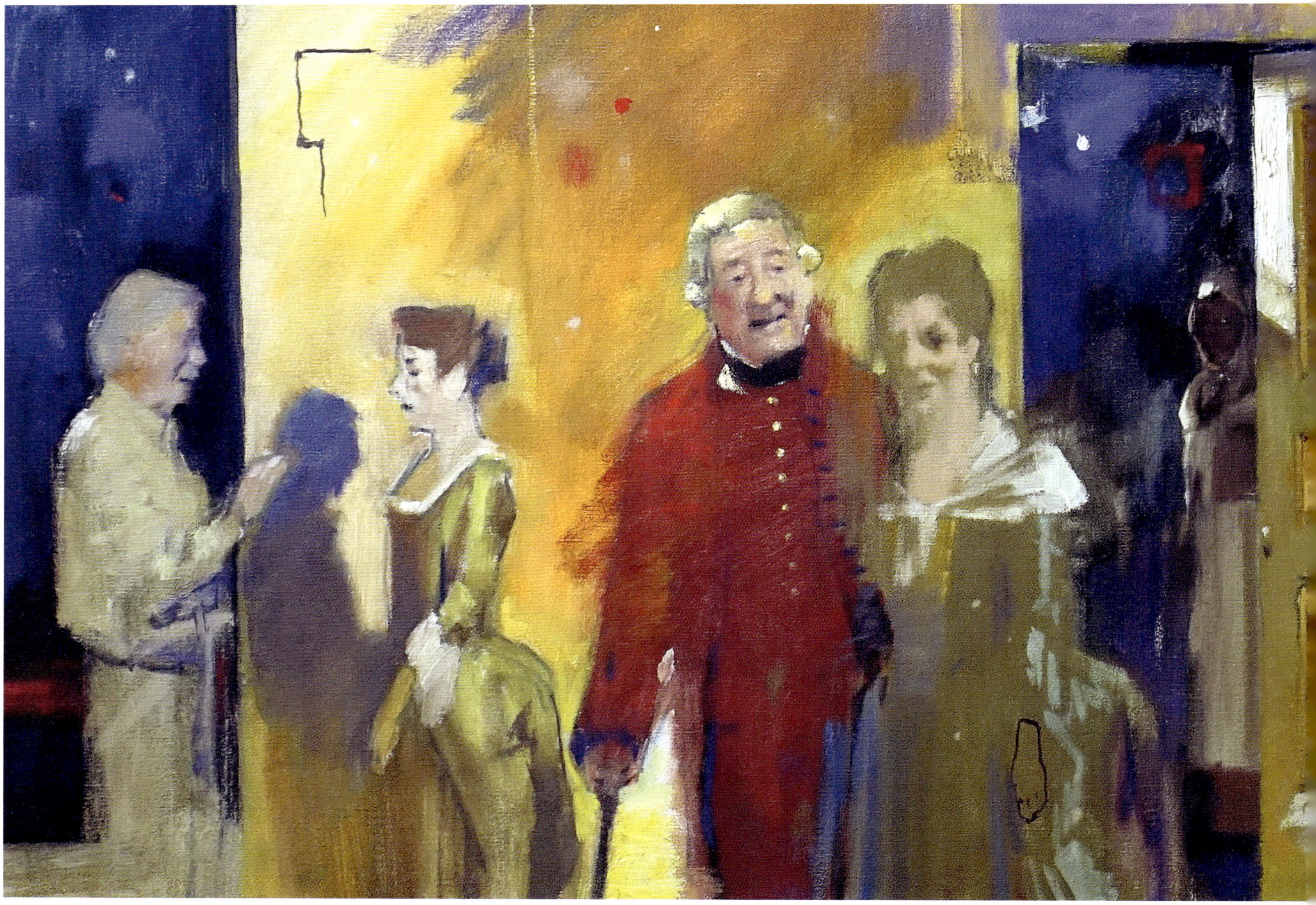

Stephanie Cole in 'The Rivals' | 2005 | oil on linen | 40.5 x 122 cm

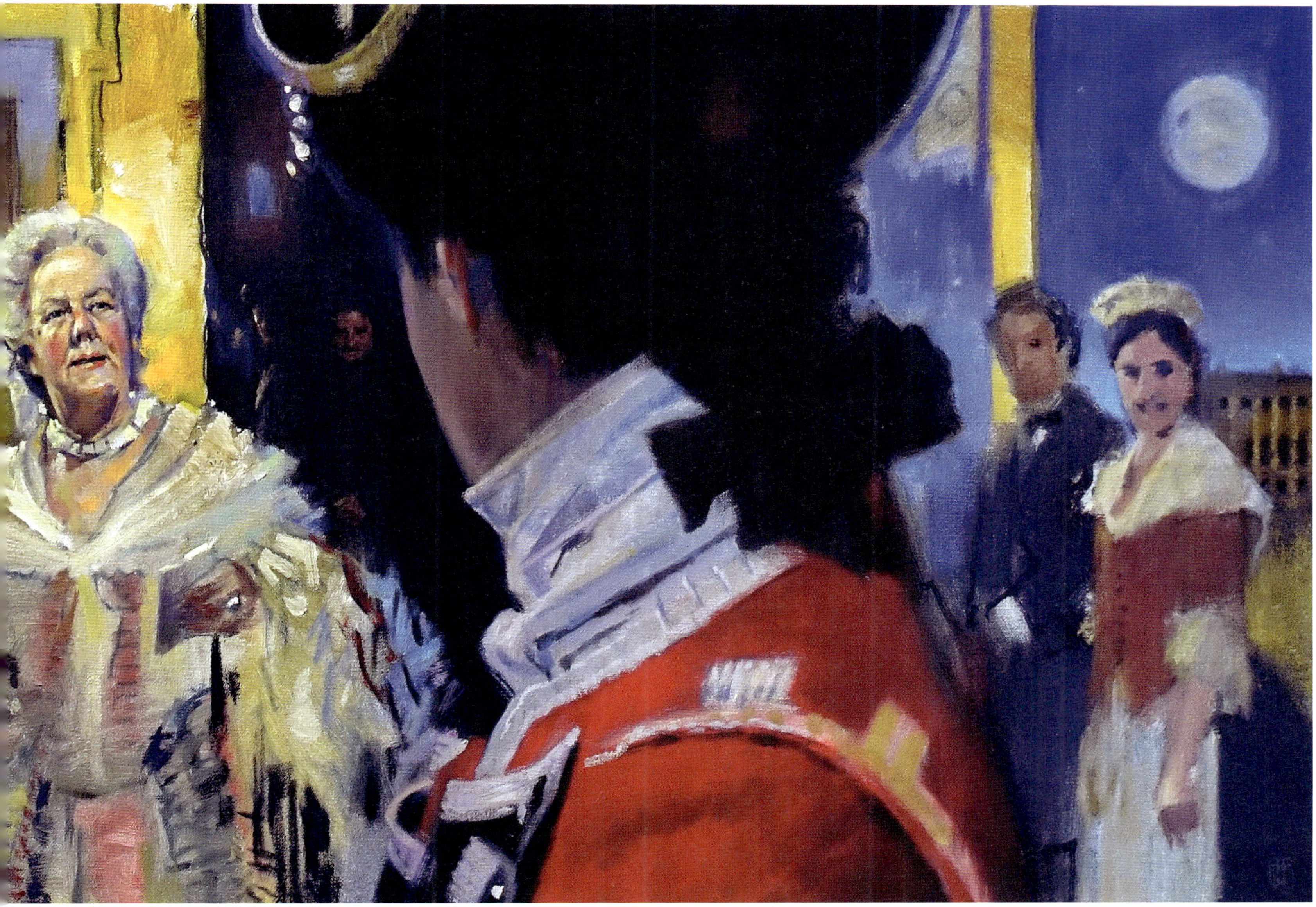

private collection

Here We All Are
2013 | oil on linen | 200 x 225 cm
collection of the artist

Life is like a circus – one that's full of comedy and tragedy at every turn. This action-packed painting contains images of beauty, cruelty, kindness, anger, love, joy, sadness, grief, fun, ecstasy, madness, pain, magic, darkness, light, struggle, hope and fear, and uses perspective, rhythm, movement and colour to create the illusion of human activity frozen in time and space.

Its subject matter is people: you, me, the bloke down the road and the little girl on the streets of Mumbai. Despite superficial differences, we are so much alike, and we are all in it together.

From time to time we have all wondered what it might be like to be someone else. With a little imagination we could be that young boy jumping, that old woman grieving or that angry young man cursing his luck. Despite our reluctance to acknowledge it, each of us is capable of great cruelty as well as great kindness. Most of us would be prepared to die for someone we cared deeply enough about, but equally prepared to kill someone if our own, or a loved one's, life depended on it. And even though we might recoil at the suggestion that we are anything like the murderers, rapists, cheats or fraudsters we read about in the news, my own view is that we have more in common with them than we care to admit.

My intention in painting this picture was to invite you, the viewer, to step into it and make the transition from onlooker to one of the crowd, leaving you as dazzled and confused, repelled and amazed, delighted and horrified, disheartened and exhilarated as I am by what I see and hear going on around me.

David Cobley, 2013

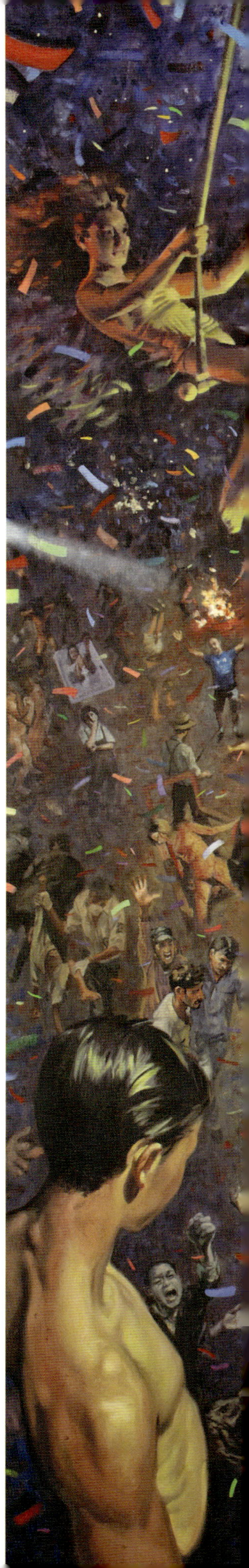

overleaf
Bandwagon to Oblivion
1992 | oil on linen | 117 x 213.5 cm
collection of the artist

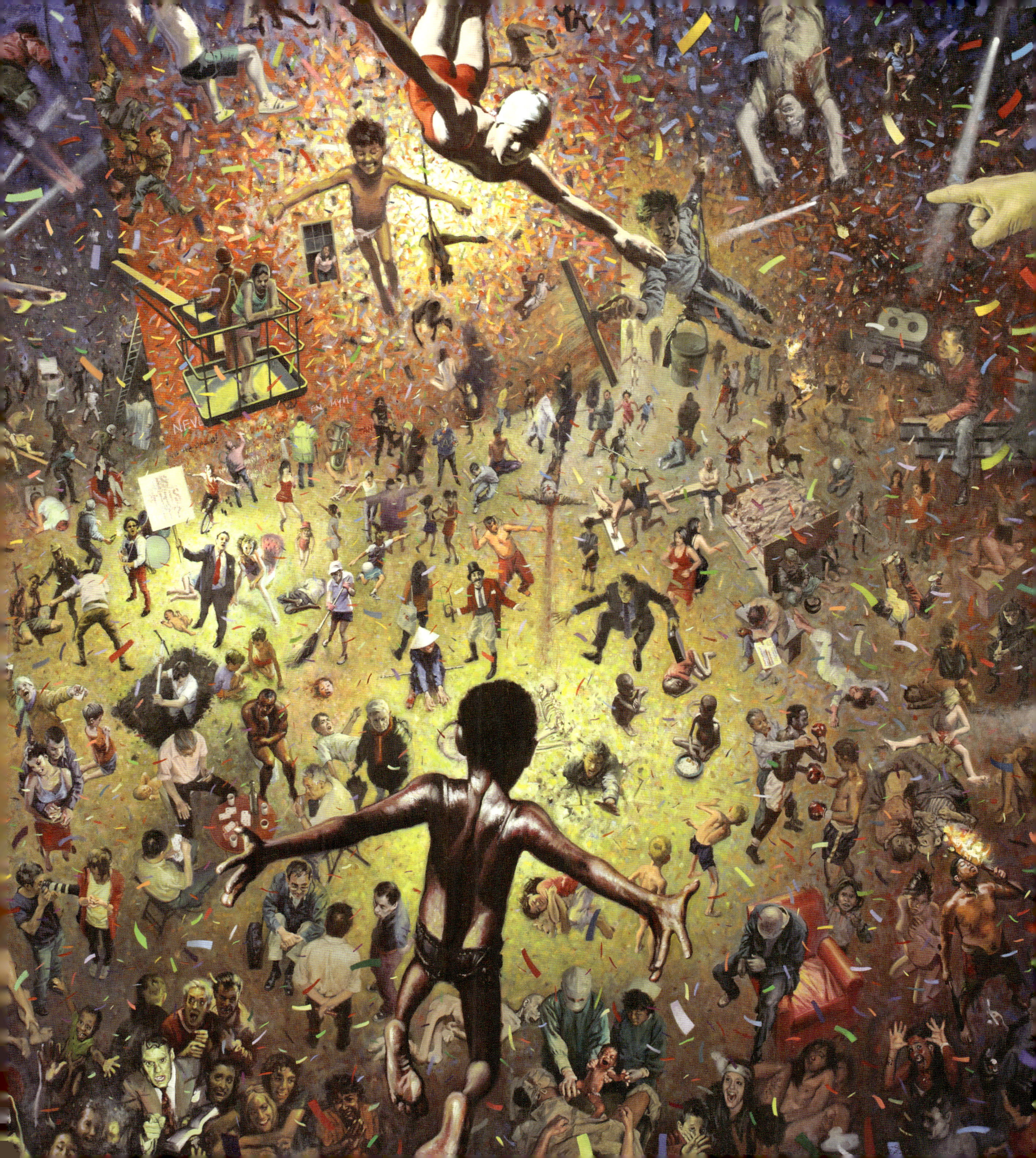

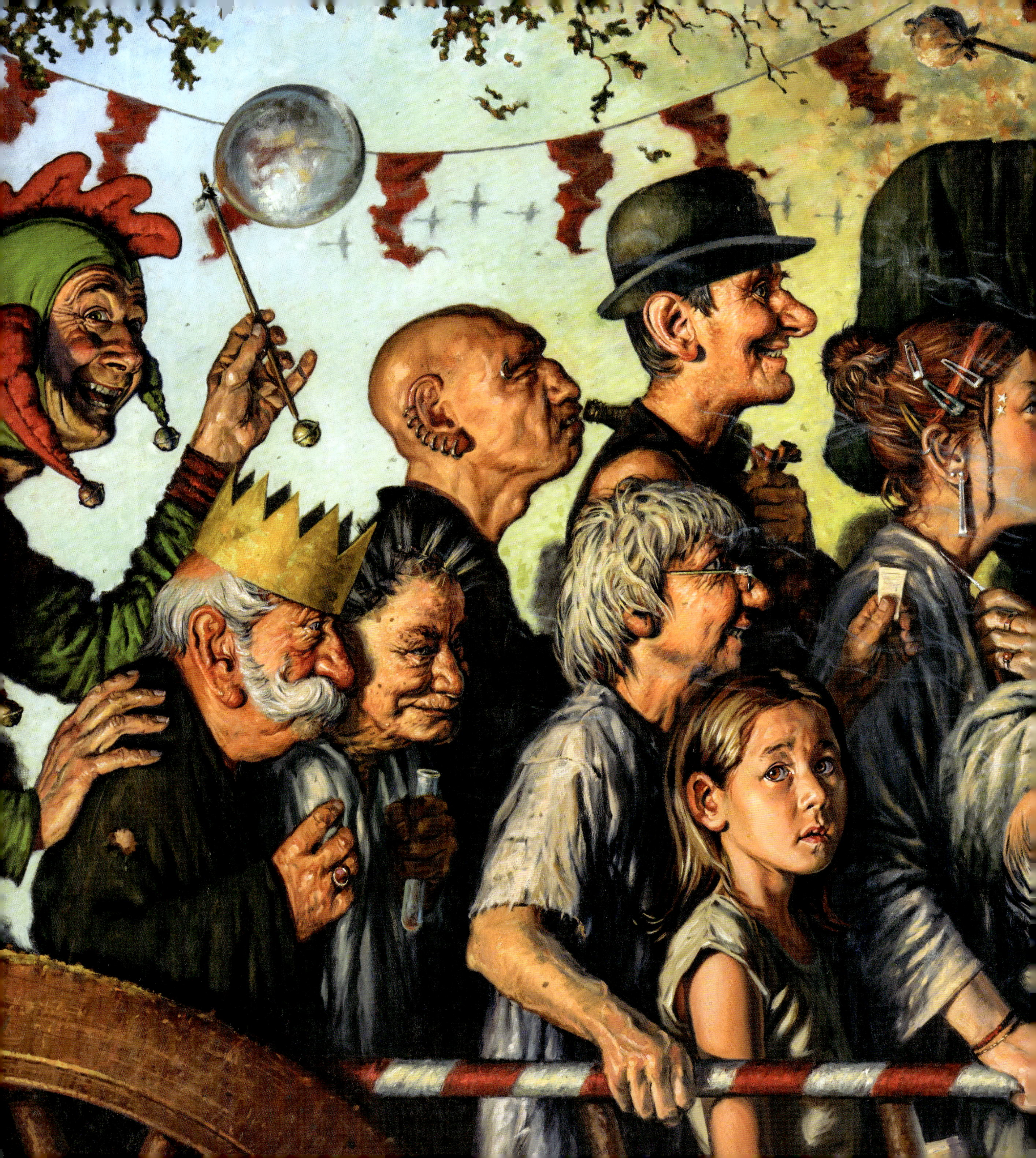

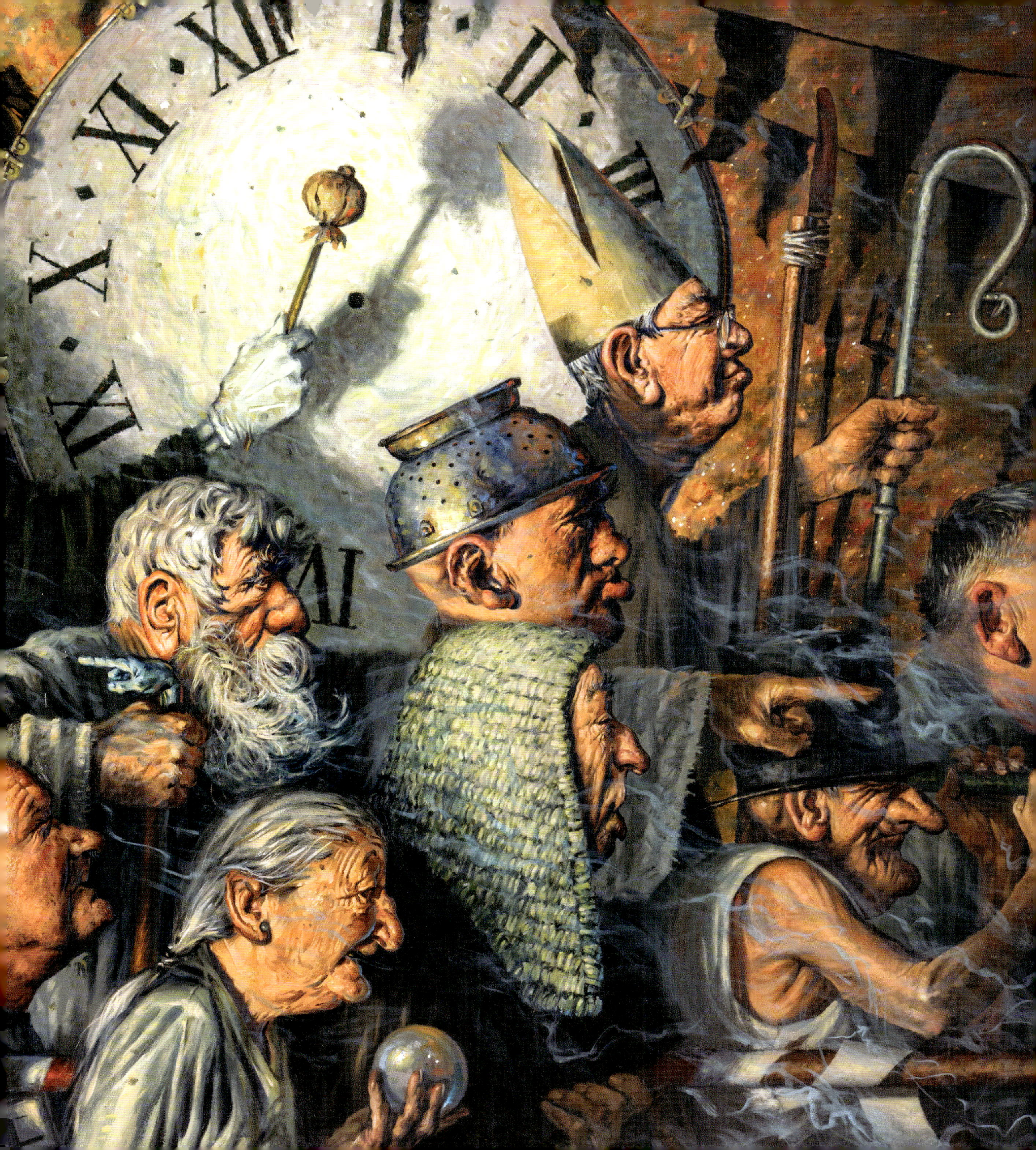

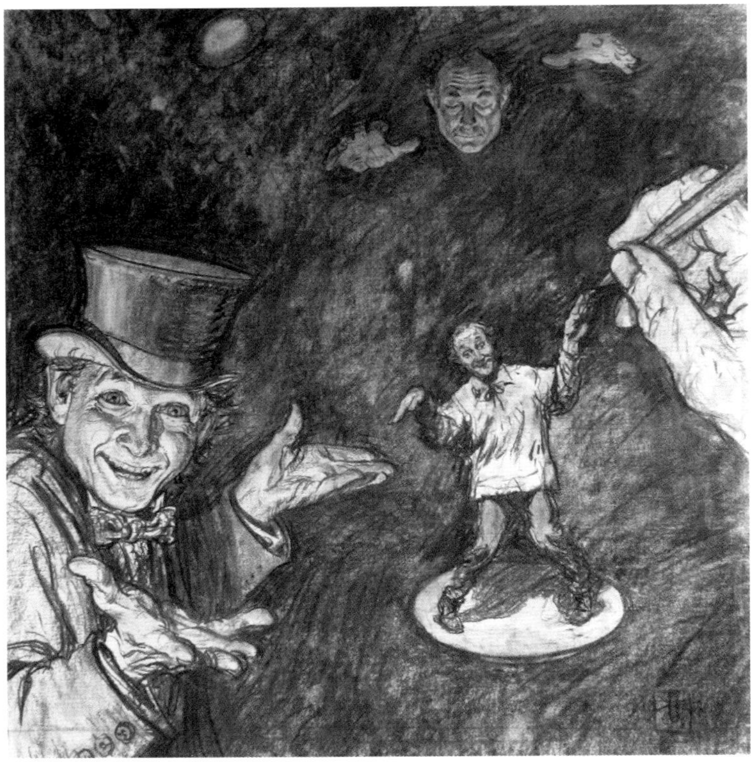

Muppets
1999 | charcoal | 63.5 x 63.5 cm
collection of the artist

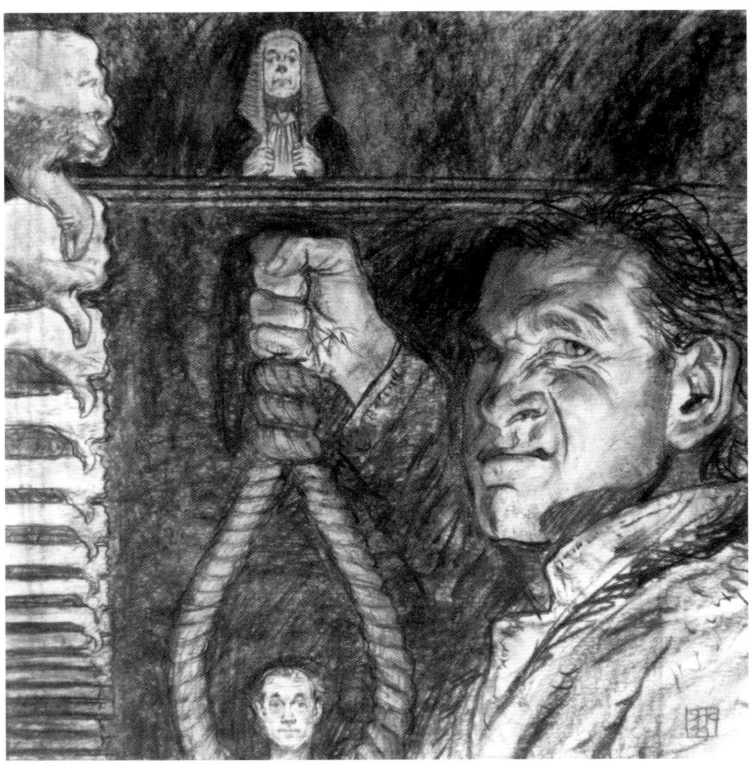

Judge and Jury
1999 | charcoal | 63.5 x 63.5 cm
collection of the artist

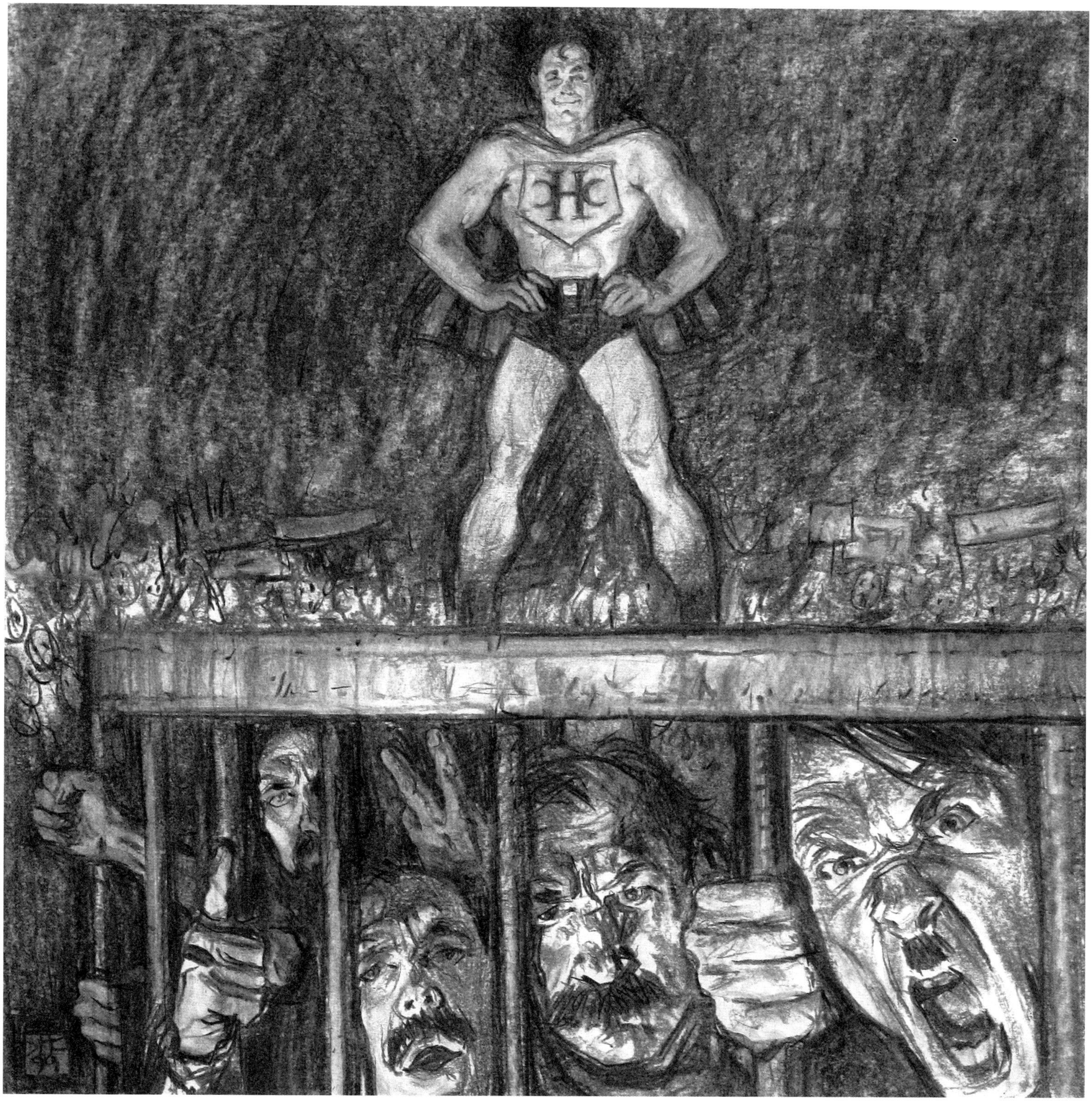

My Hero | 1999 | charcoal | 63.5 x 63.5 cm

collection of the artist

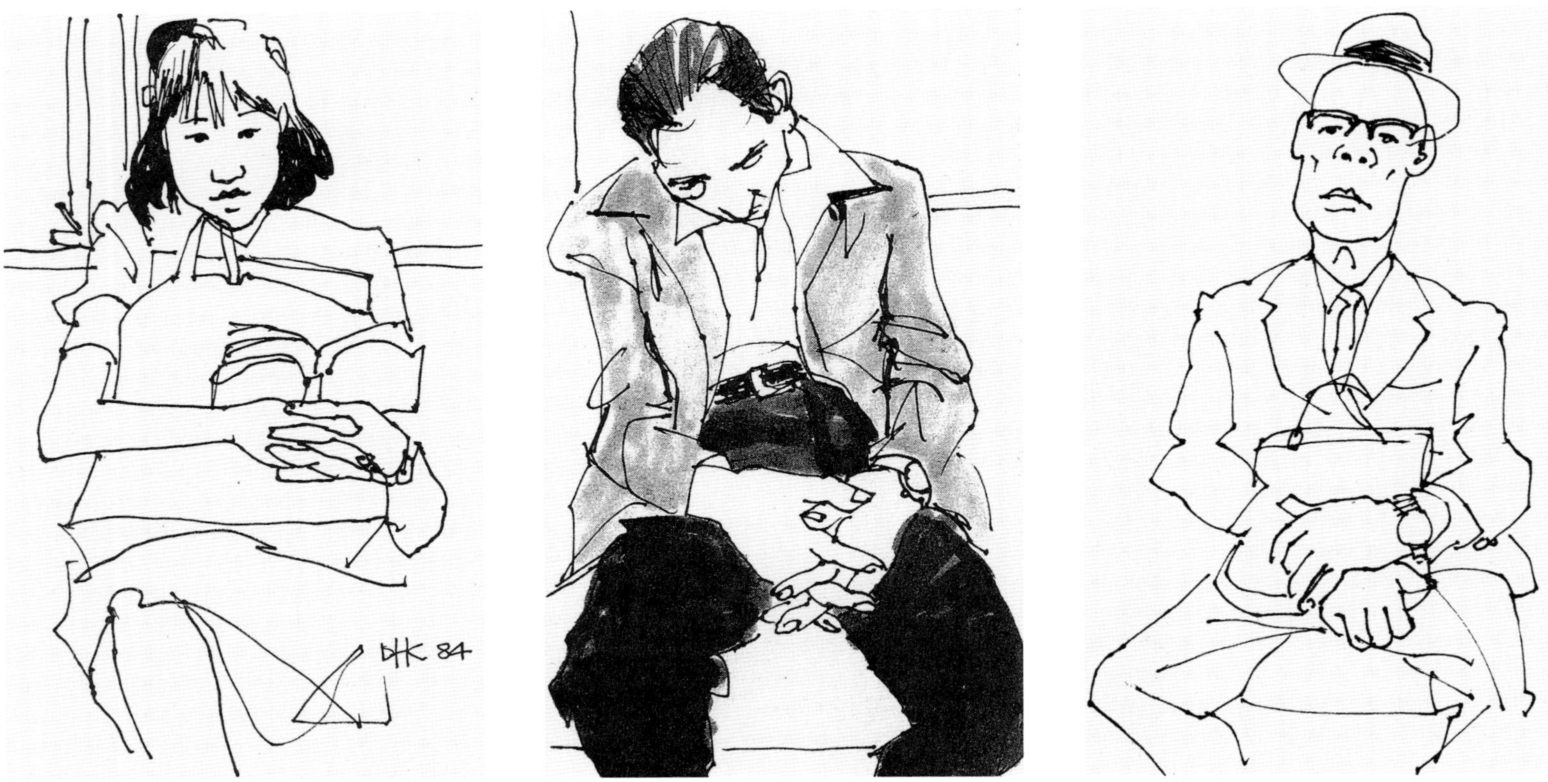

On the Subway I–III | 1984 | magic marker | 20.5 x 15.5 cm

private collection

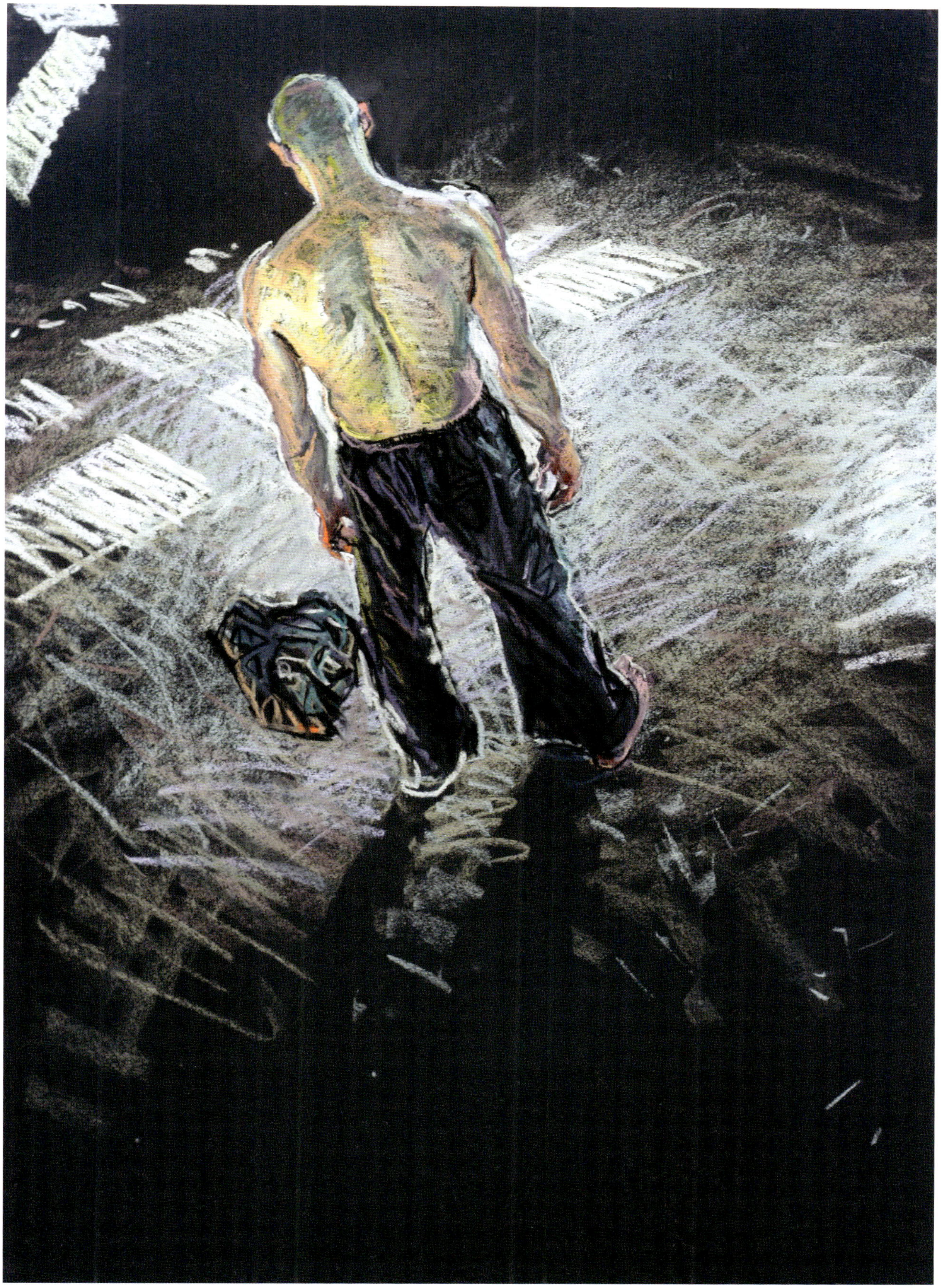

Fighter | 1997 | pastel | 75 x 54.5 cm

collection of the artist

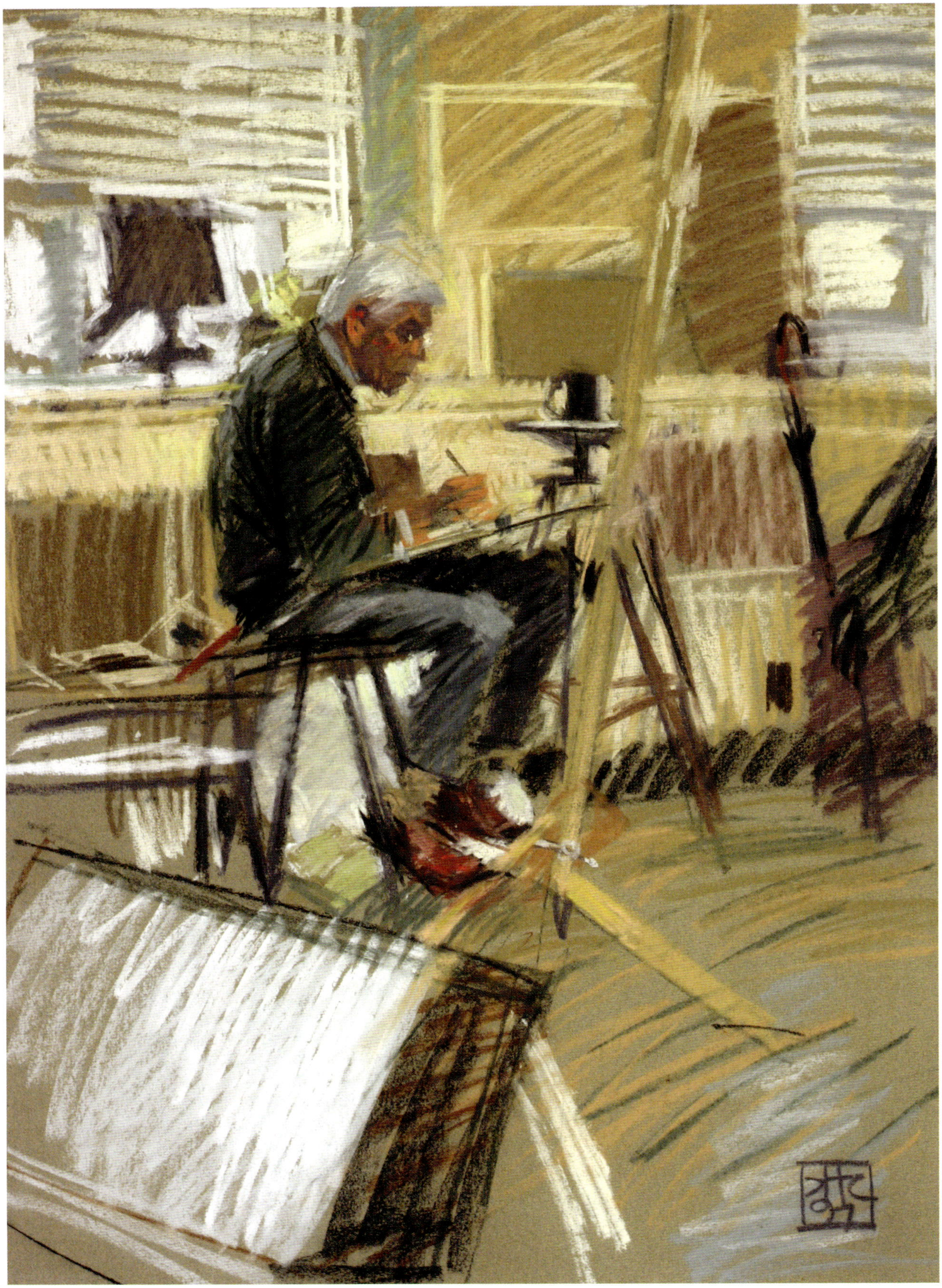

Drawing in the Schoolroom I | 1997 | pastel | 68 x 51 cm collection of the artist

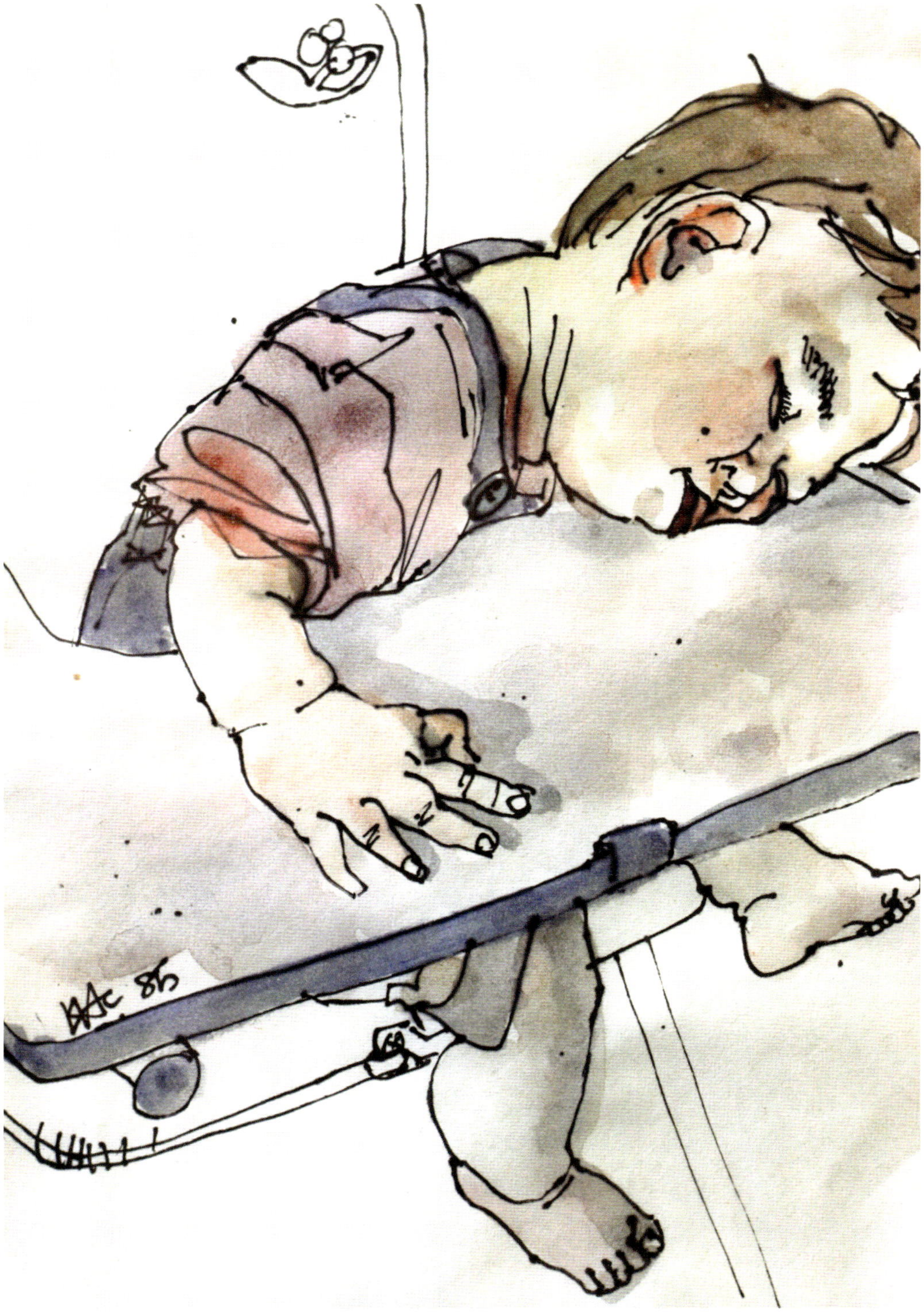

So Tired | 1985 | magic marker and wash | 20.5 x 15.5 cm collection of the artist

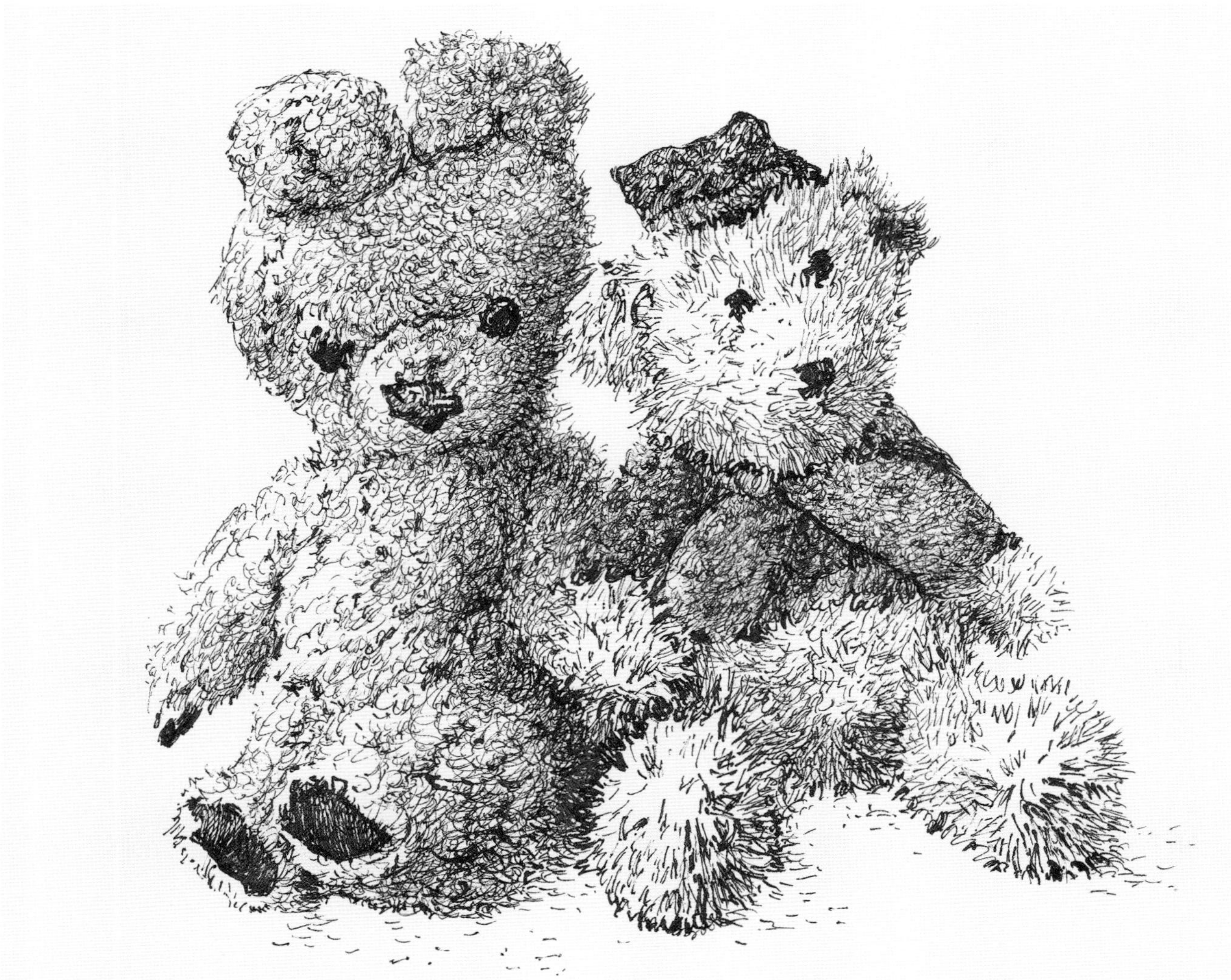

Two Teddy Bears | 2014 | rollerball pen | 20.5 x 25.5 cm

private collection

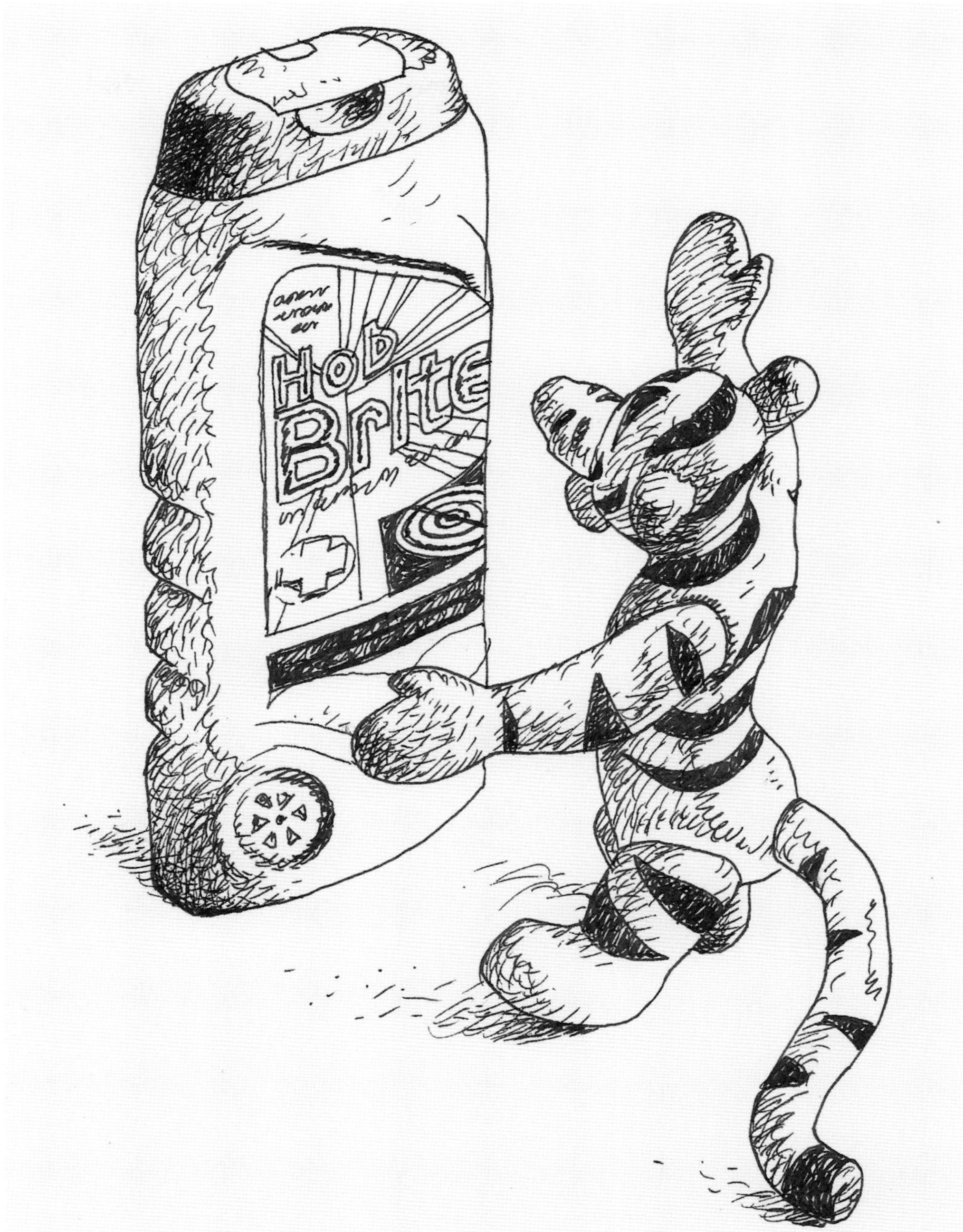

Tigger, on Discovering He's the Same Colour as a Well-known Hob Cleaner
2017 | rollerball pen | 25.5 x 20.5 cm
collection of the artist

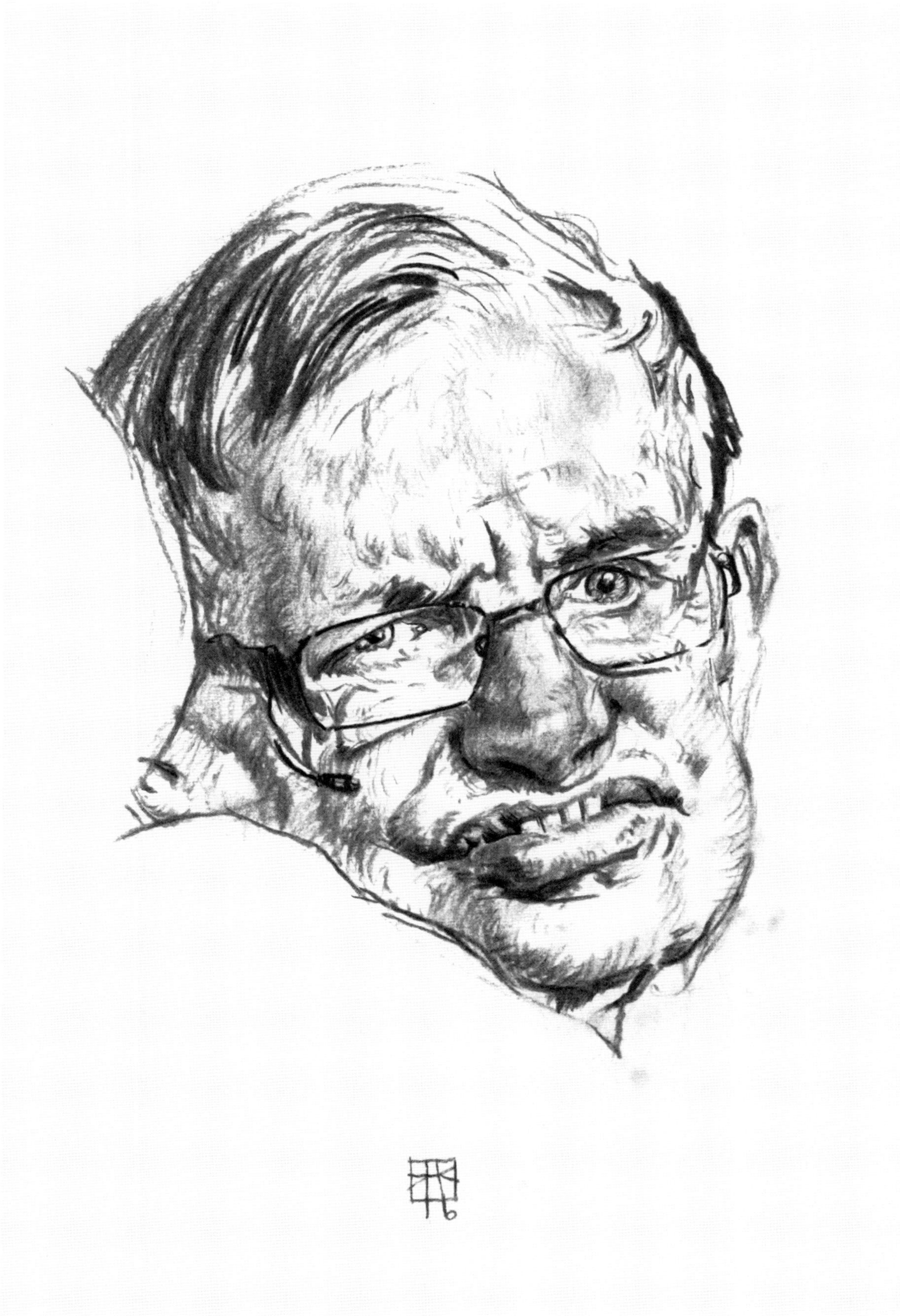

Stephen Hawking | 2016 | charcoal | 42 x 29.5 cm

University College Oxford

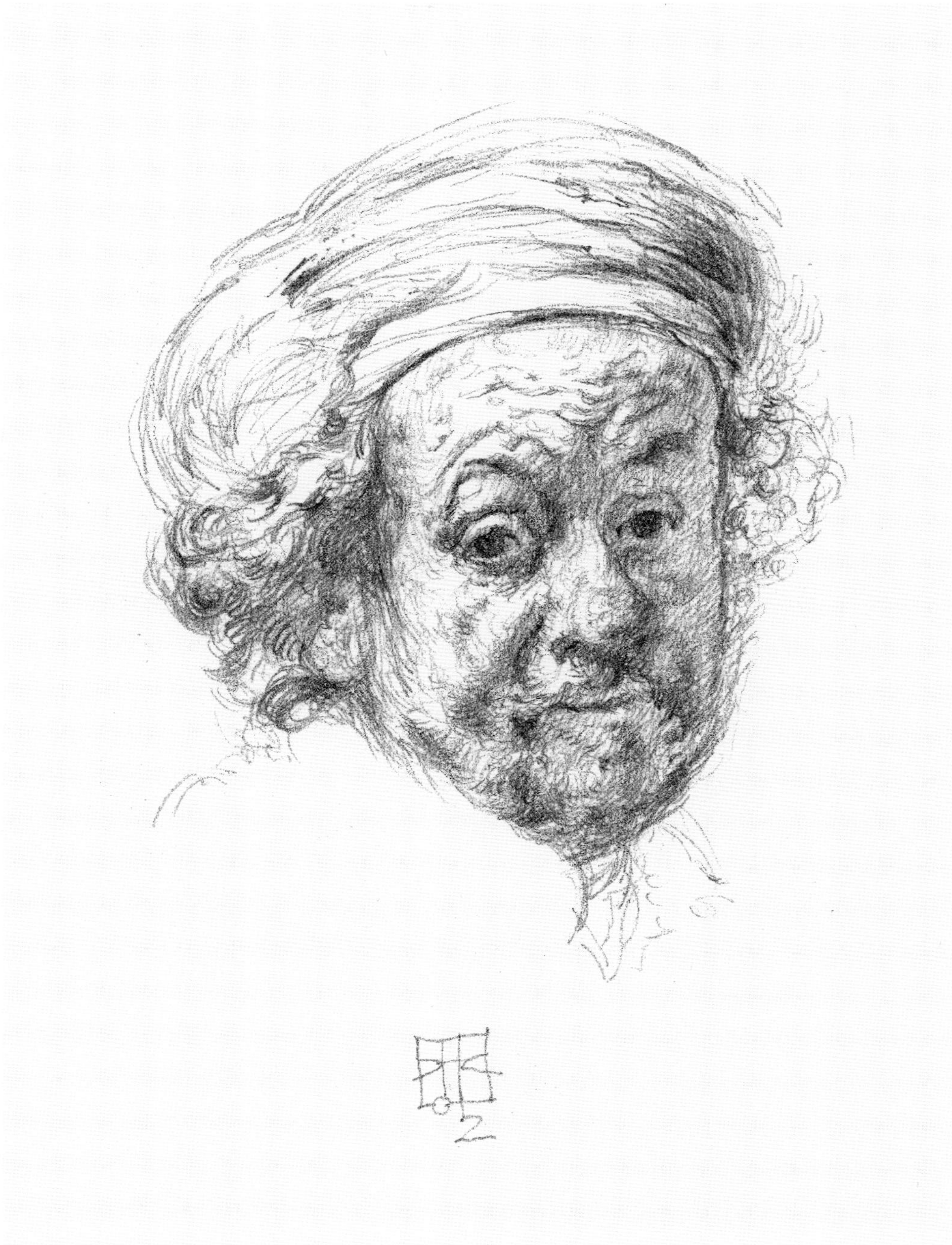

Self Portrait as the Apostle Paul by Rembrandt
2012 | pencil | 25.5 x 20.5 cm
collection of the artist

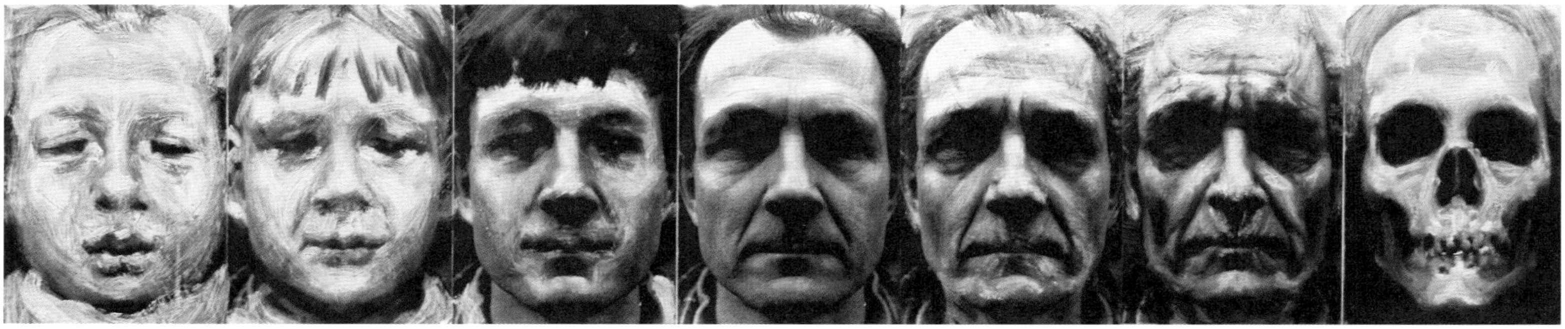

The Seven Ages of Man | 1997 | mixed media | 8.5 x 47.5 cm collection of the artist

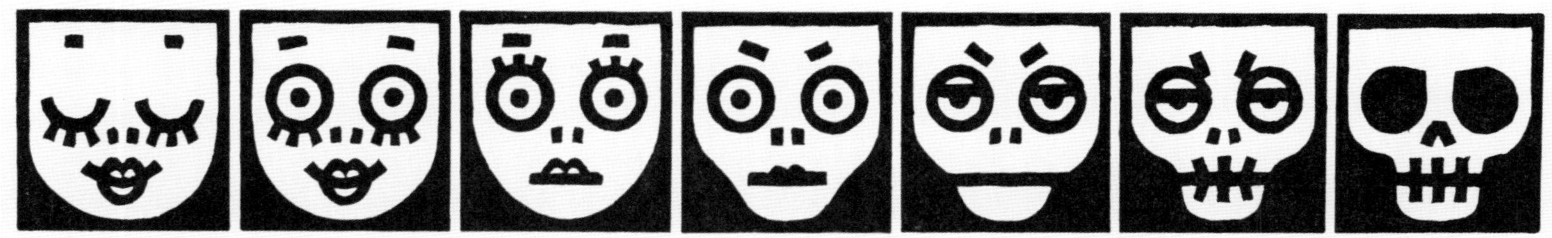

The Seven Ages of Man | 1999 | linocut | 12.5 x 60 cm collection of the artist

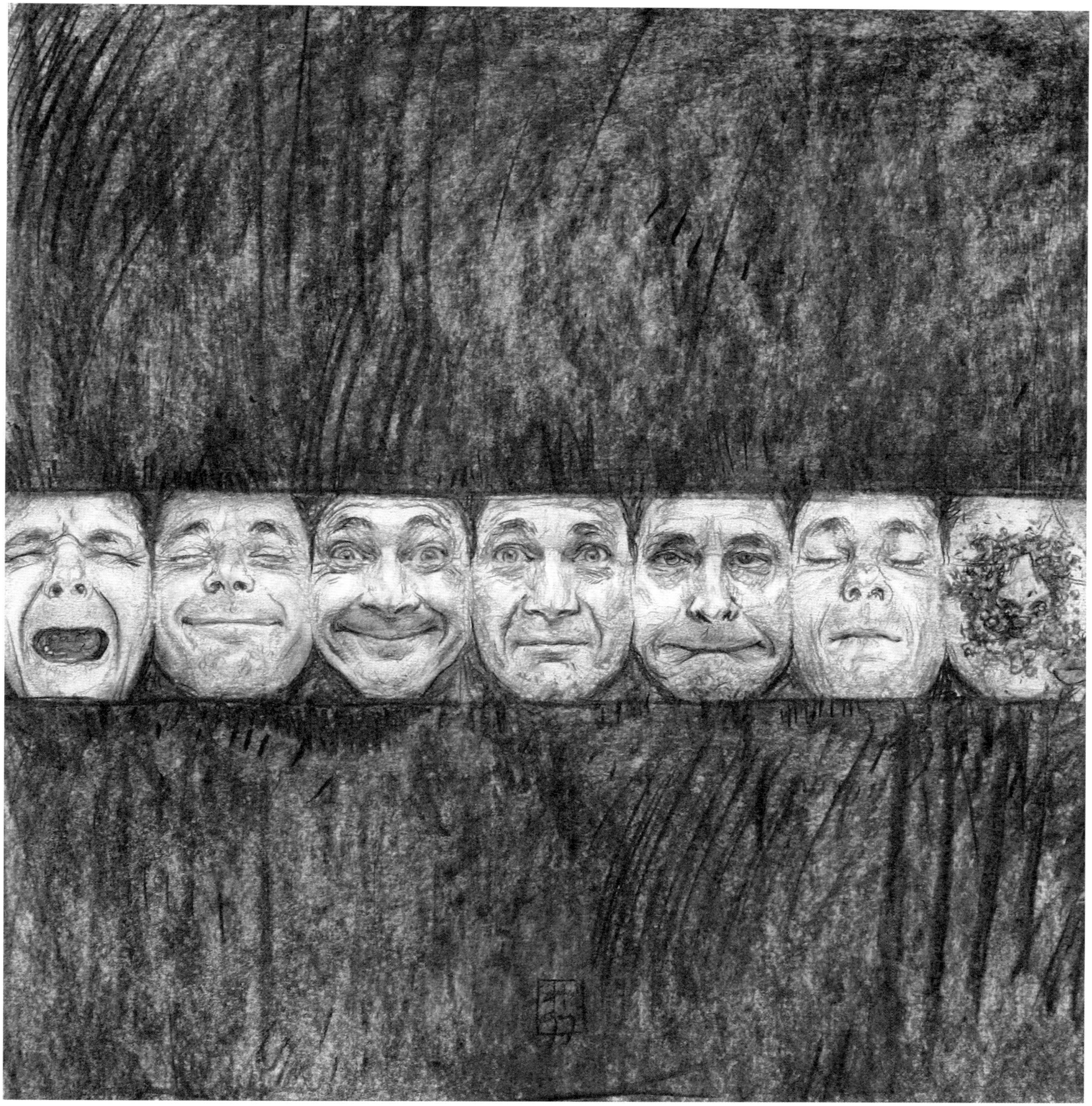

That's Life | 1997 | charcoal | 63.5 x 63.5 cm

collection of the artist

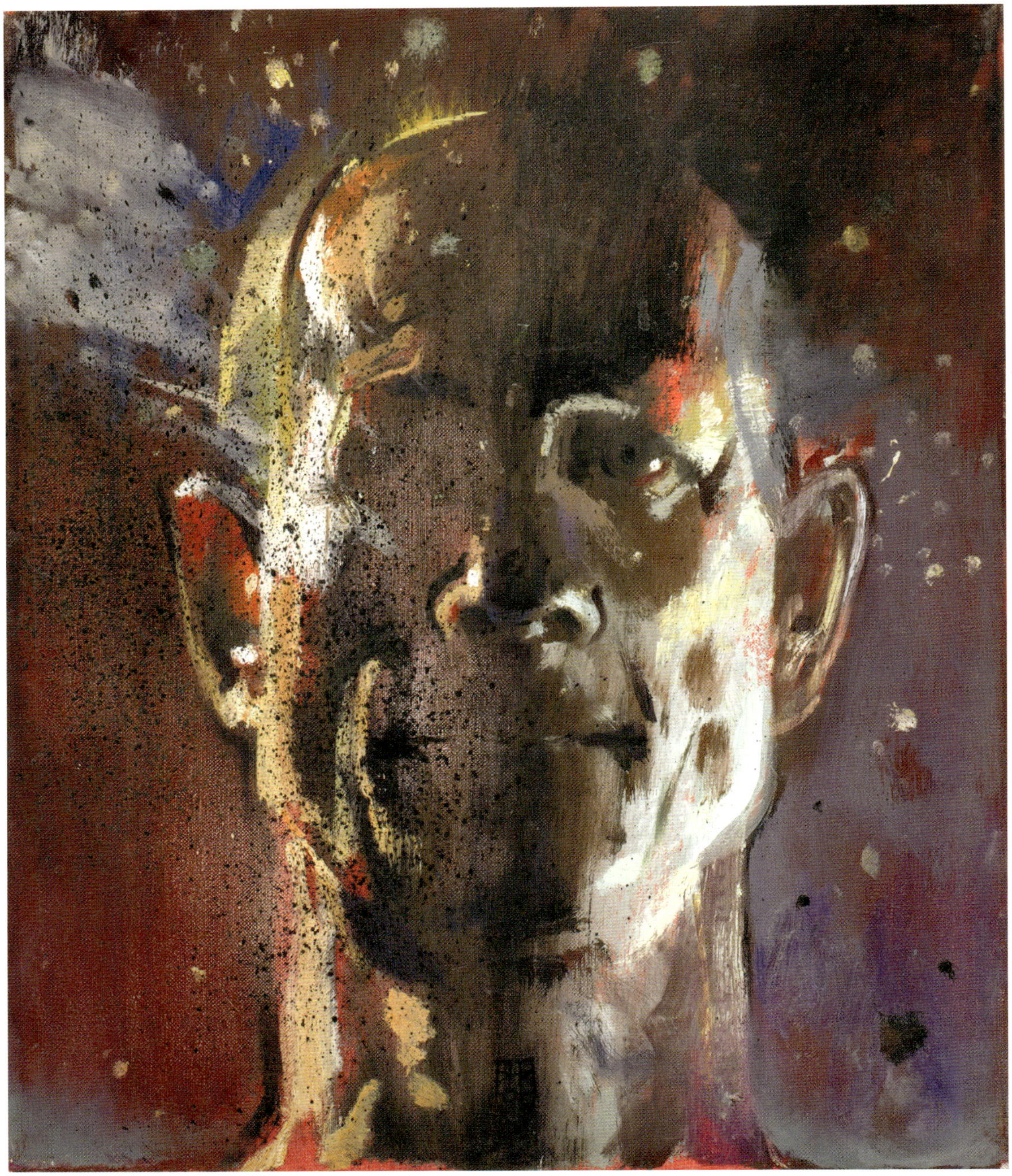

Fragile Hero II | 2001 | oil on linen | 35.5 x 30.5 cm collection of the artist

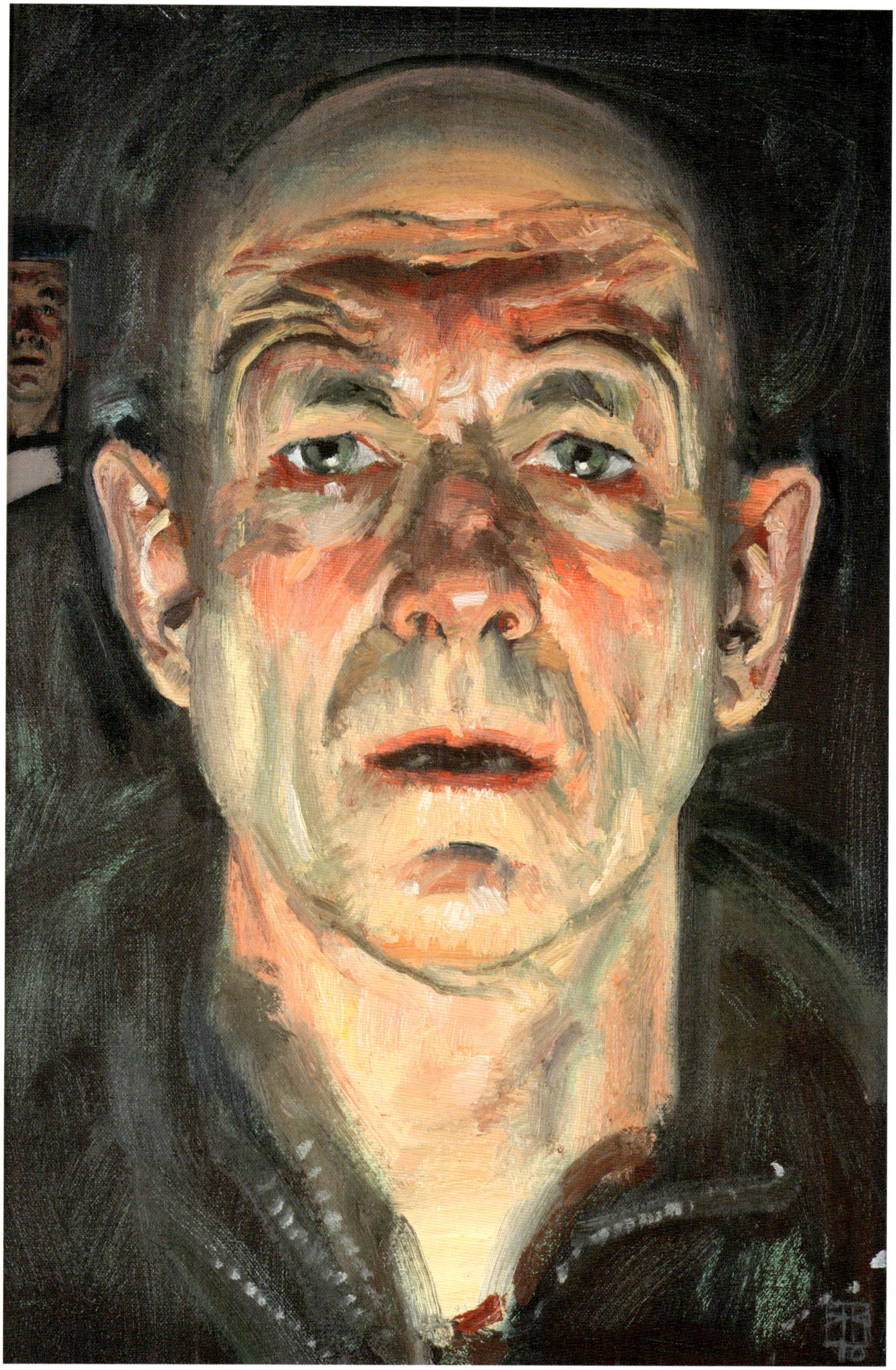

WTF | 2010 | oil on linen | 45.5 x 30.5 cm

private collection

What Are You Doing Here?
2010 | oil on linen | 61 x 61 cm
collection of the artist

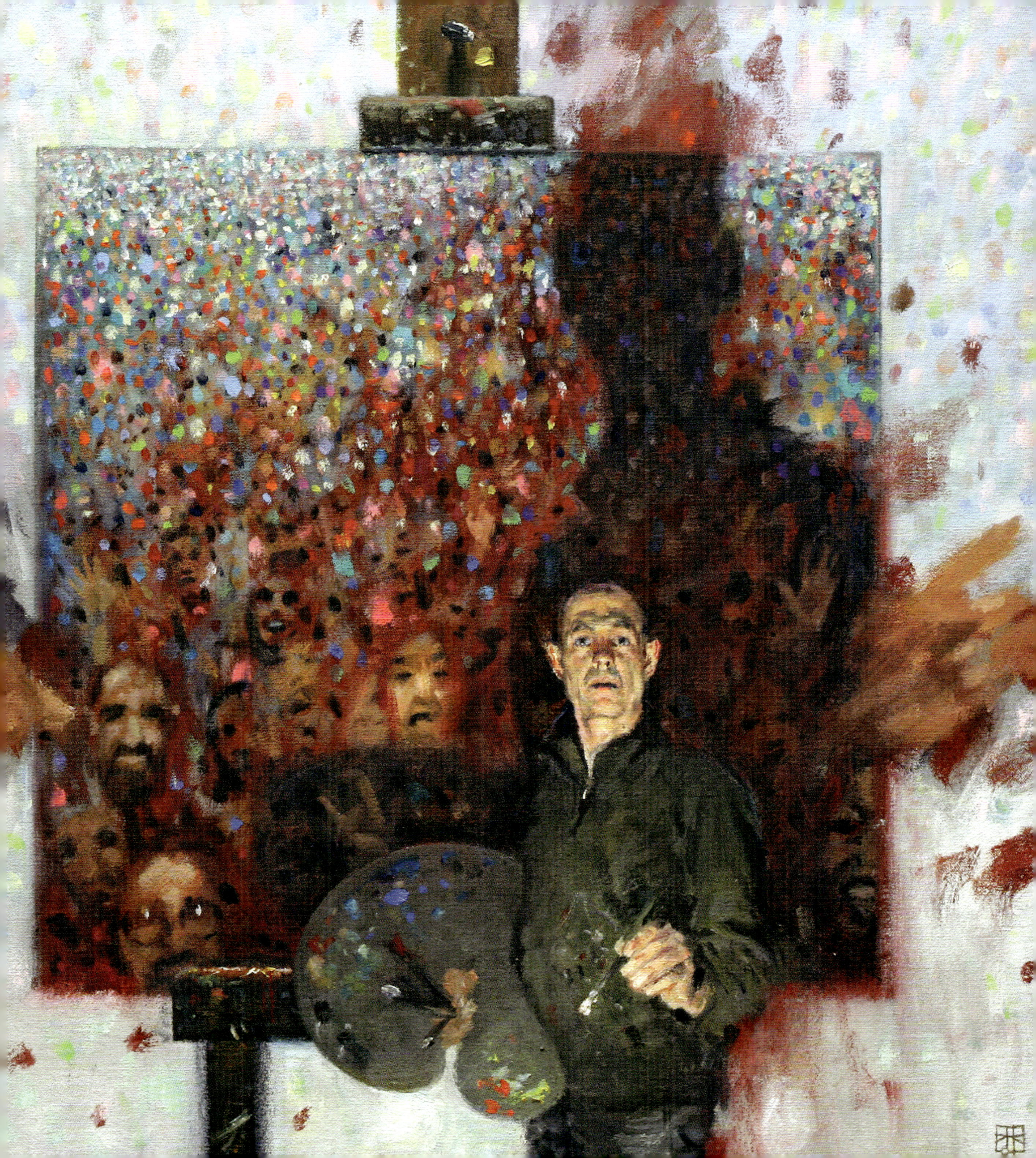

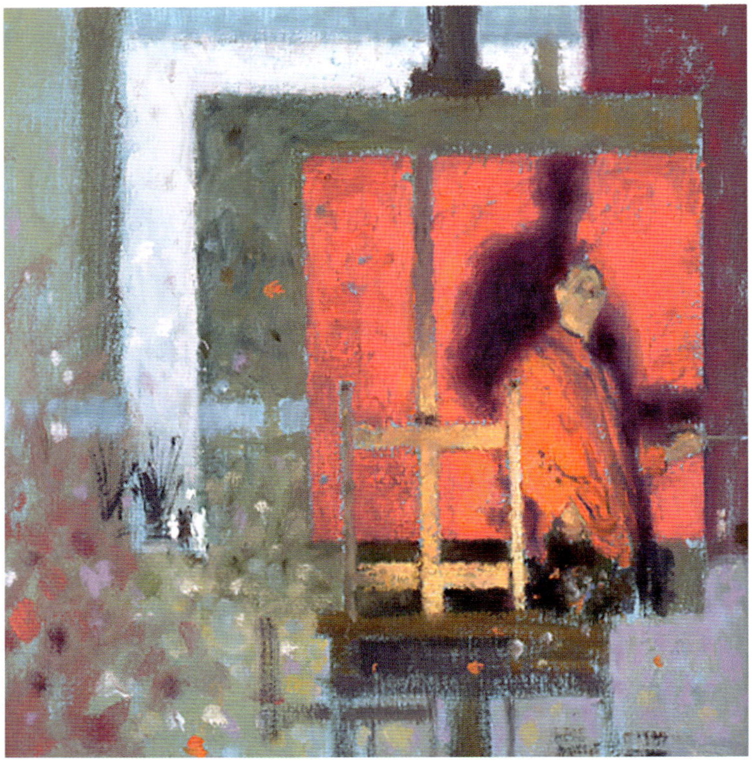

Studio in Pink
2004 | oil on linen | 30.5 x 30.5 cm
private collection

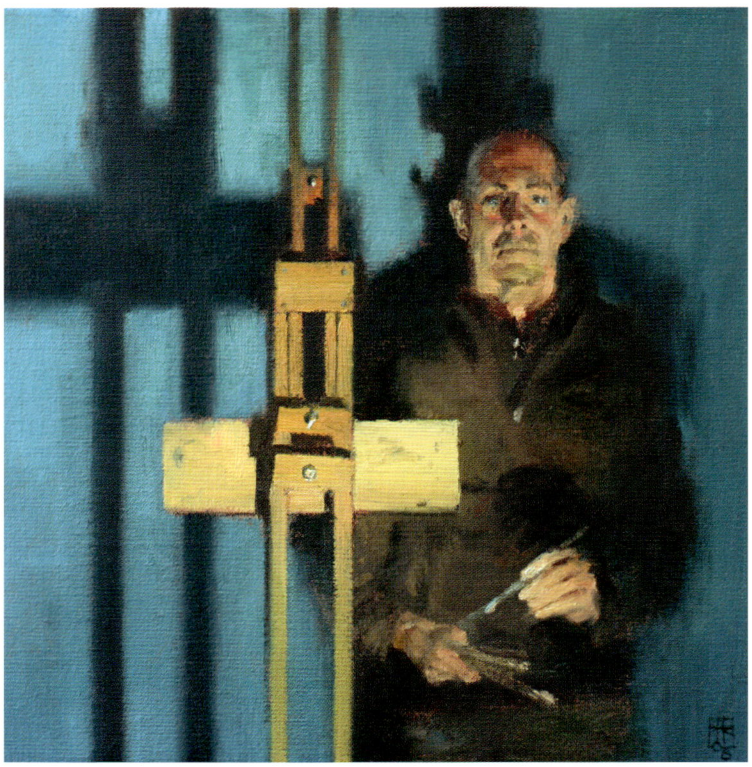

In Turquoise I
2008 | oil on linen | 30.5 x 30.5 cm
collection of the artist

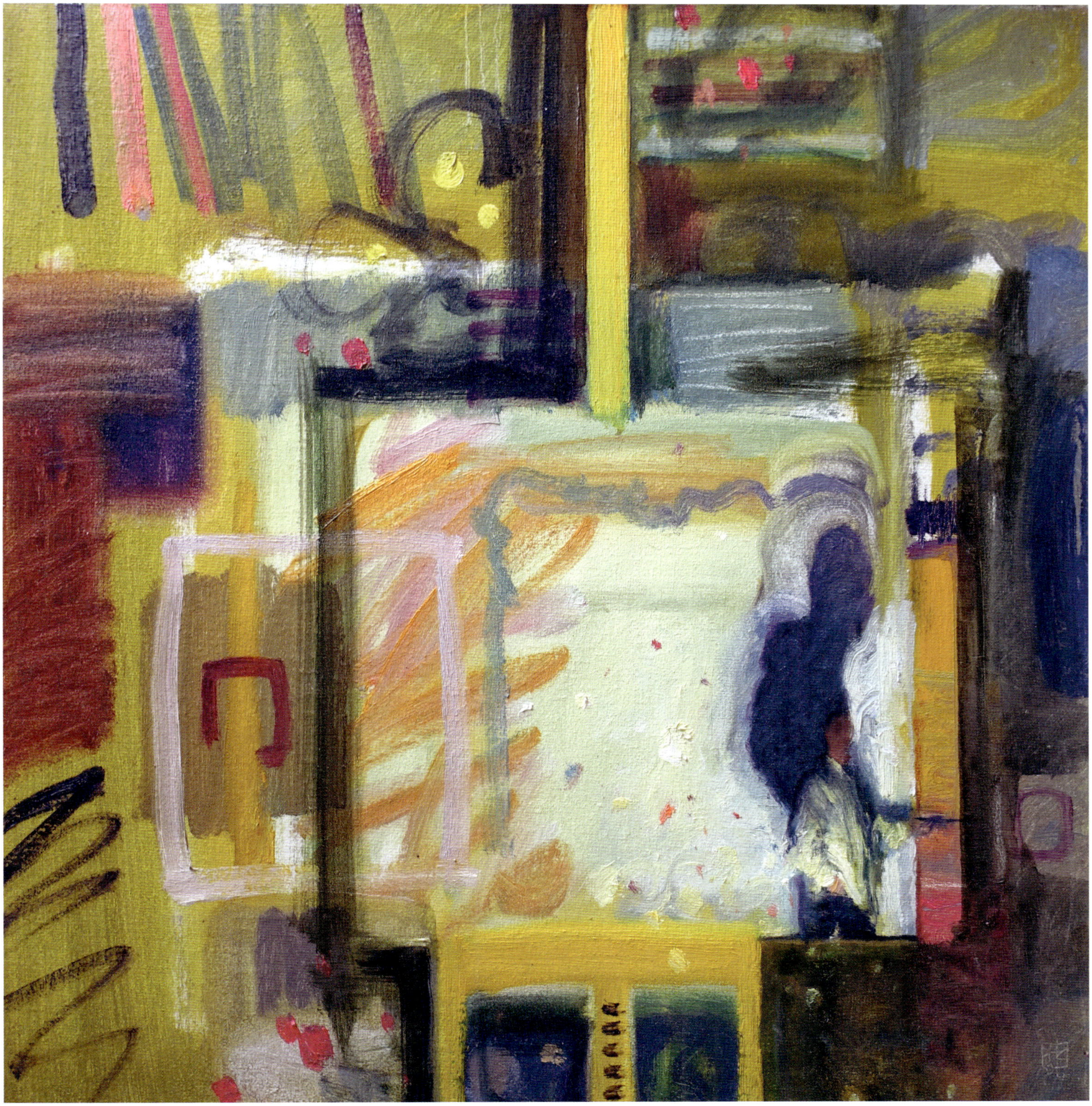

The Yellow Easel | 2004 | oil cn linen | 41 x 41 cm

collection of the artist

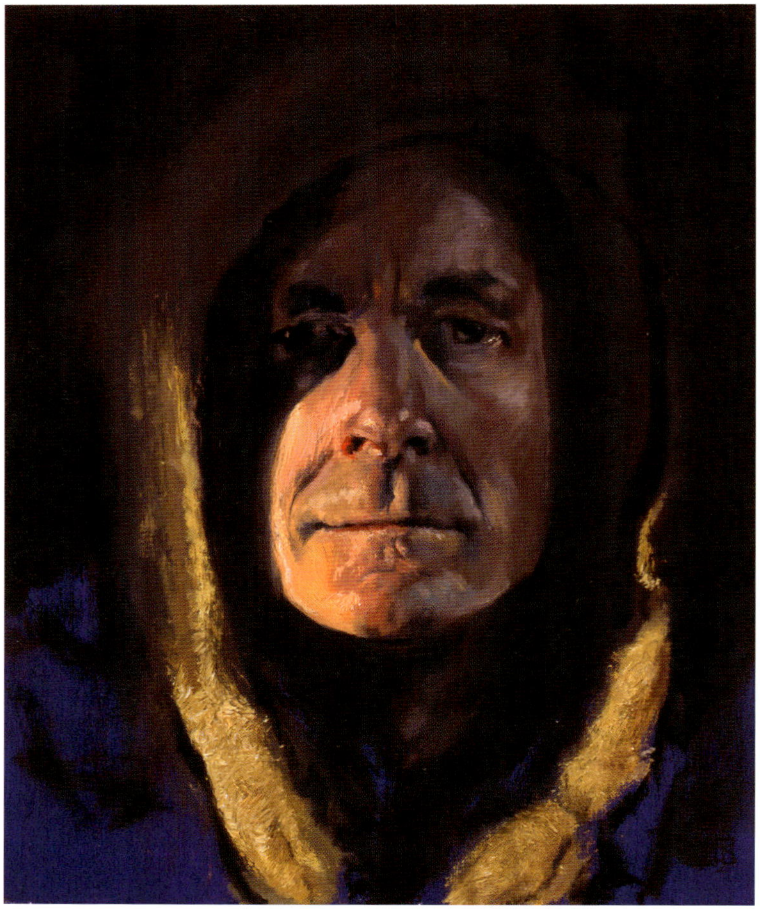

Hoody
2002 | oil on linen | 45.5 x 30.5 cm
private collection

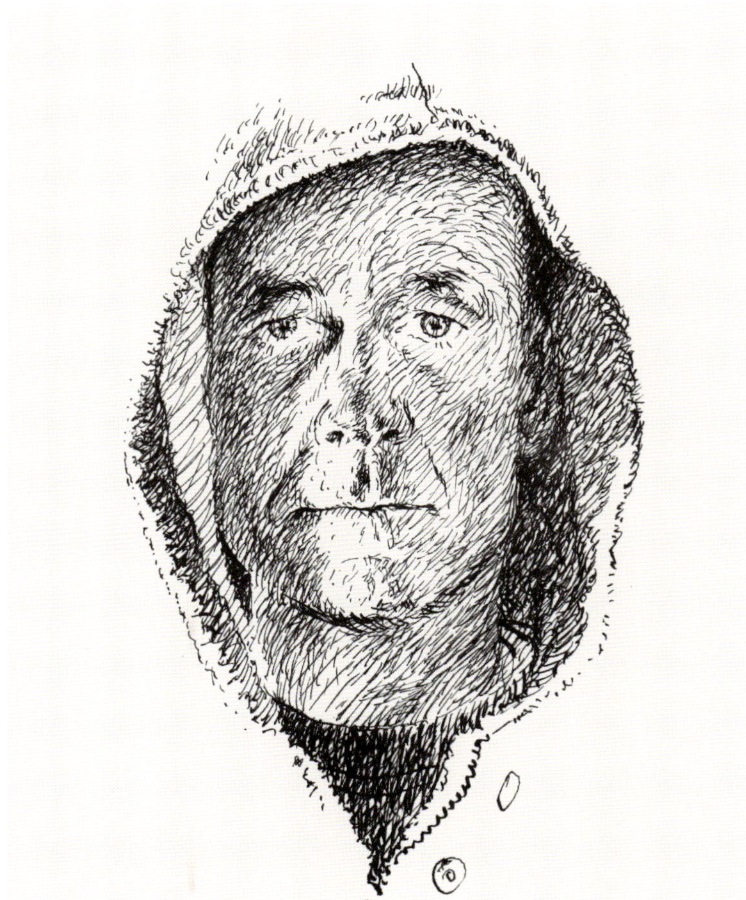

Hoody
2002 | pen and ink | 30 x 21 cm
private collection

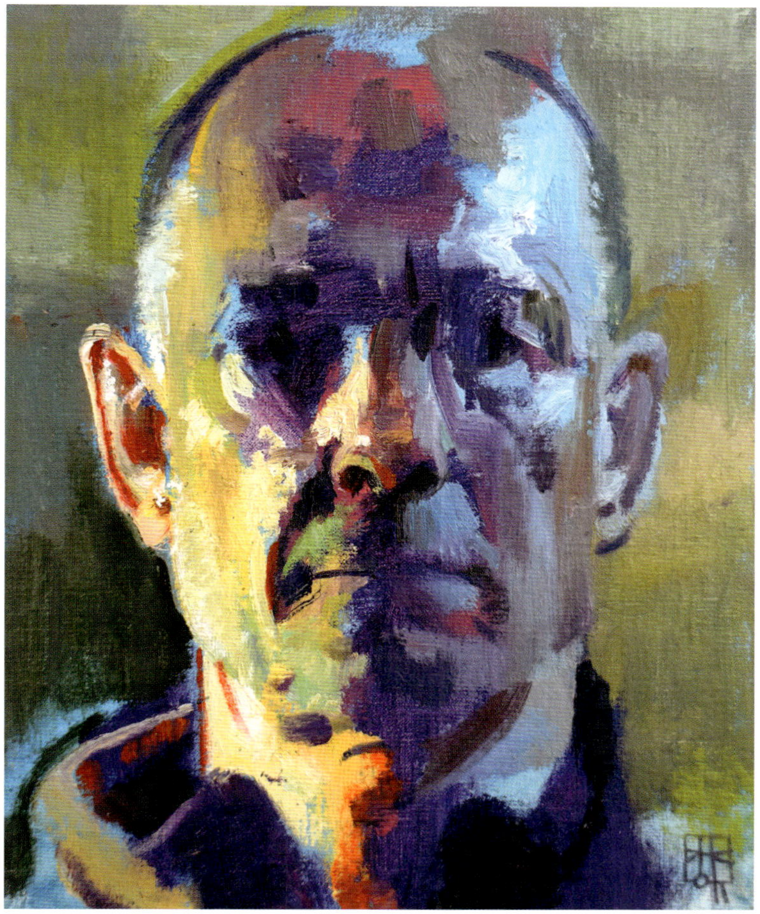

In Gold and Purple
2011 | oil on panel | 24 x 20 cm
collection of the artist

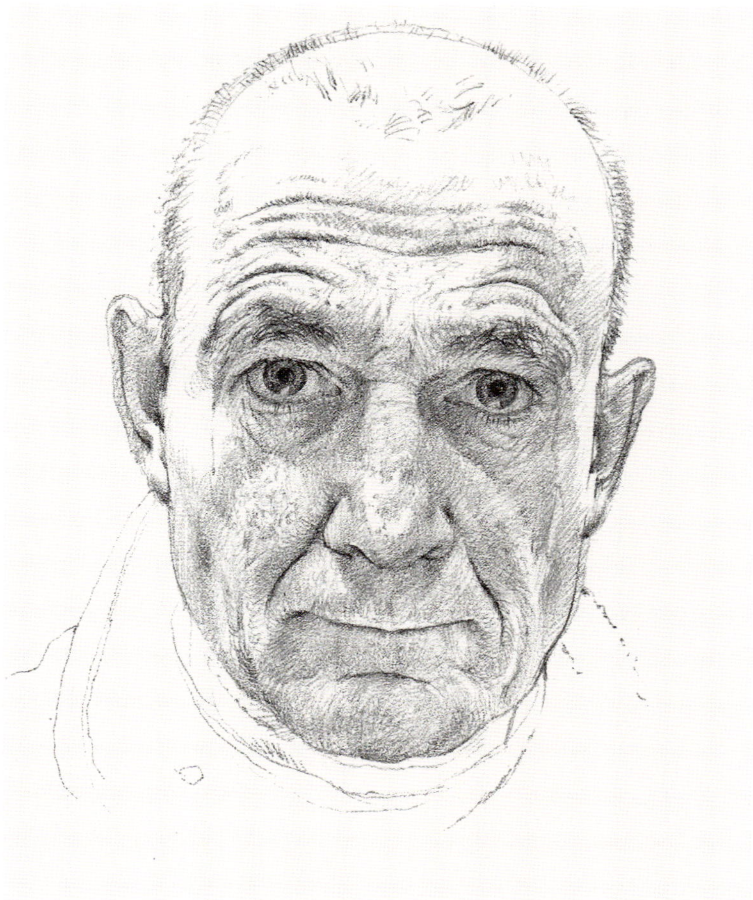

I Was Here
2007 | pencil | 30.5 x 25.5 cm
collection of the artist

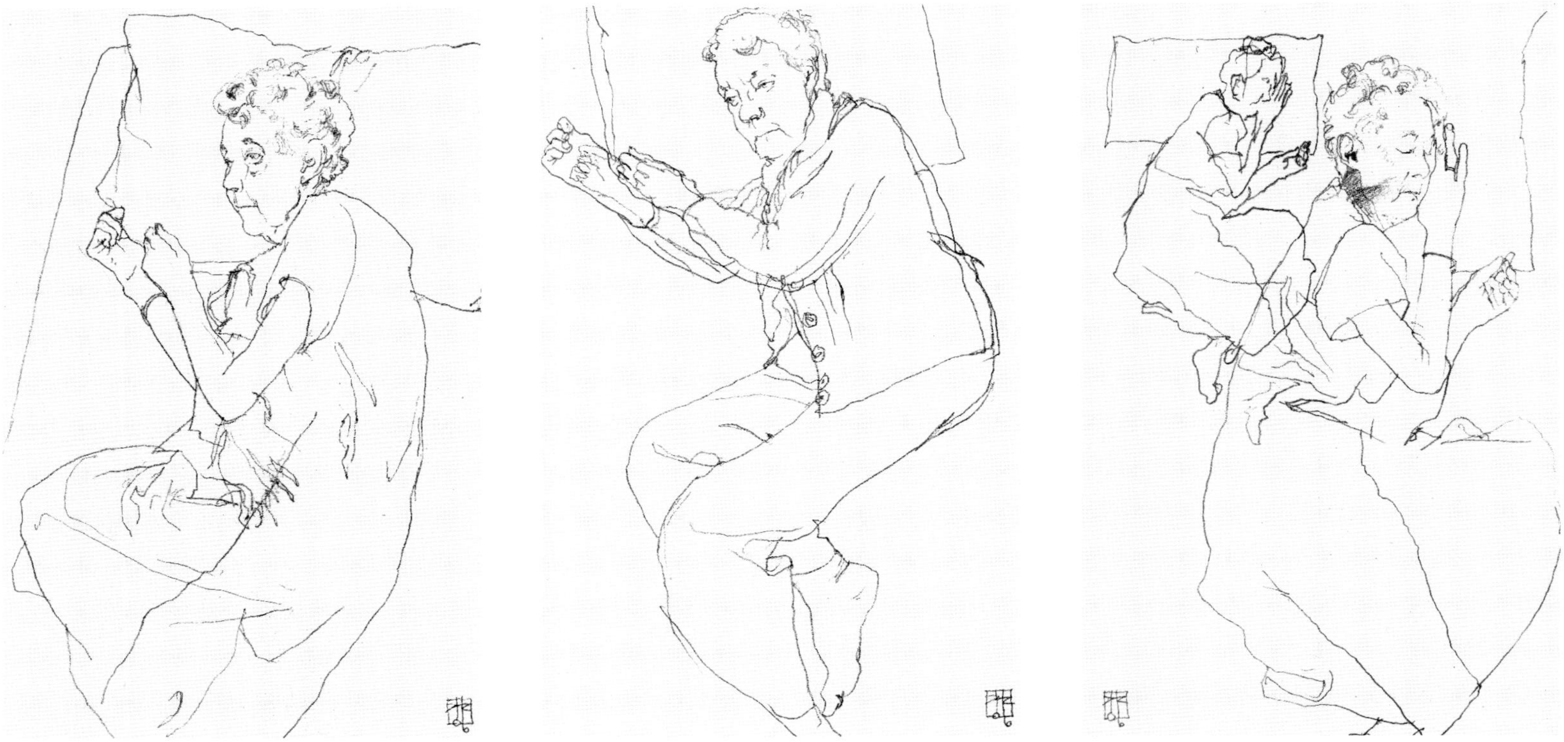

Mum Resting I–III | 2006 | pencil | 30.5 x 20.5cm

collection of the artist

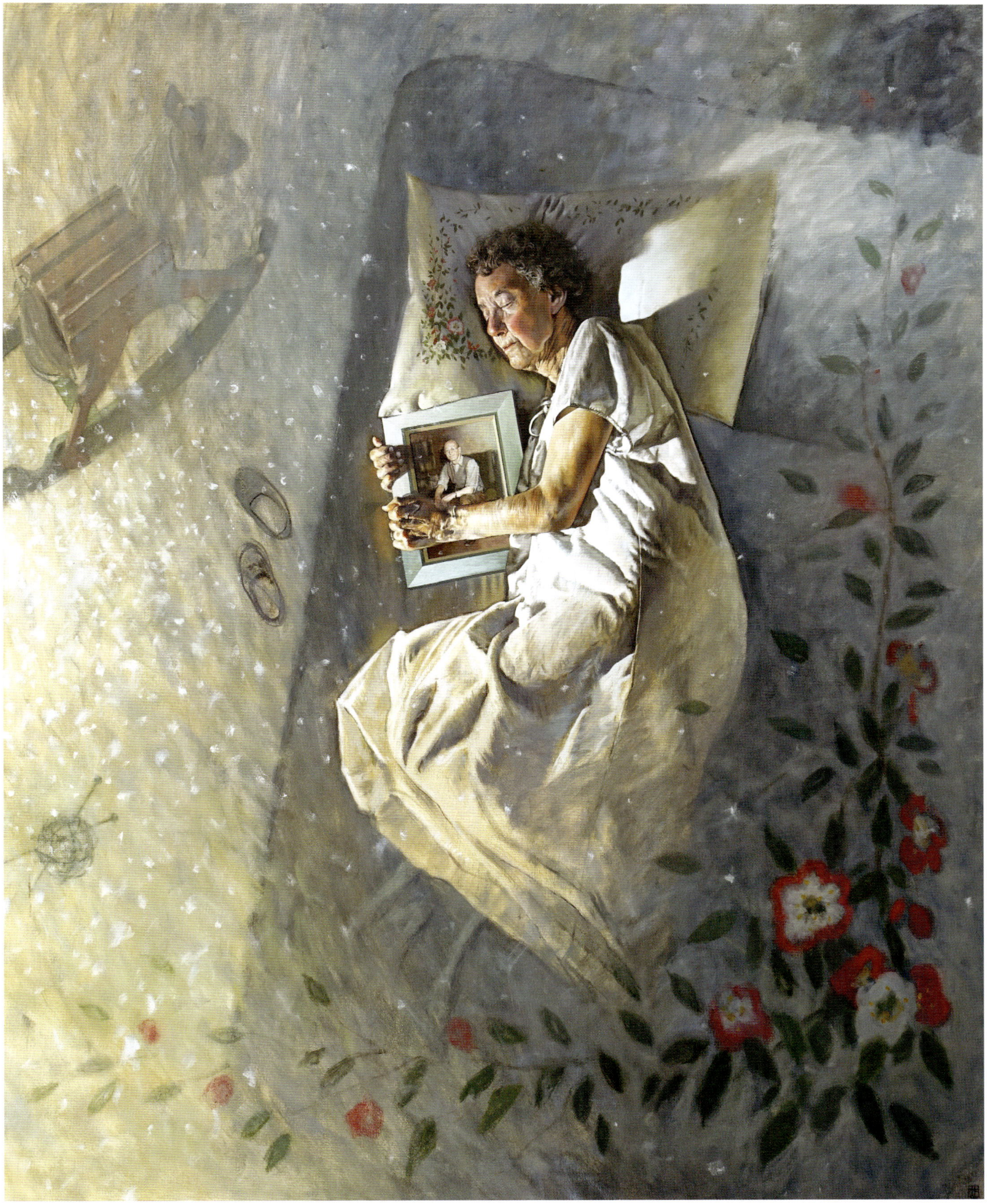

Not Fade Away | 2009 | oil on linen | 183 x 152.5 cm

collection of the artist

Empty Bed
2004 | oil on linen | 91.5 x 91.5 cm
private collection

The Bed

Where life comes screaming into
the world bloodied and bewildered
by the ferocity of its first breath.

Where it awakes in excitement at
the possibilities of the day before it

And where it returns from its
exhaustion for replenishment.

A place of solace from the pain
of betrayal and deceitfulness,

And a place where the world of
dreams transports it from the dull
tedium of a day's uneventfulness.

Where it stirs unhurriedly to days
of quiet reflection,

Curls for comfort

And finds expression for its passion.

Where illness is nursed,

Where weariness is eased

And where freedom finally
welcomes it home.

David Cobley, July 2004

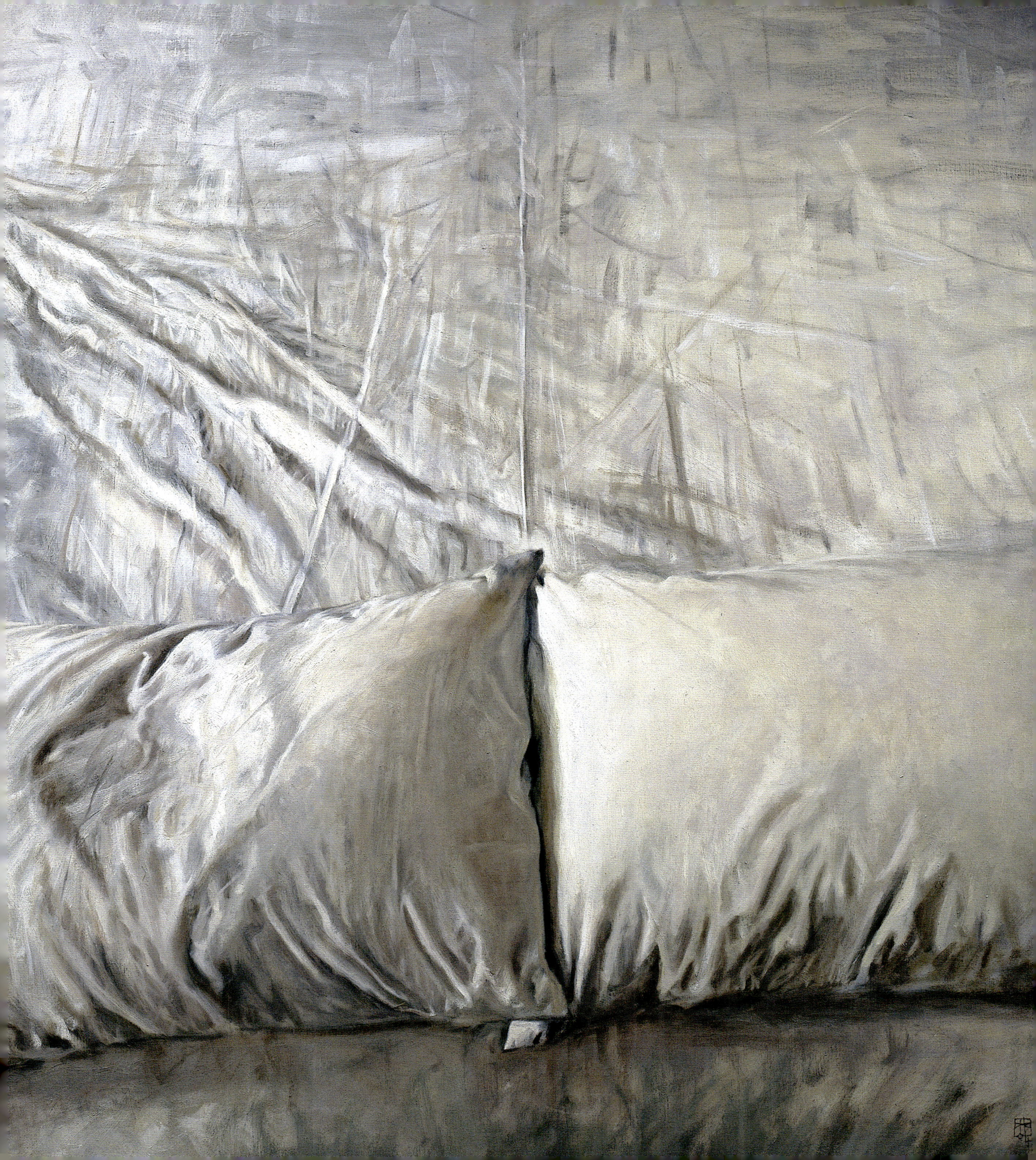

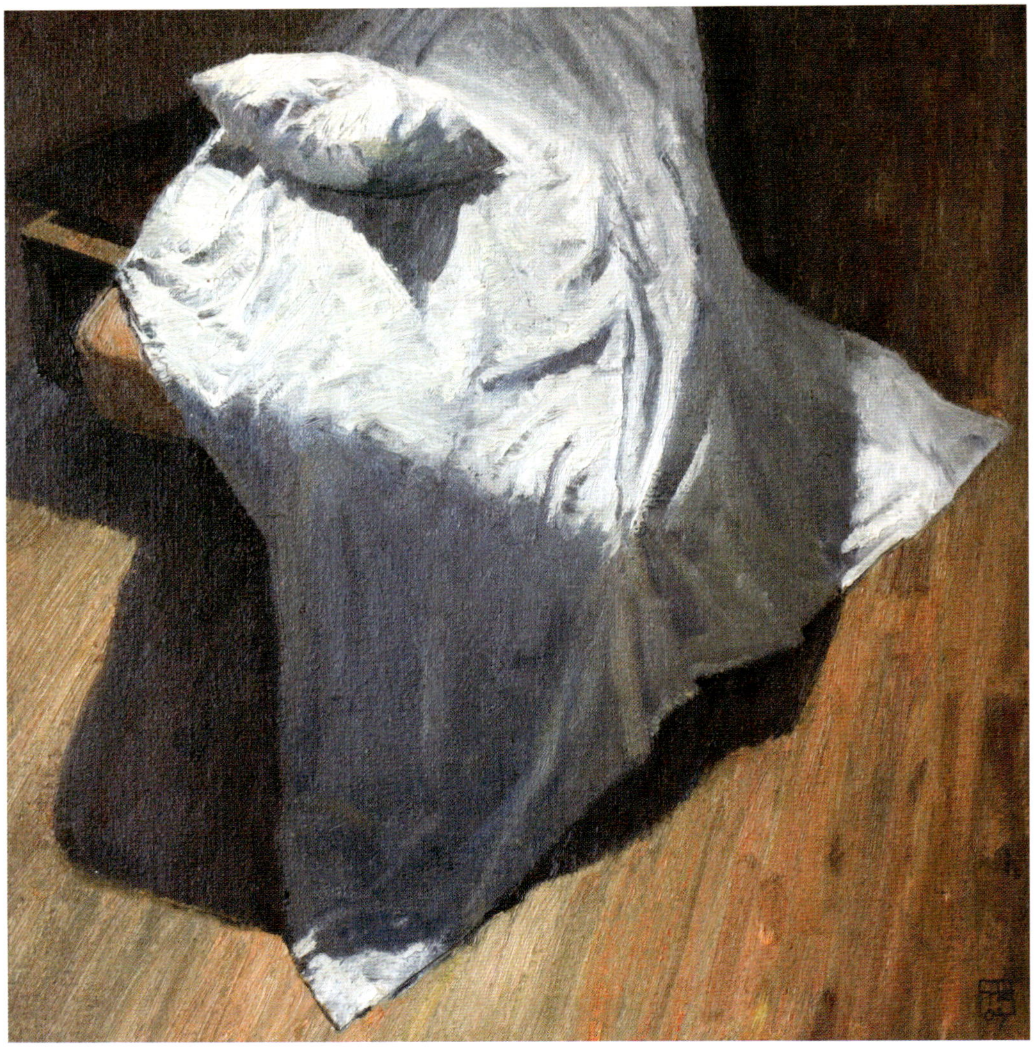

Strange Bed | 2007 | oil on linen | 30.5 x 30.5 cm collection of the artist

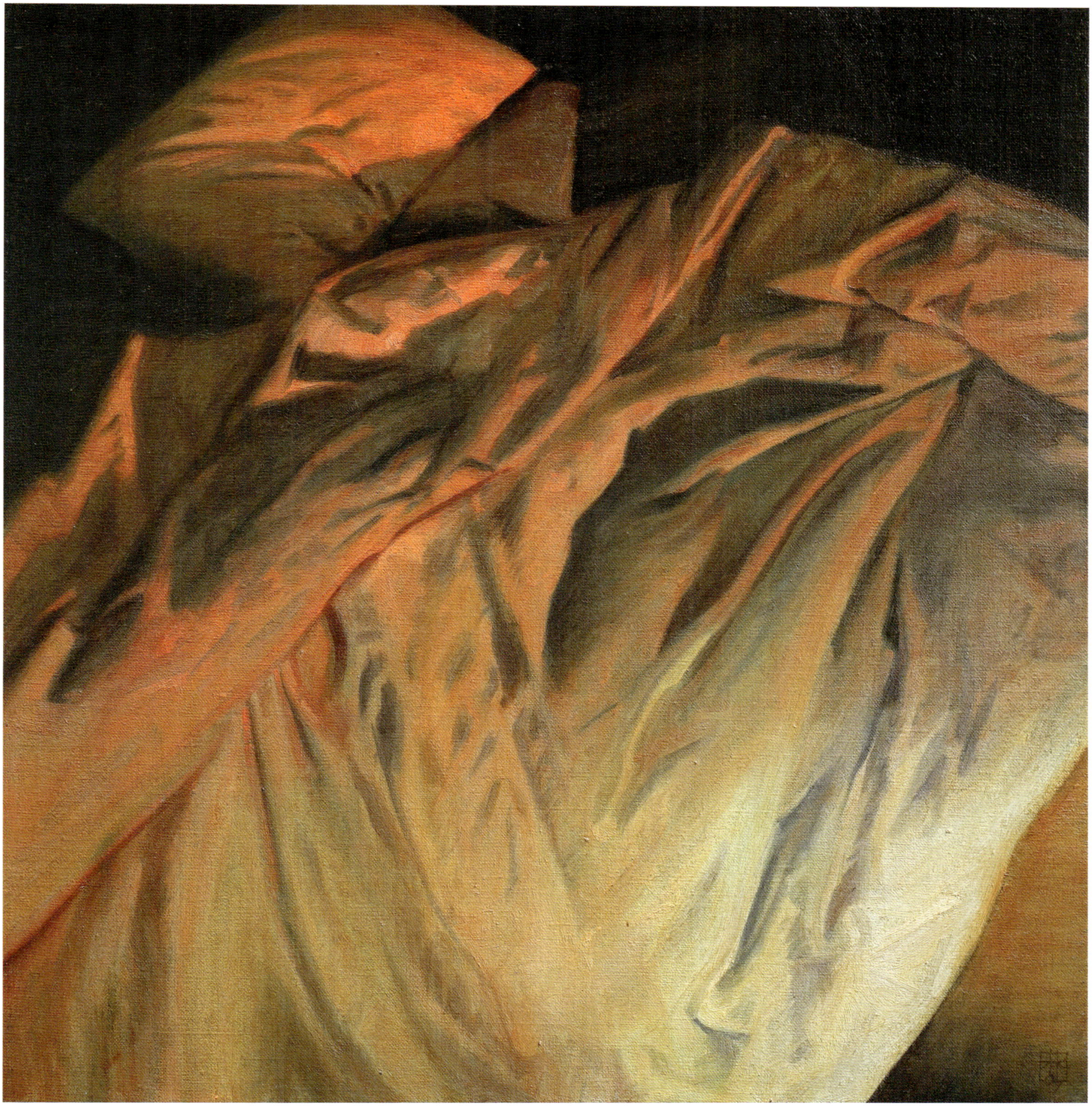

Unmade Bed | 2007 | oil on linen | 45.5 x 45.5 cm private collection

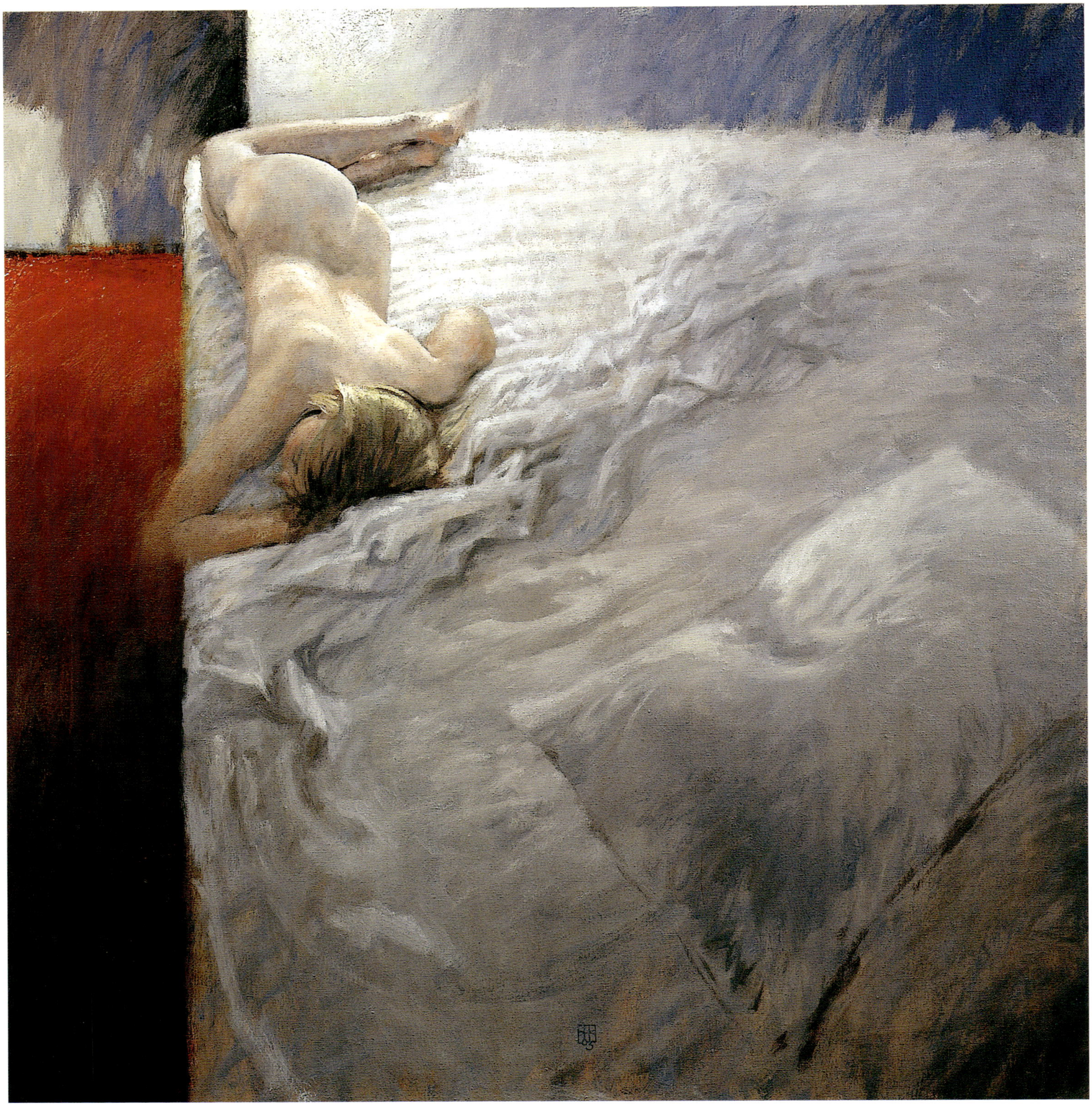

On the Edge | 2002 | oil on linen | 183 x 183 cm

private collection

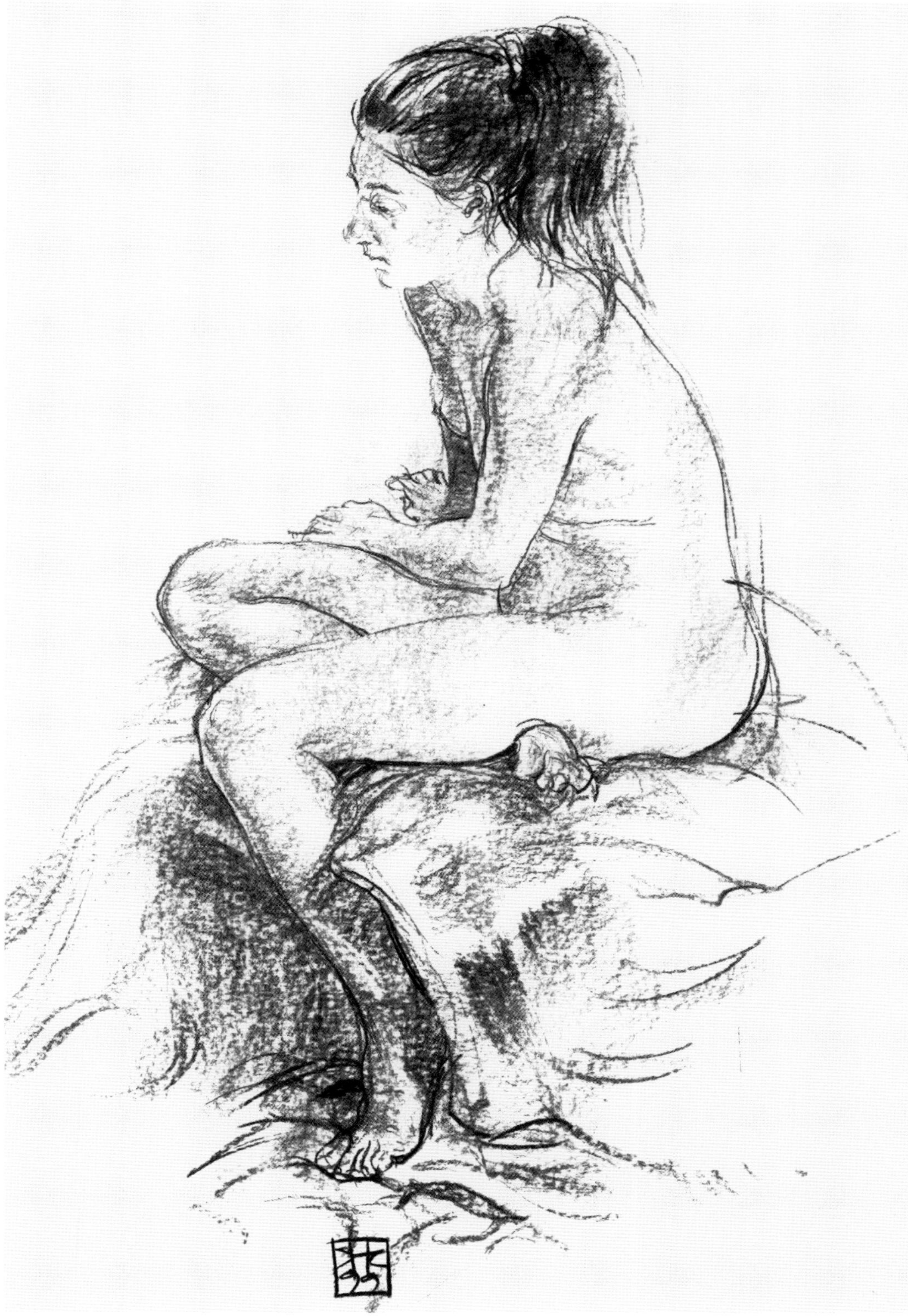

Susie | 1999 | charcoal | 56 x 38 cm collection of the artist

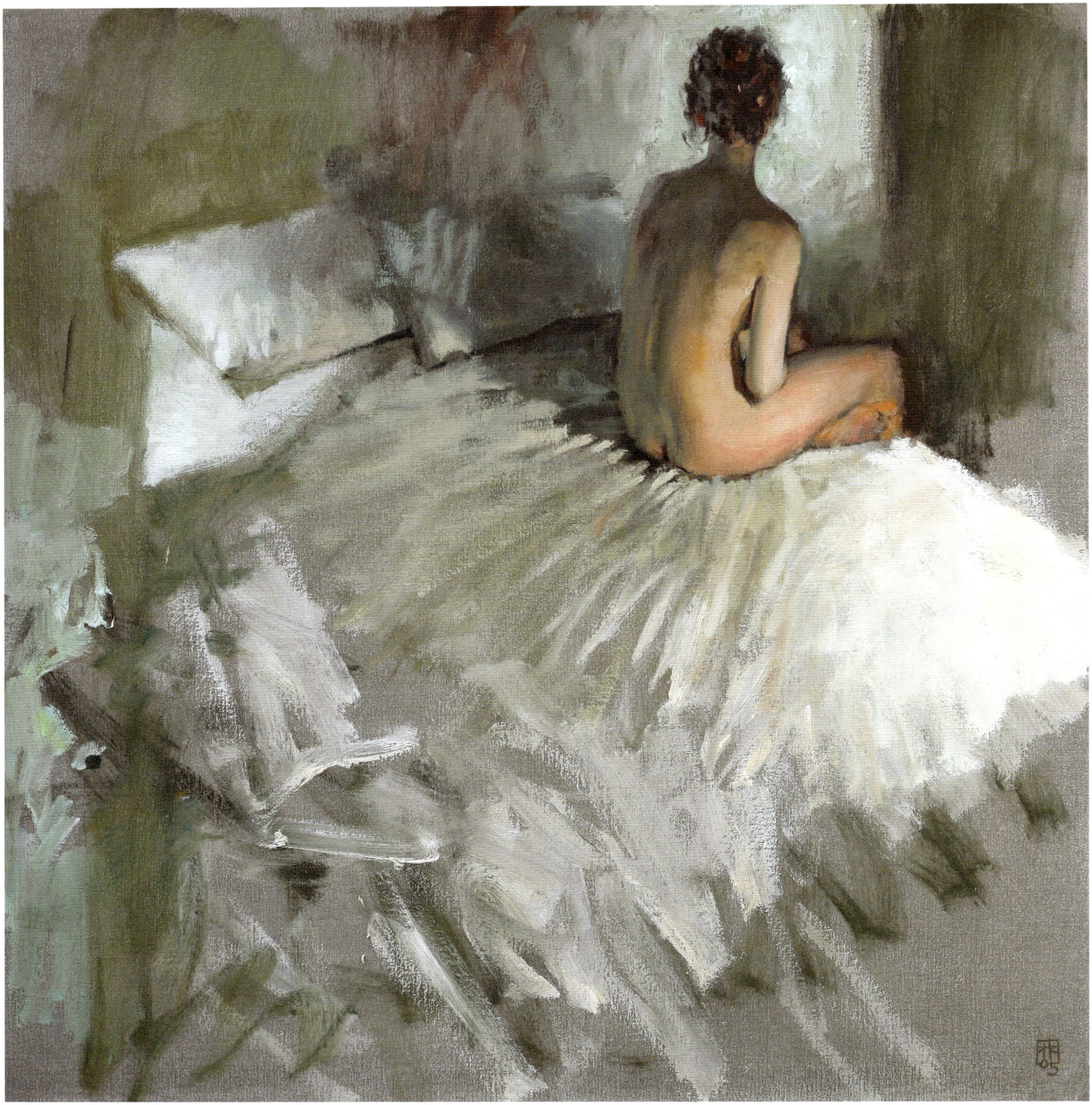

Seated II | 2005 | oil on linen | 61 x 61 cm private collection

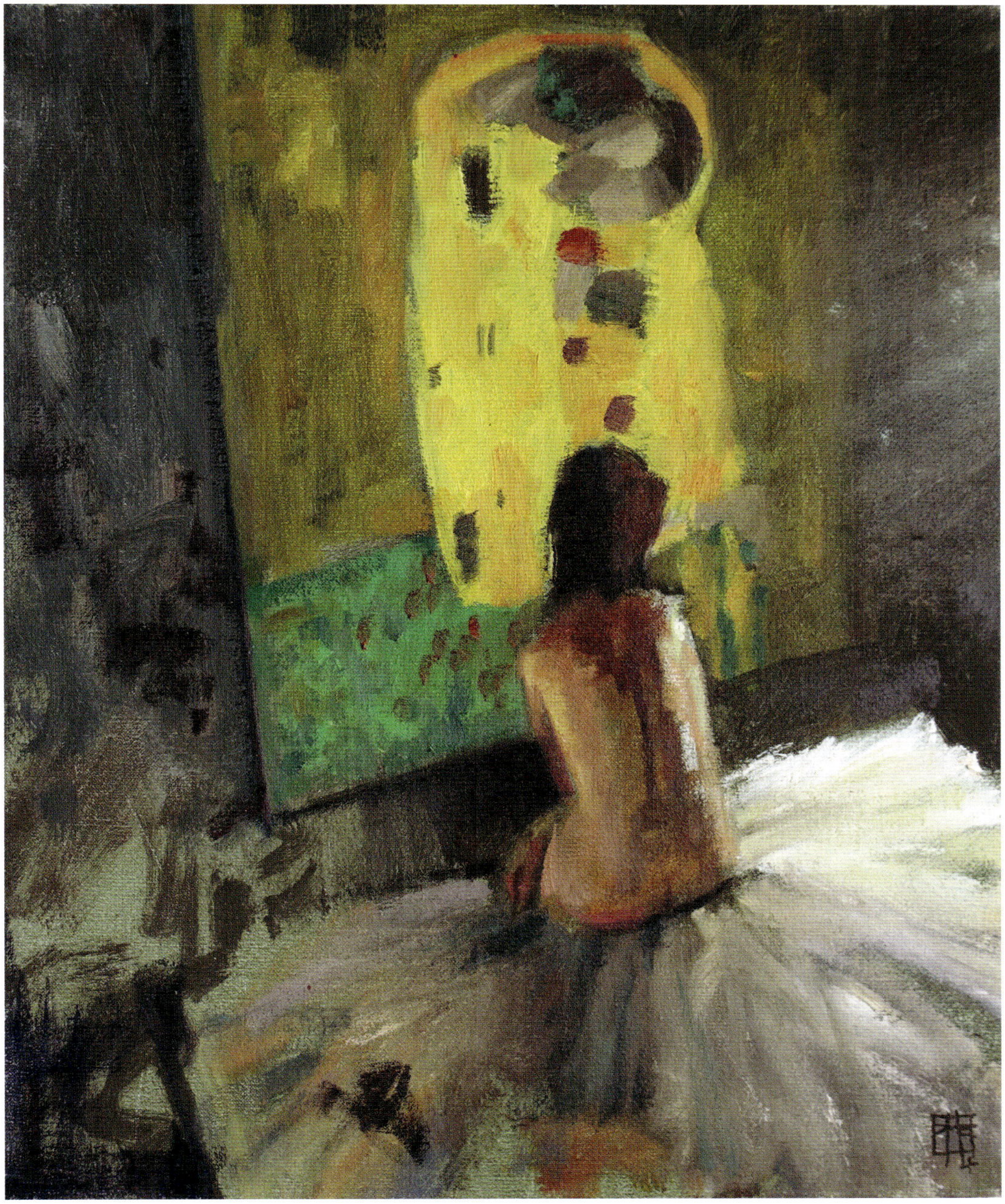

With The Kiss | 2014 | oil on linen | 40.5 x 30.5 cm collection of the artist

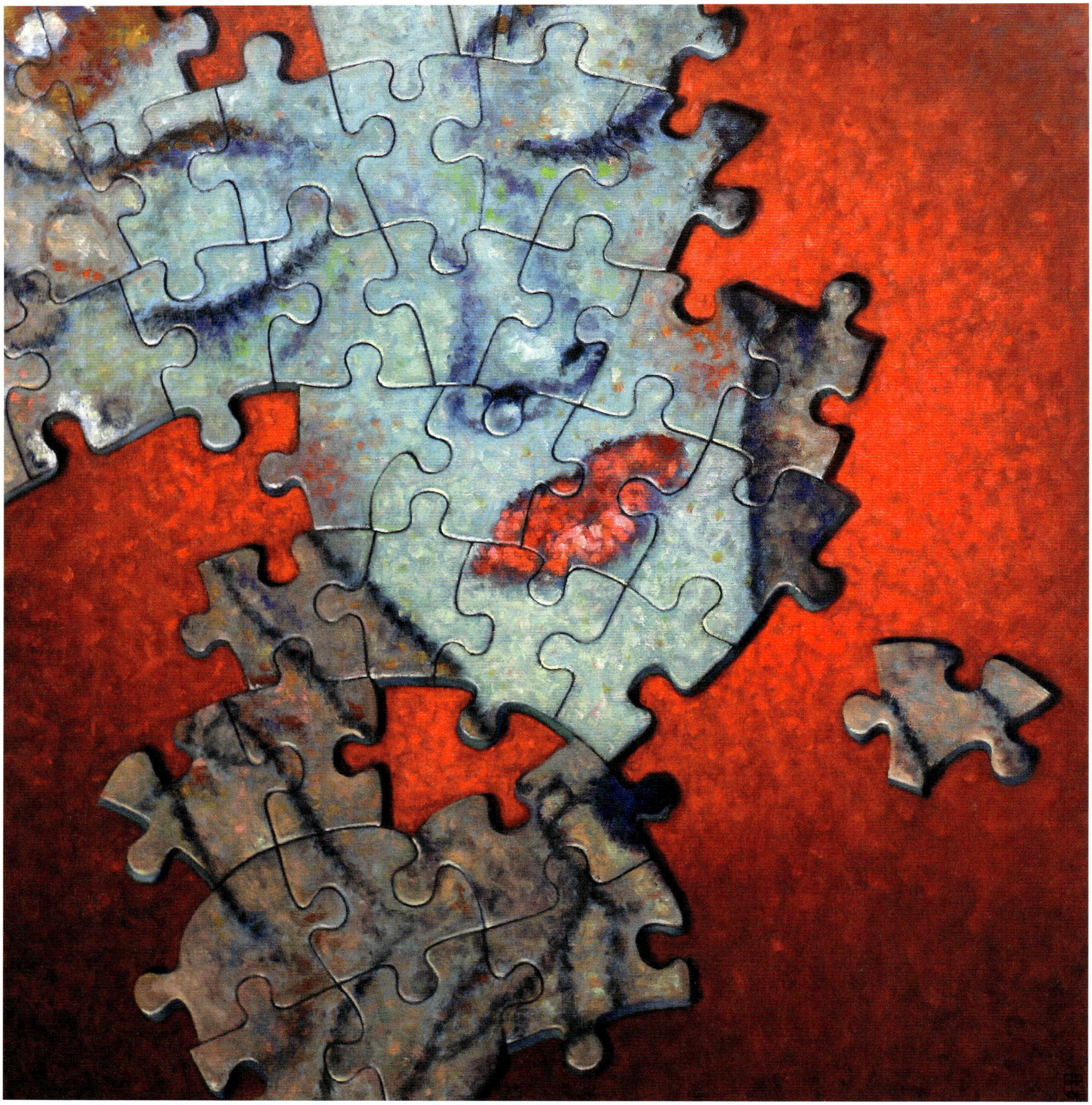

The Klimt Conspiracy | 2010 | oil on linen | 91.5 x 91.5 cm private collection

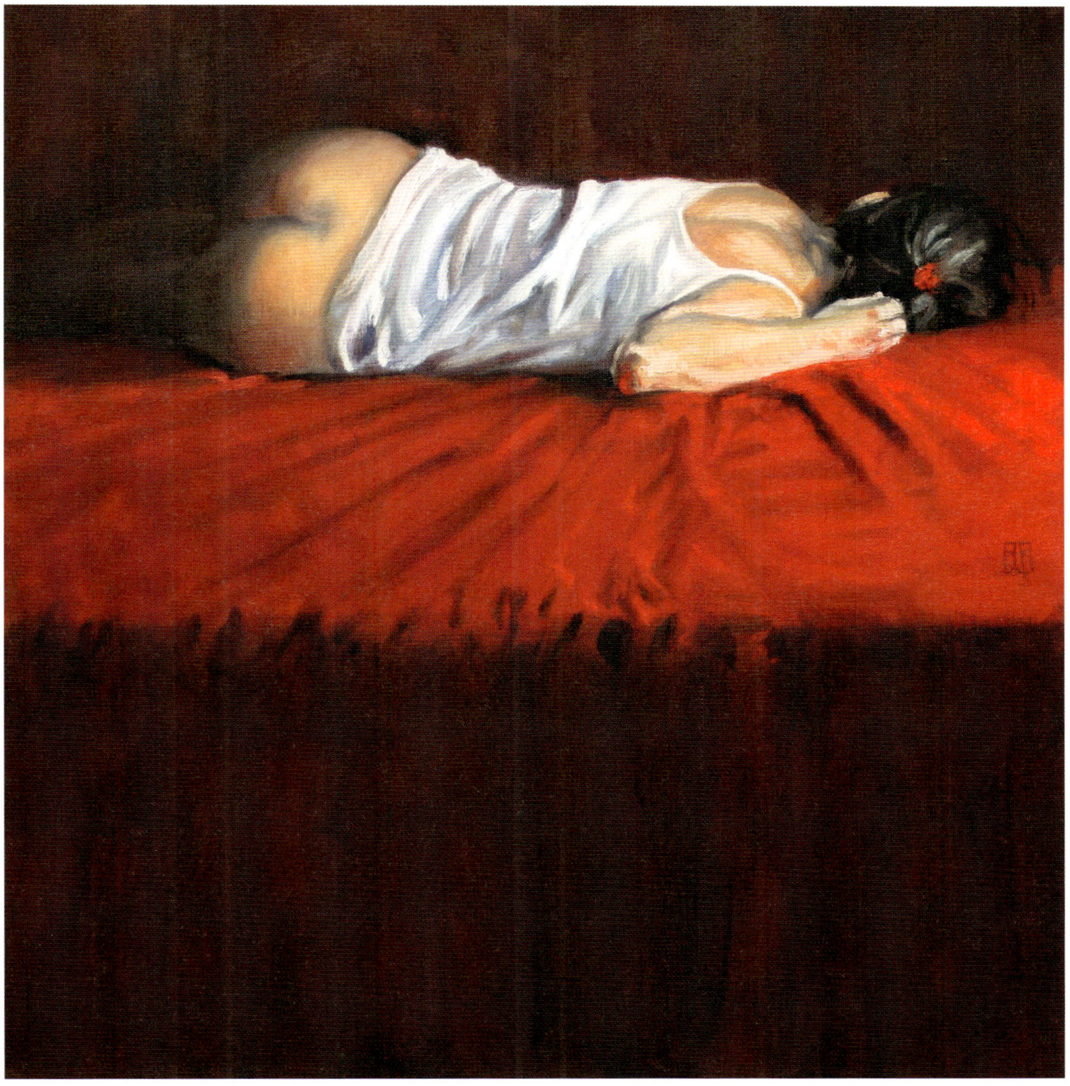

The White Top | 2003 | oil on linen | 41 x 41 cm private collection

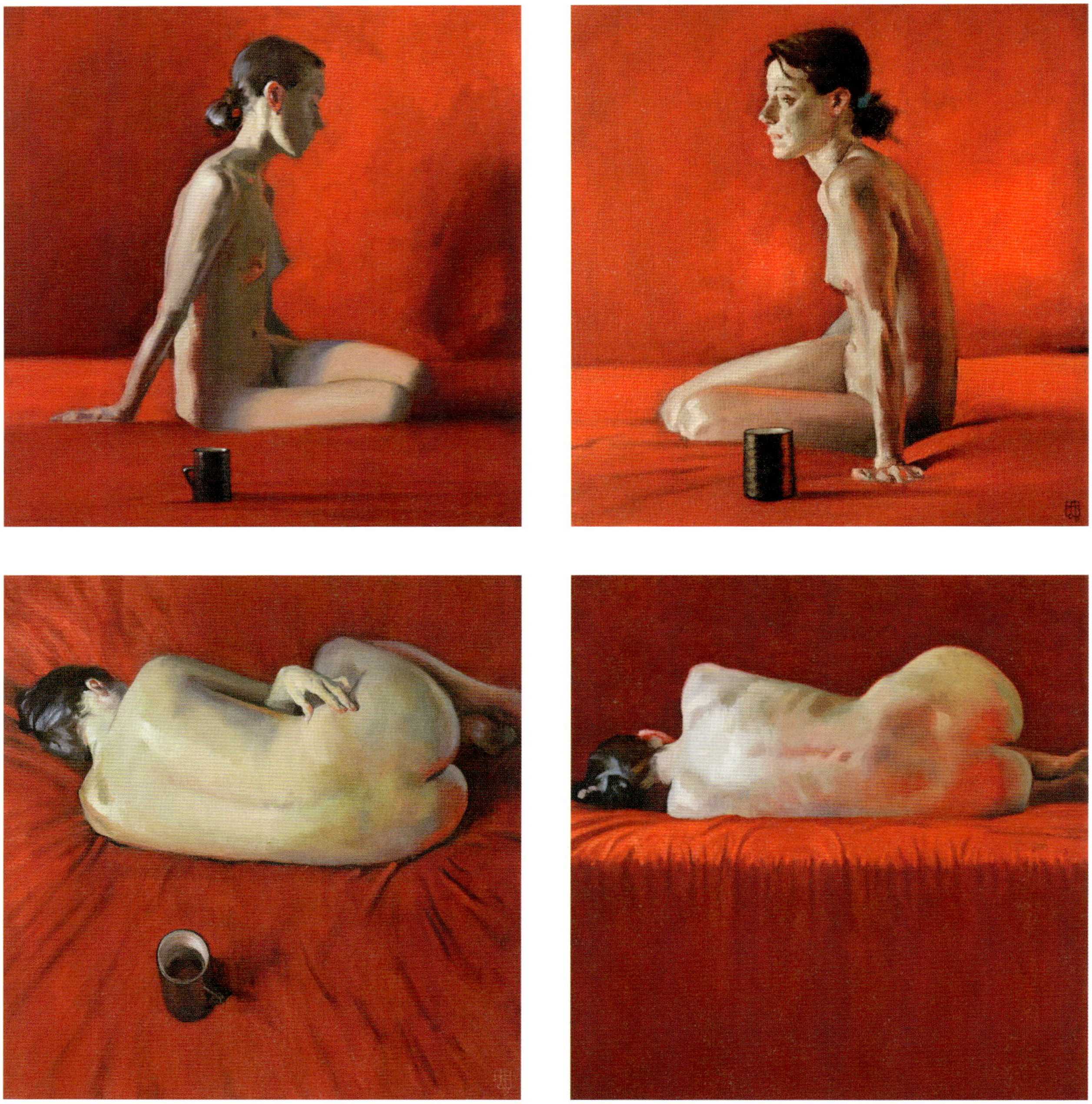

On Red (clockwise from top right) **I** / **VII*** / **IV** / **V** | 2009/*2011 | oil on linen | 45.5 x 45.5 cm private collection

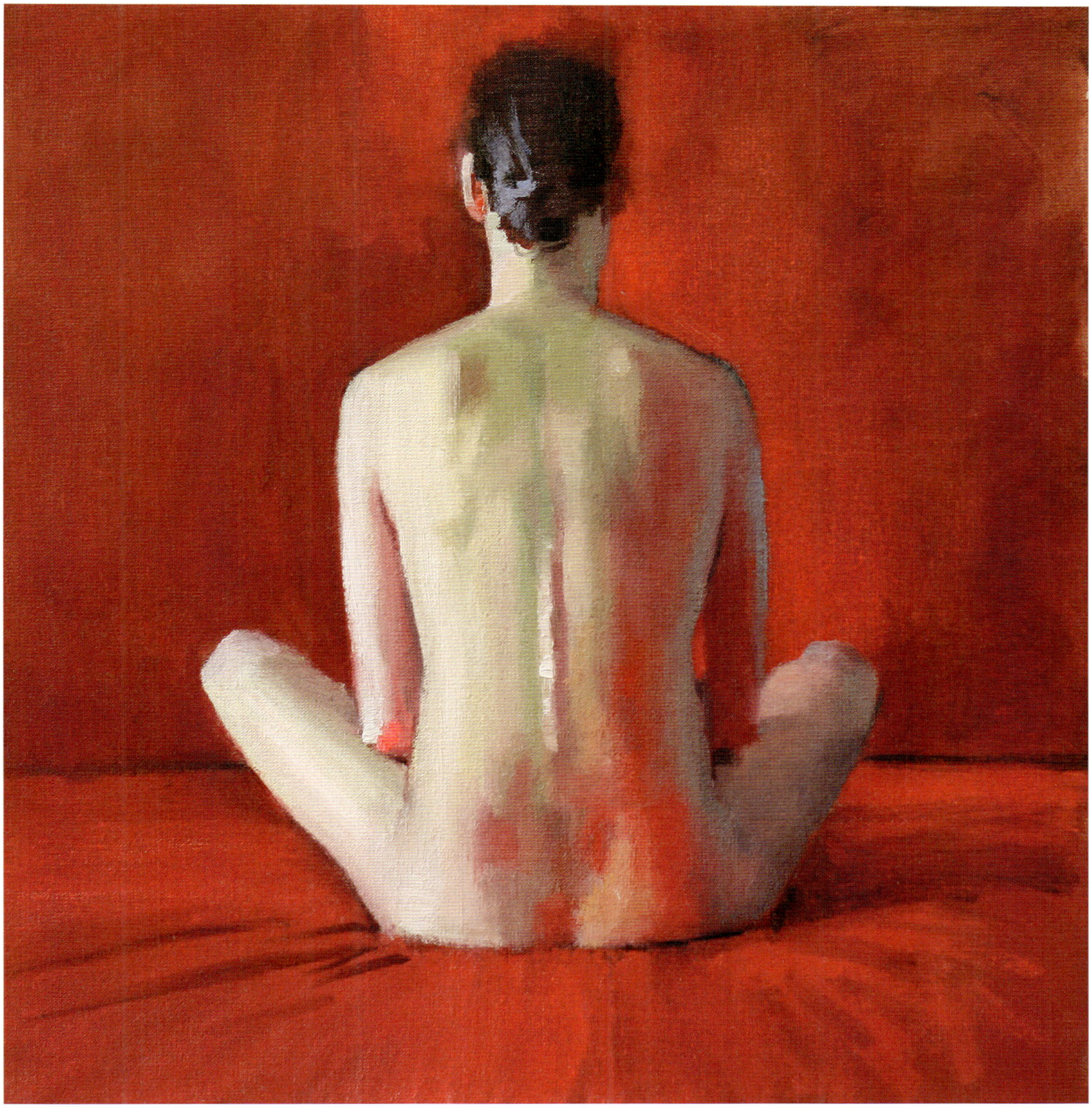

On Red III | 2009 | oil on linen | 45.5 x 45.5 cm private collection

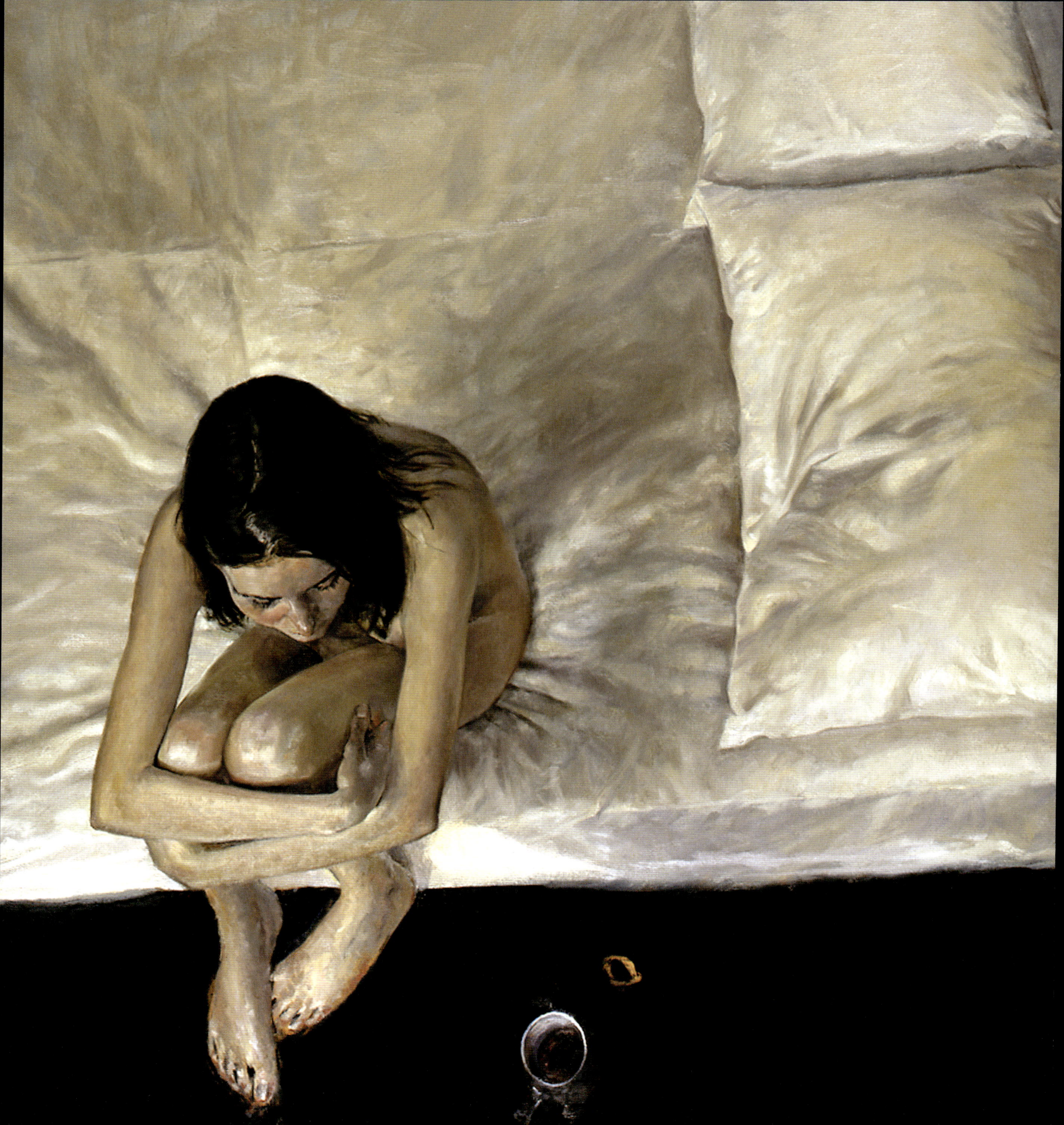

Seated Figure
2002 | oil on linen | 91.5 x 91.5 cm
private collection

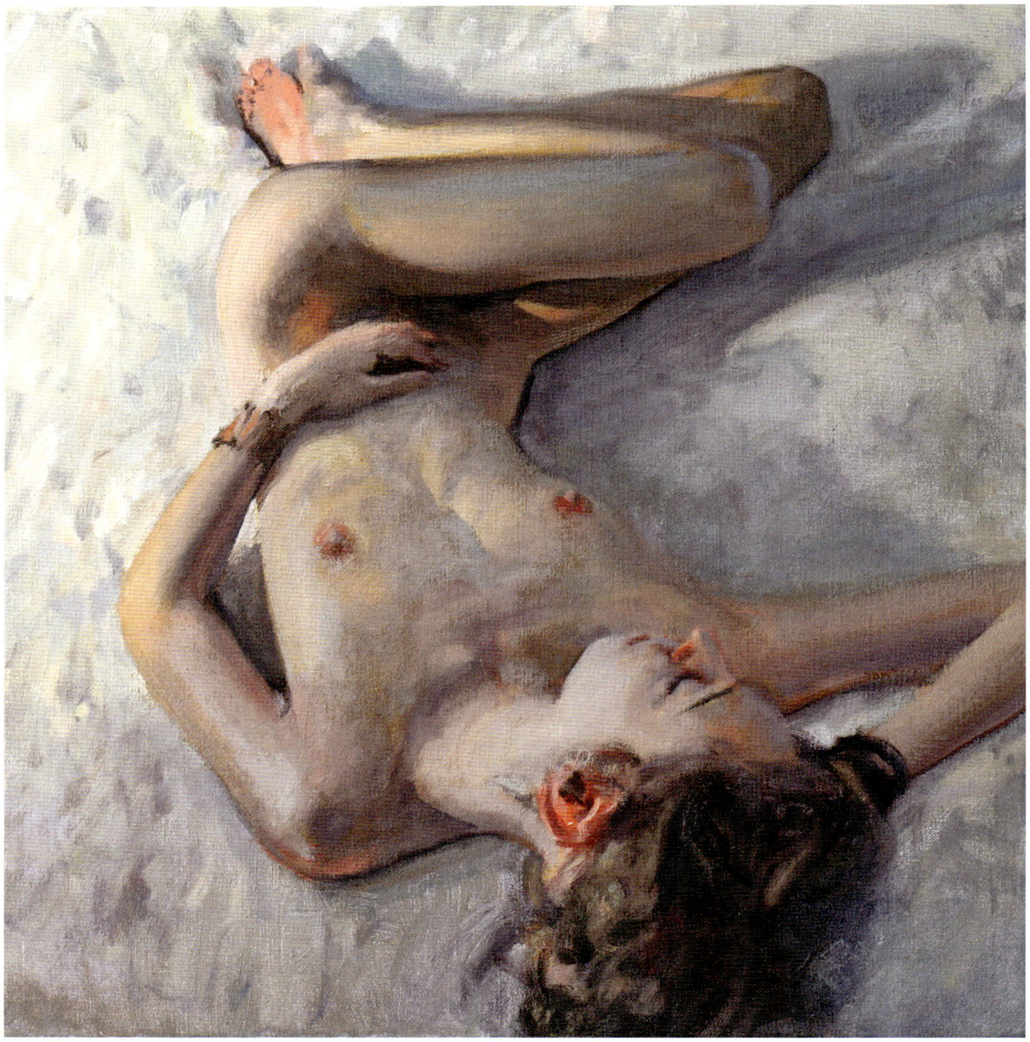

Within a Square | 2010 | pencil | 45.5 x 45.5 cm private collection

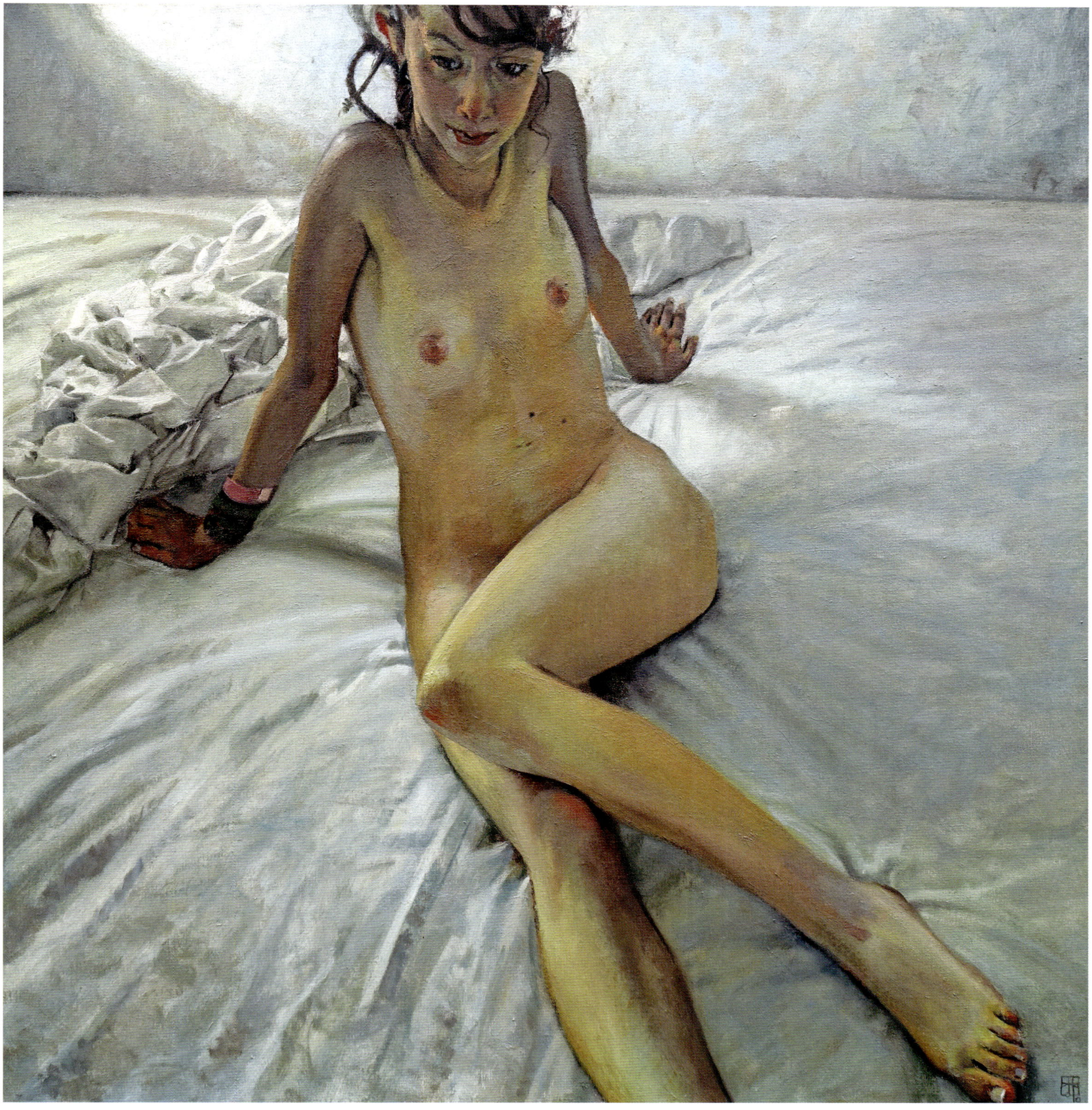

Big Bed | 2010 | oil on linen | 91.5 x 91.5 cm collection of the artist

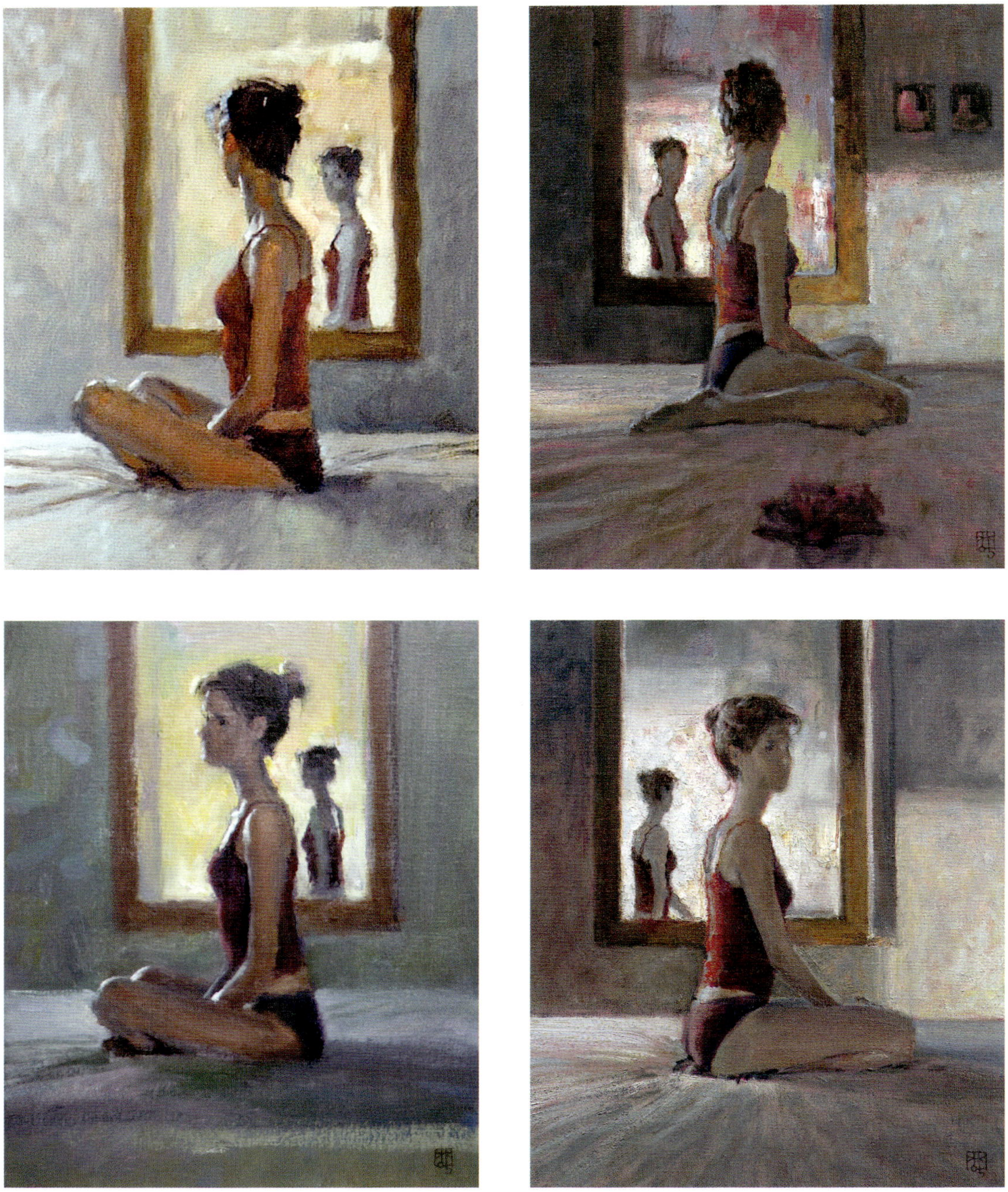

Mirror (clockwise from top right) **II–V** | 2005 | oil on linen | 40.5 x 35.5 cm private collection

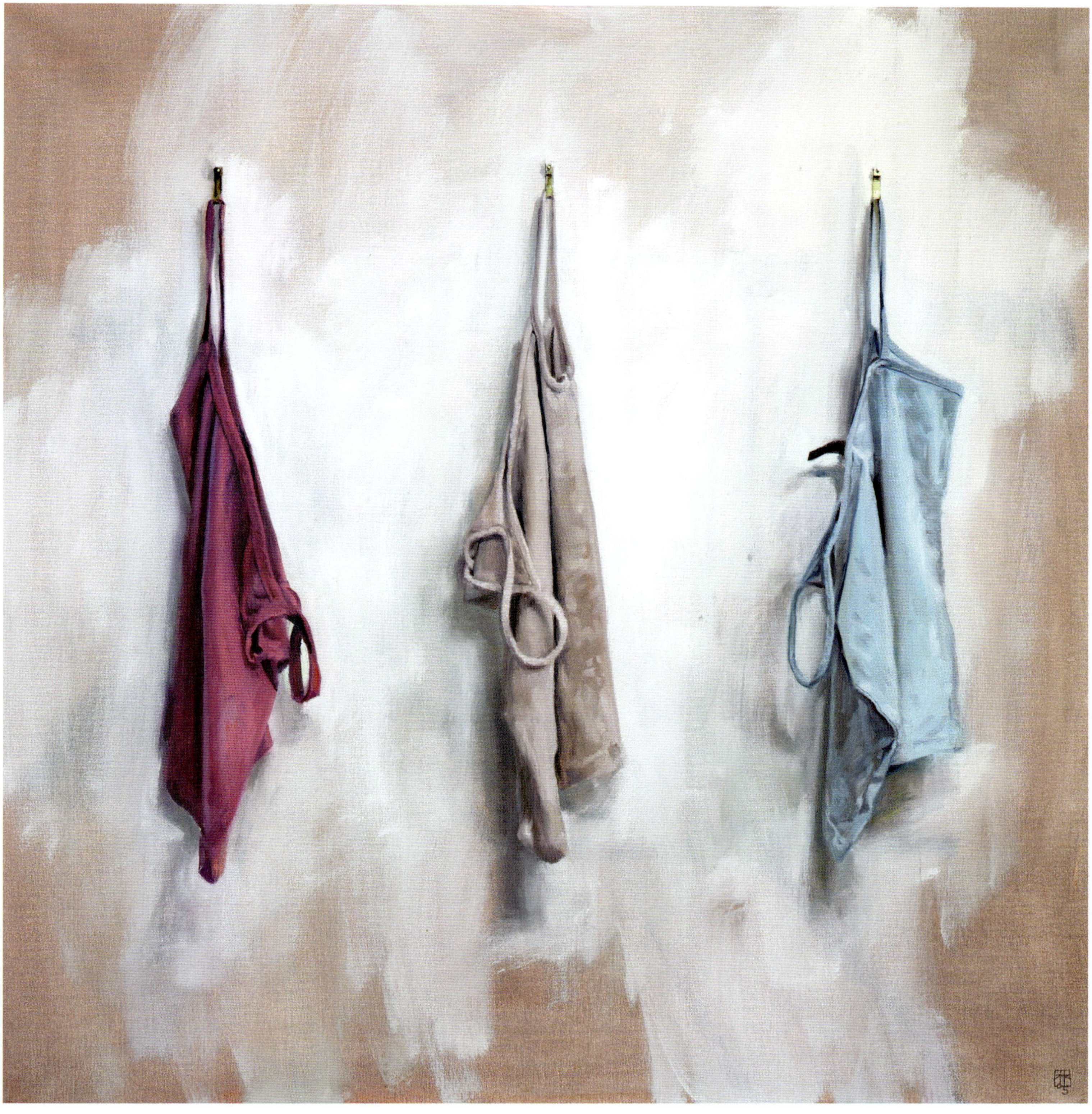

Now Just Rags | 2005 | oil on linen | 91.5 x 91.5 cm

private collection

A Kind of Equilibrium
2004 | oil on linen | 183 x 183 cm
collection of the artist

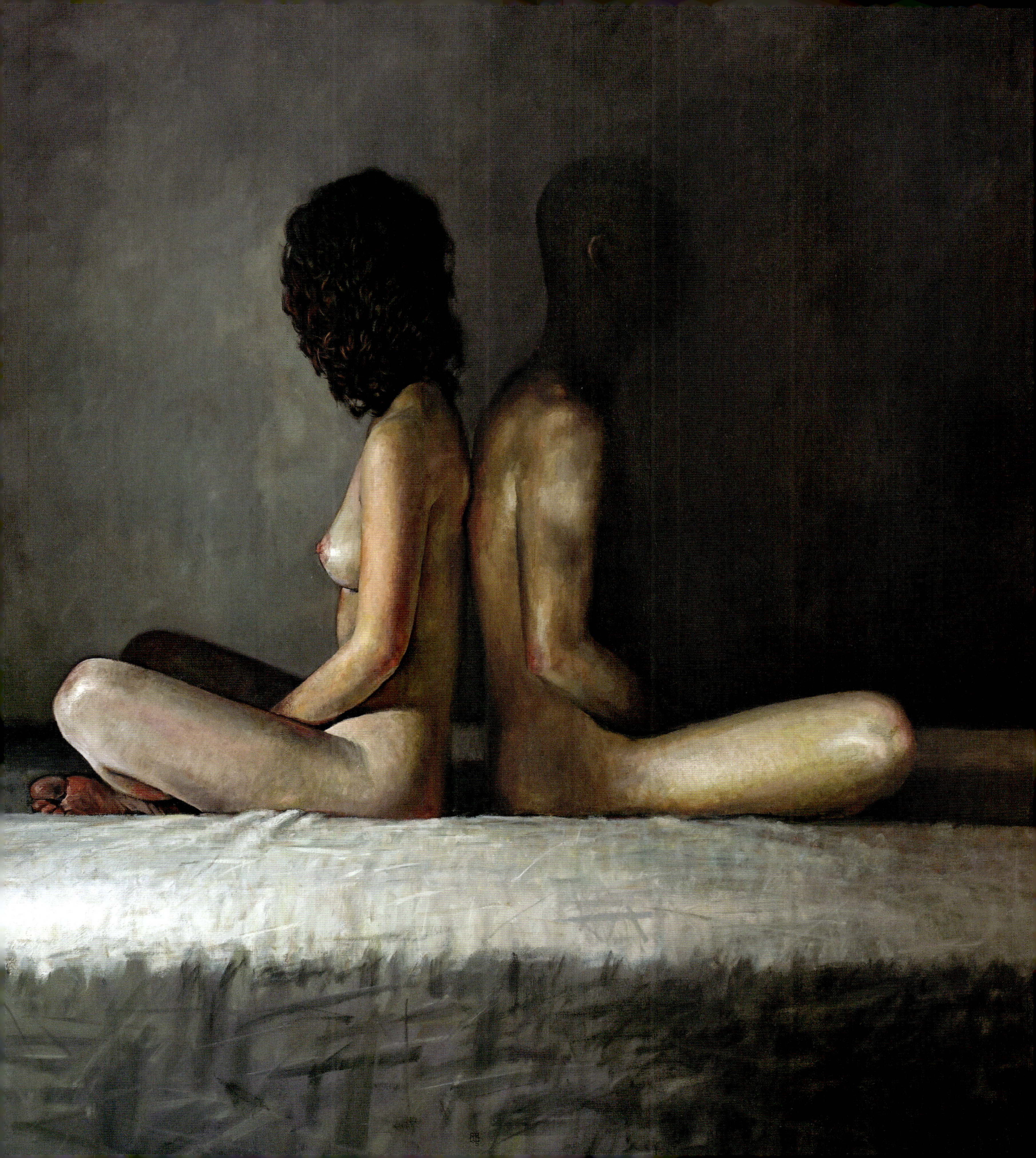

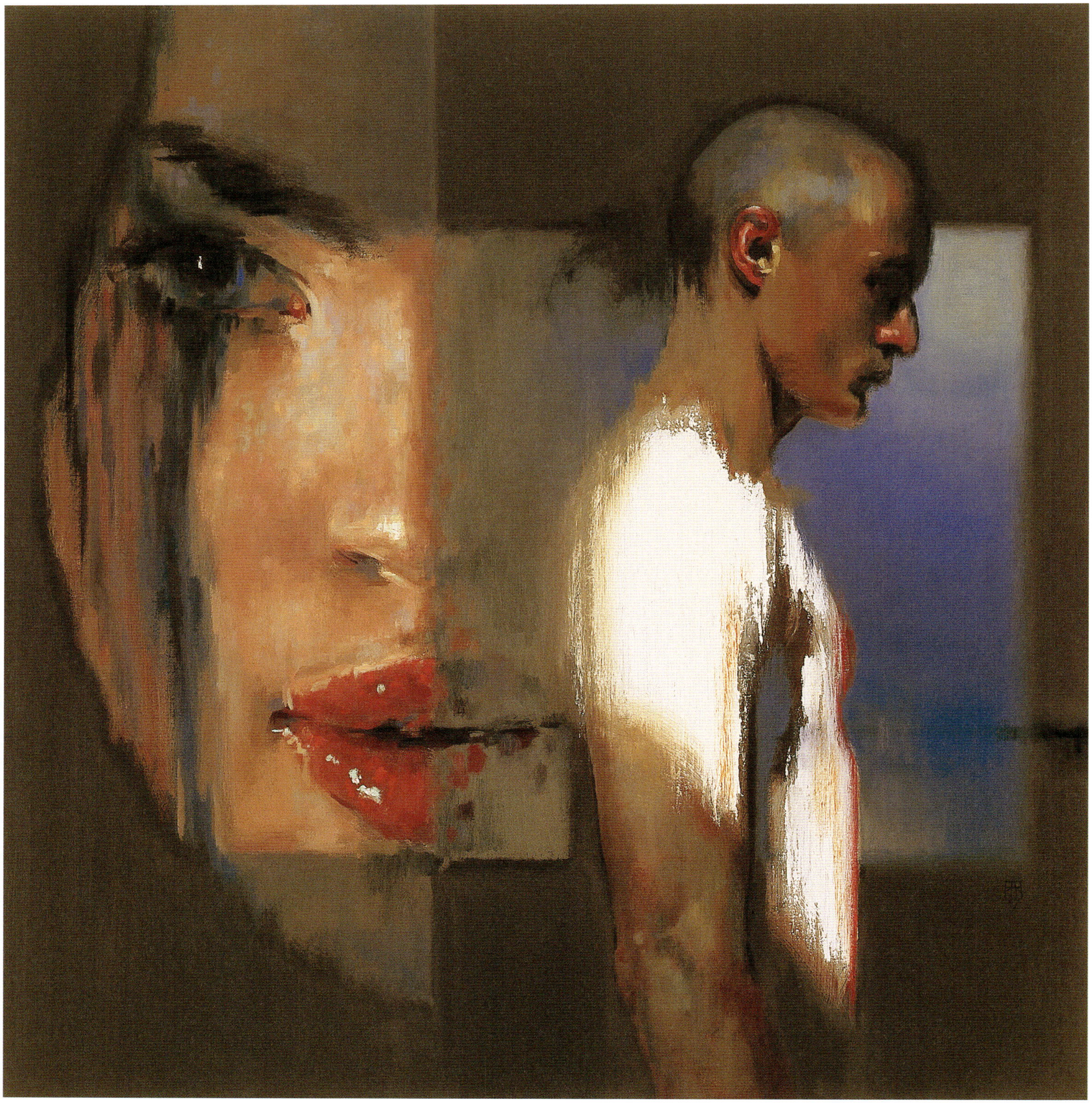

Lost Horizon | 2007 | oil on linen | 91.5 x 91.5 cm private collection

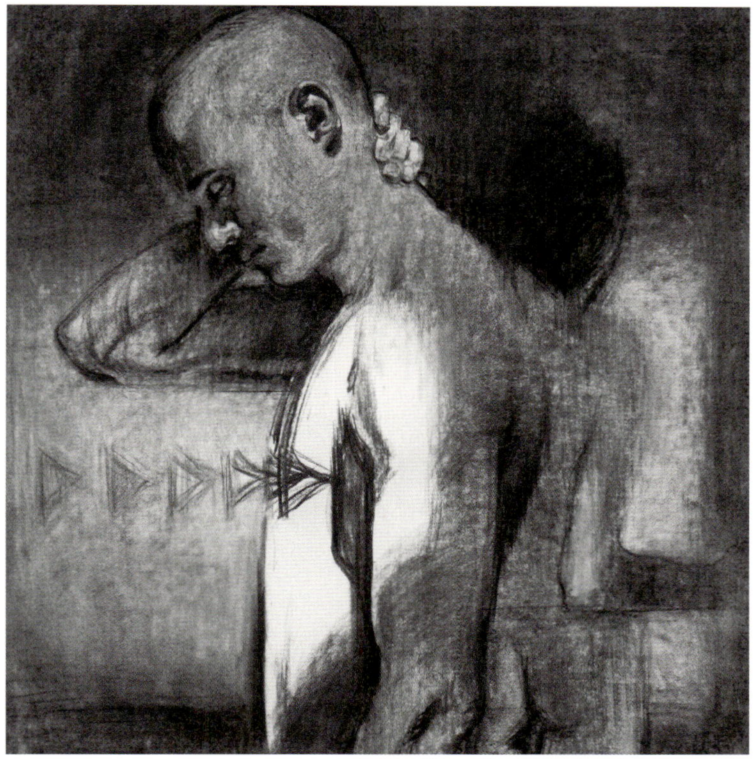

Study for By Themselves
2006 | charcoal | 63.5 x 63.5 cm
collection of the artist

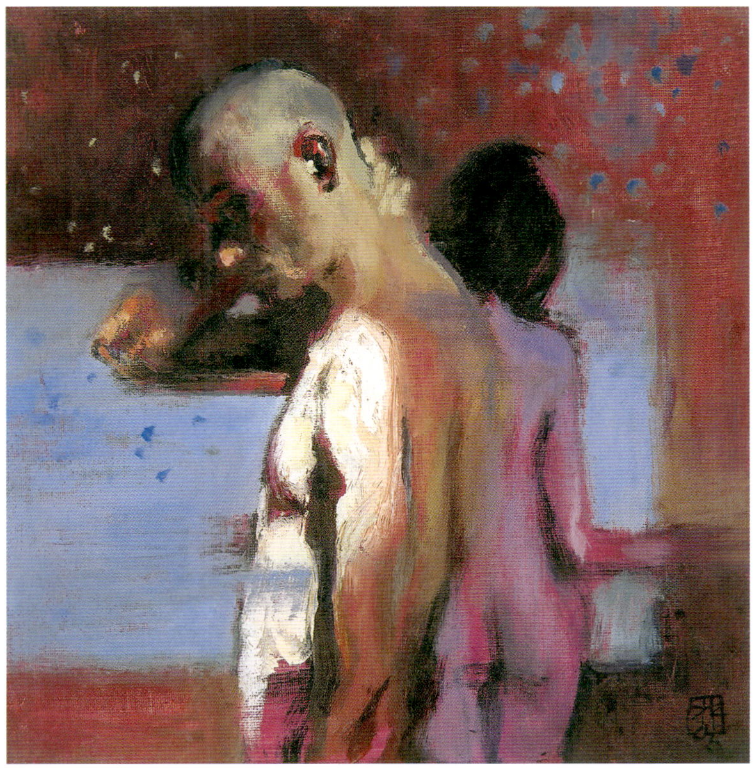

Study for By Themselves
2006 | oil on panel | 20.5 x 20.5 cm
collection of the artist

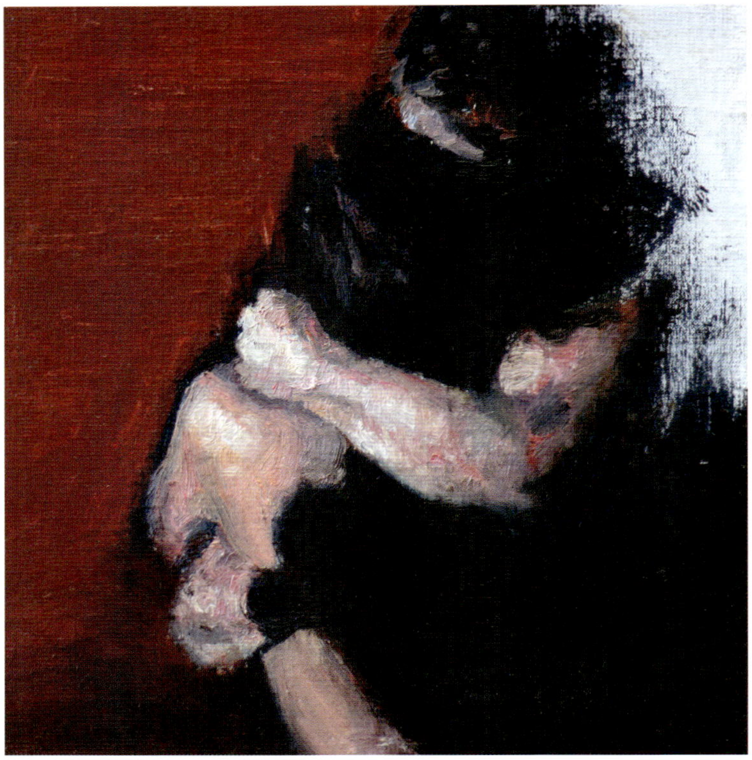

Wild Embrace
2004 | oil on panel | 20.5 x 20.5 cm
private collection

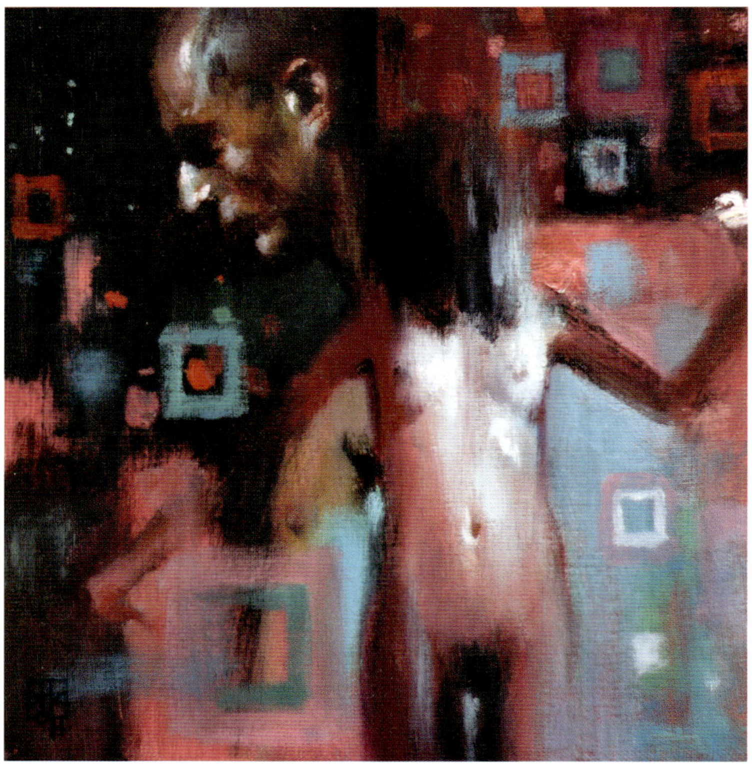

Study for Strange Tango
2005 | oil on linen | 20.5 x 20.5 cm
collection of the artist

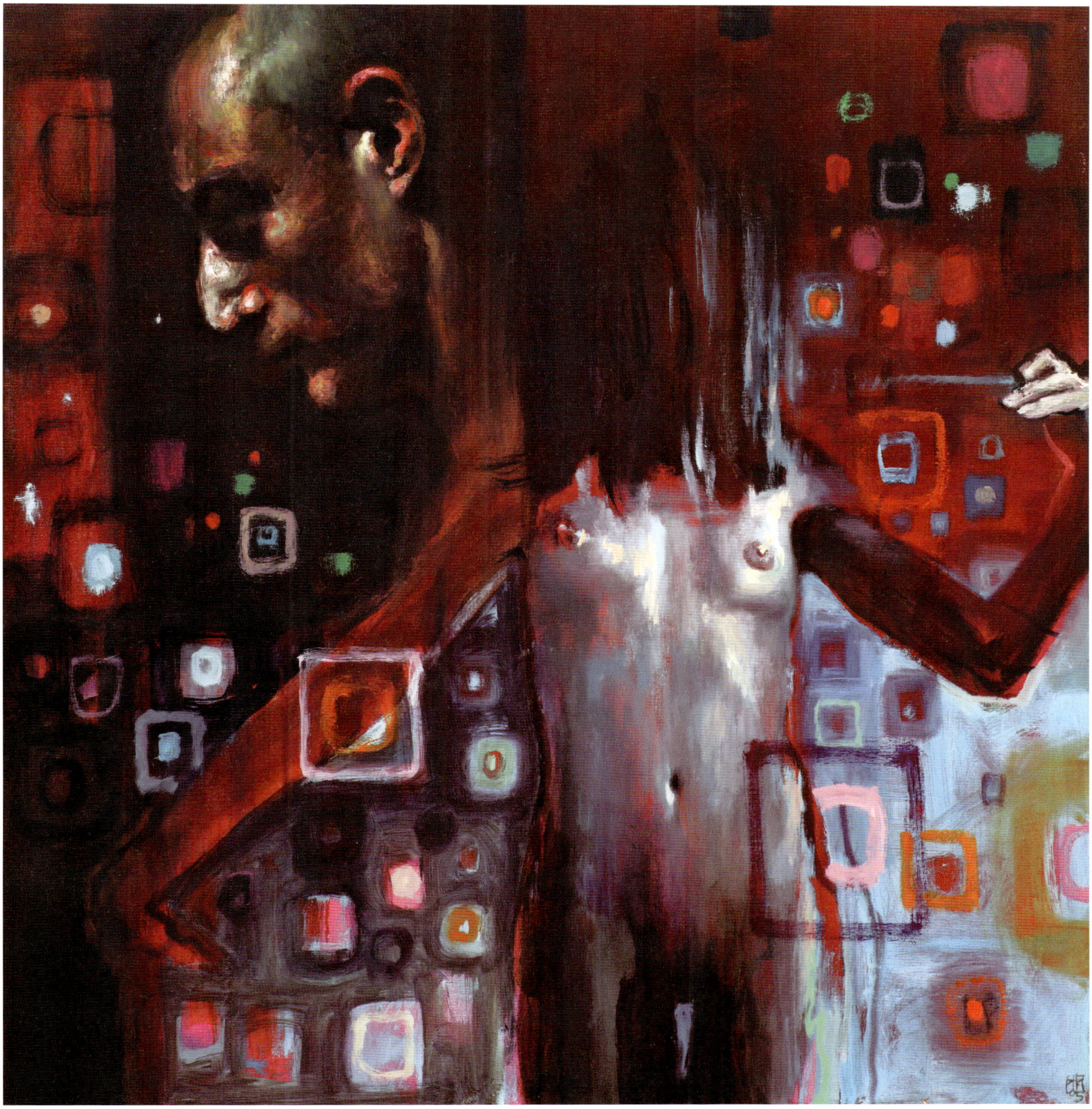

Strange Tango | 2005 | oil on linen | 91.5 x 91.5 cm

private collection

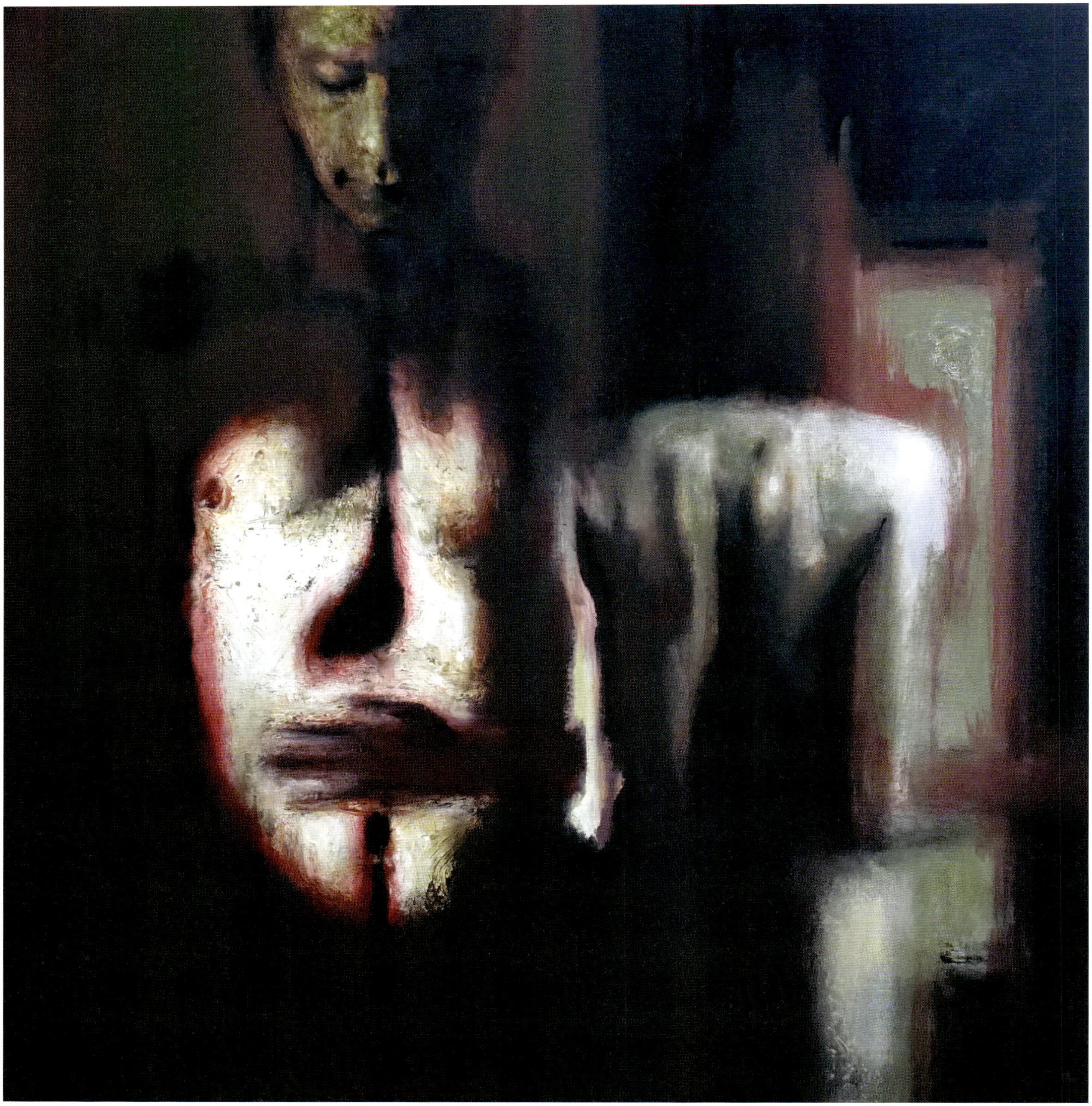

Deep Inside | 2004 | oil on linen | 91.5 x 91.5 cm collection of the artist

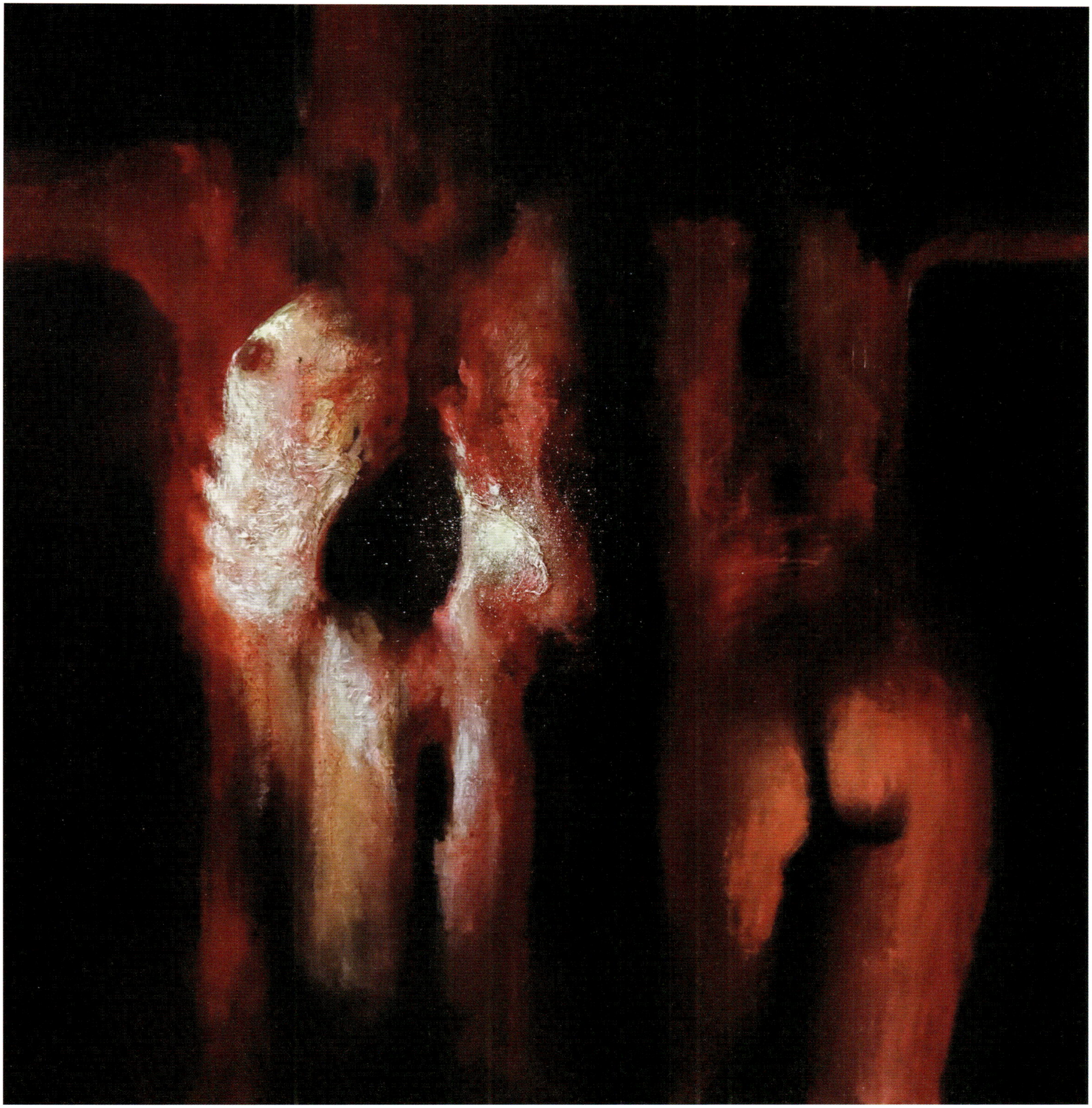

Into One | 2007 | oil on linen | 91.5 x 91.5 cm private collection

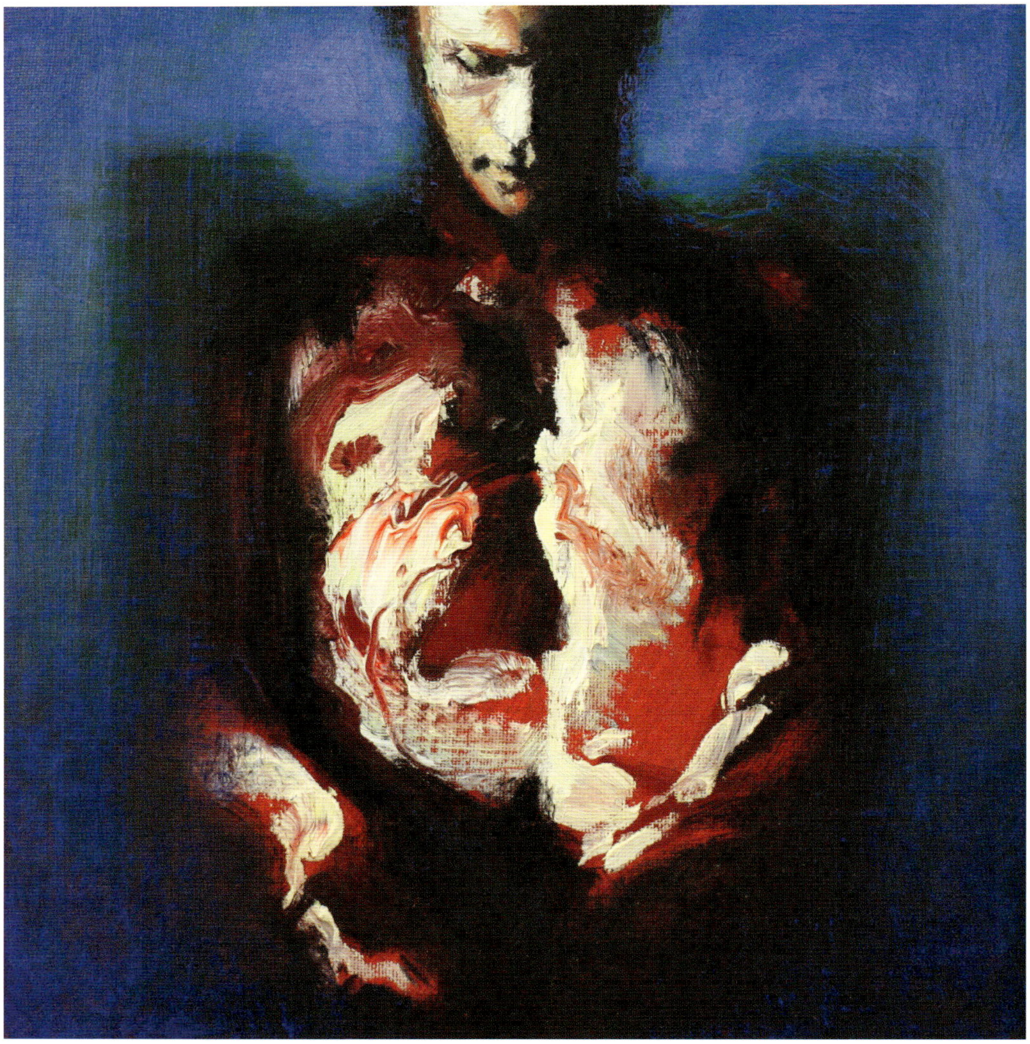

The Gift | 2005 | oil on linen | 25.5 x 25.5 cm private collection

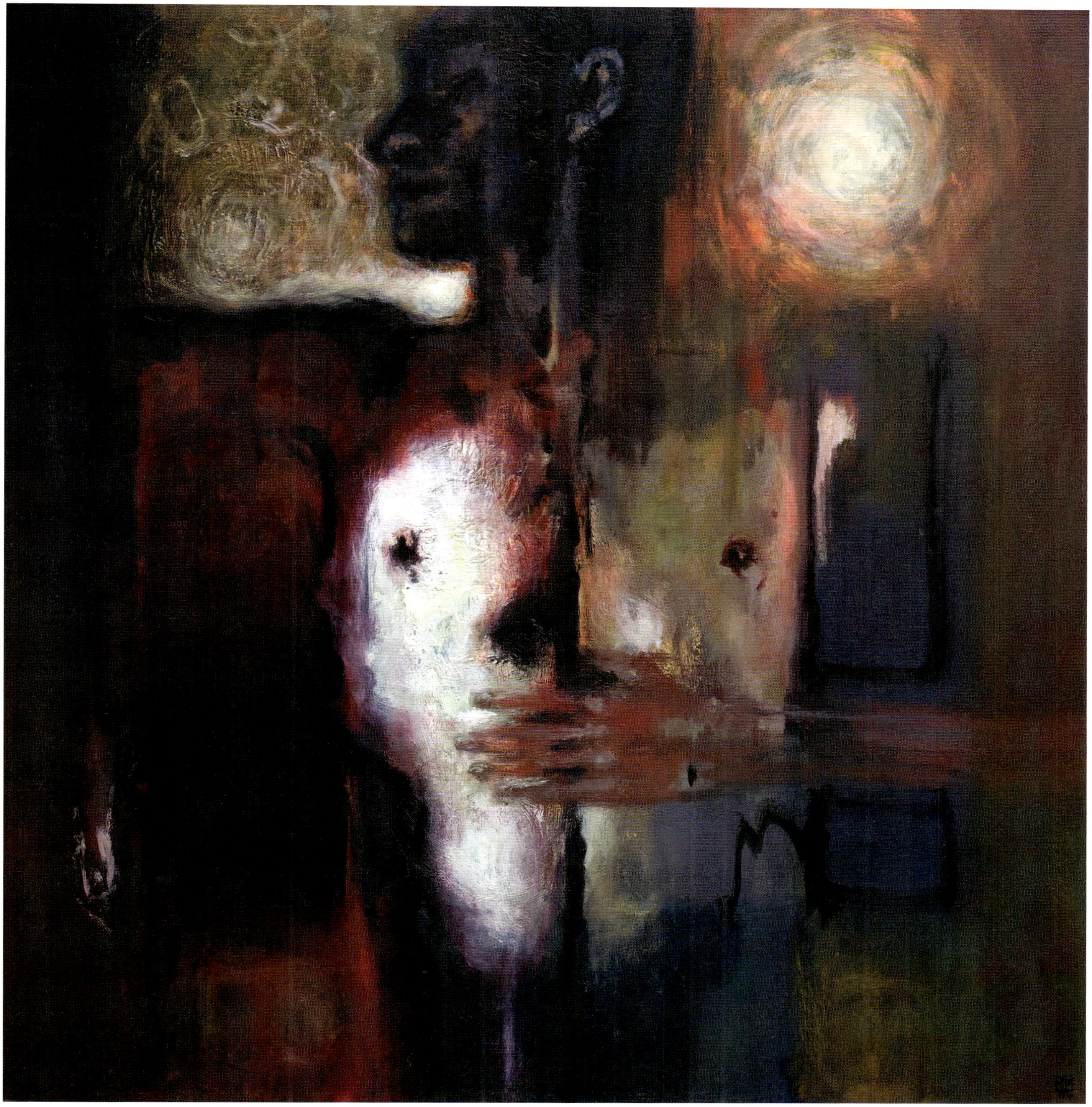

Wound | 2004 | oil on linen | 91.5 x 91.5 cm collection of the artist

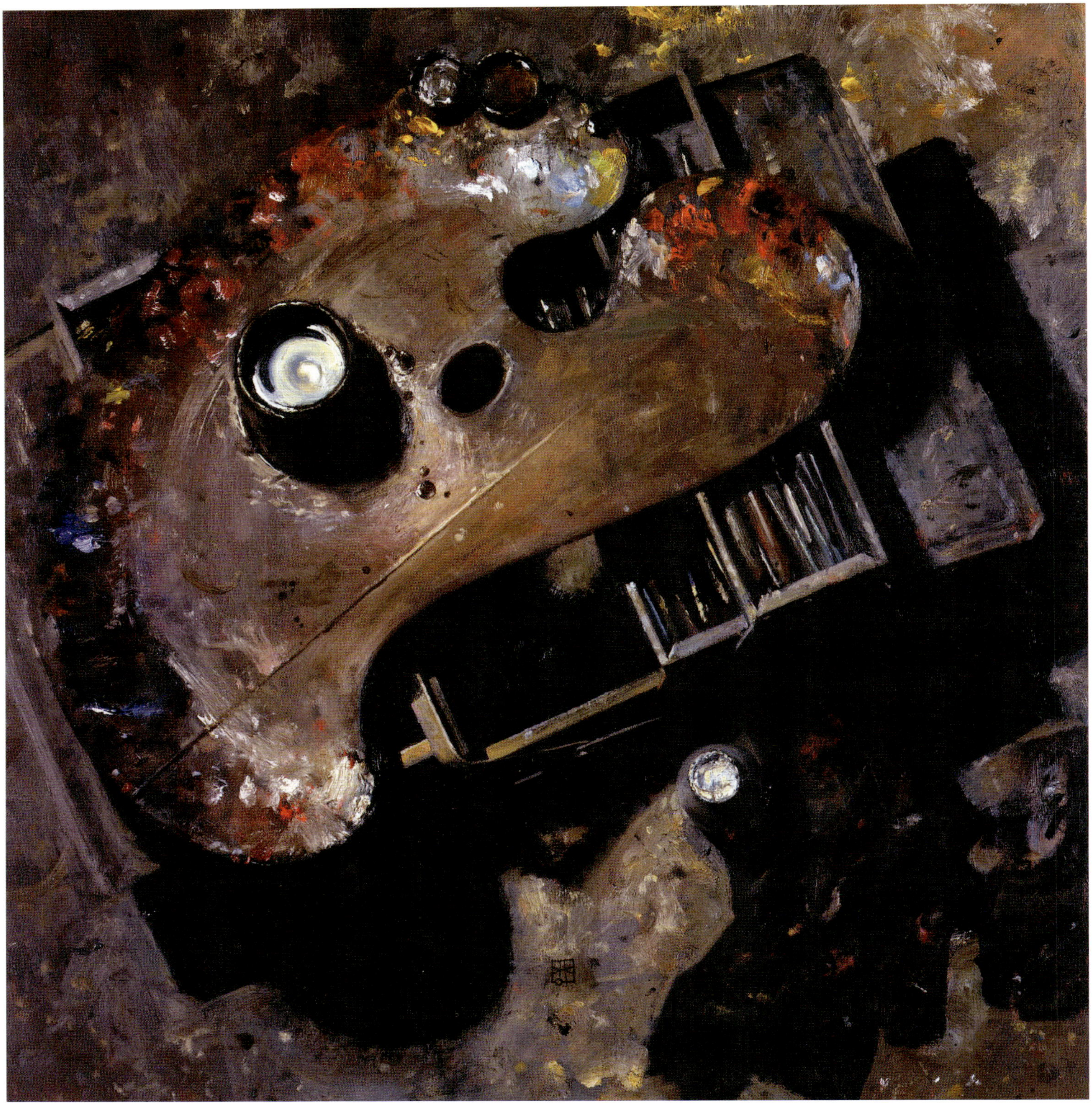

The Smell of Turps | 2001 | oil on linen | 61 x 61 cm   Victoria Art Gallery, Bath

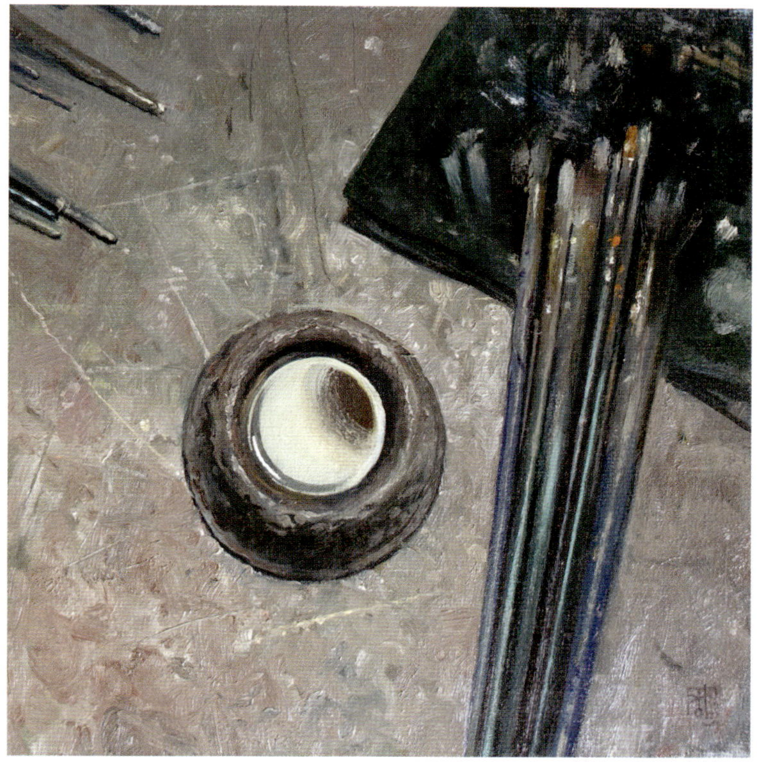

After the Event
2006 | oil on panel | 30.5 x 30.5 cm
collection of the artist

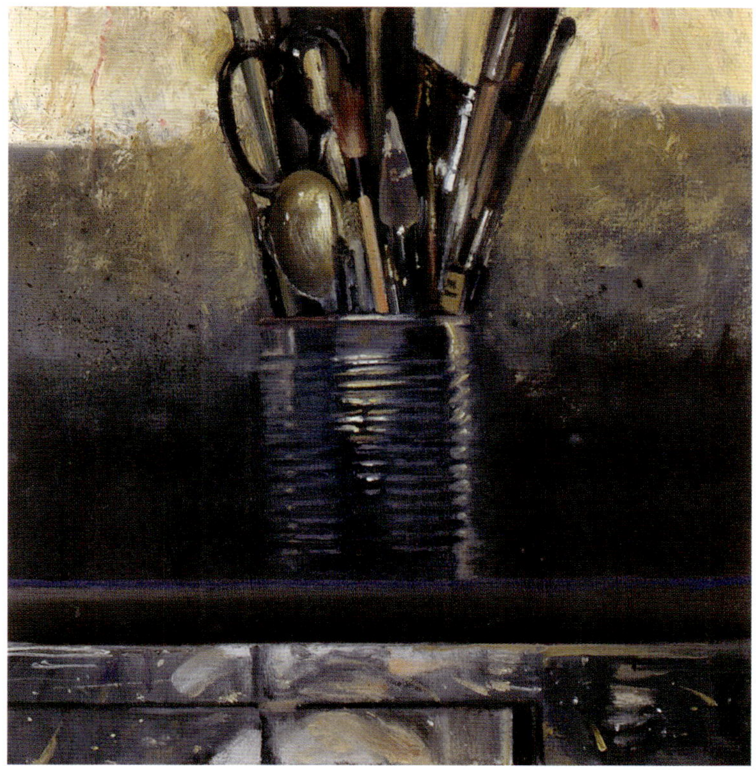

Paraphernalia
2002 | oil on linen | 40.5 x 40.5 cm
private collection

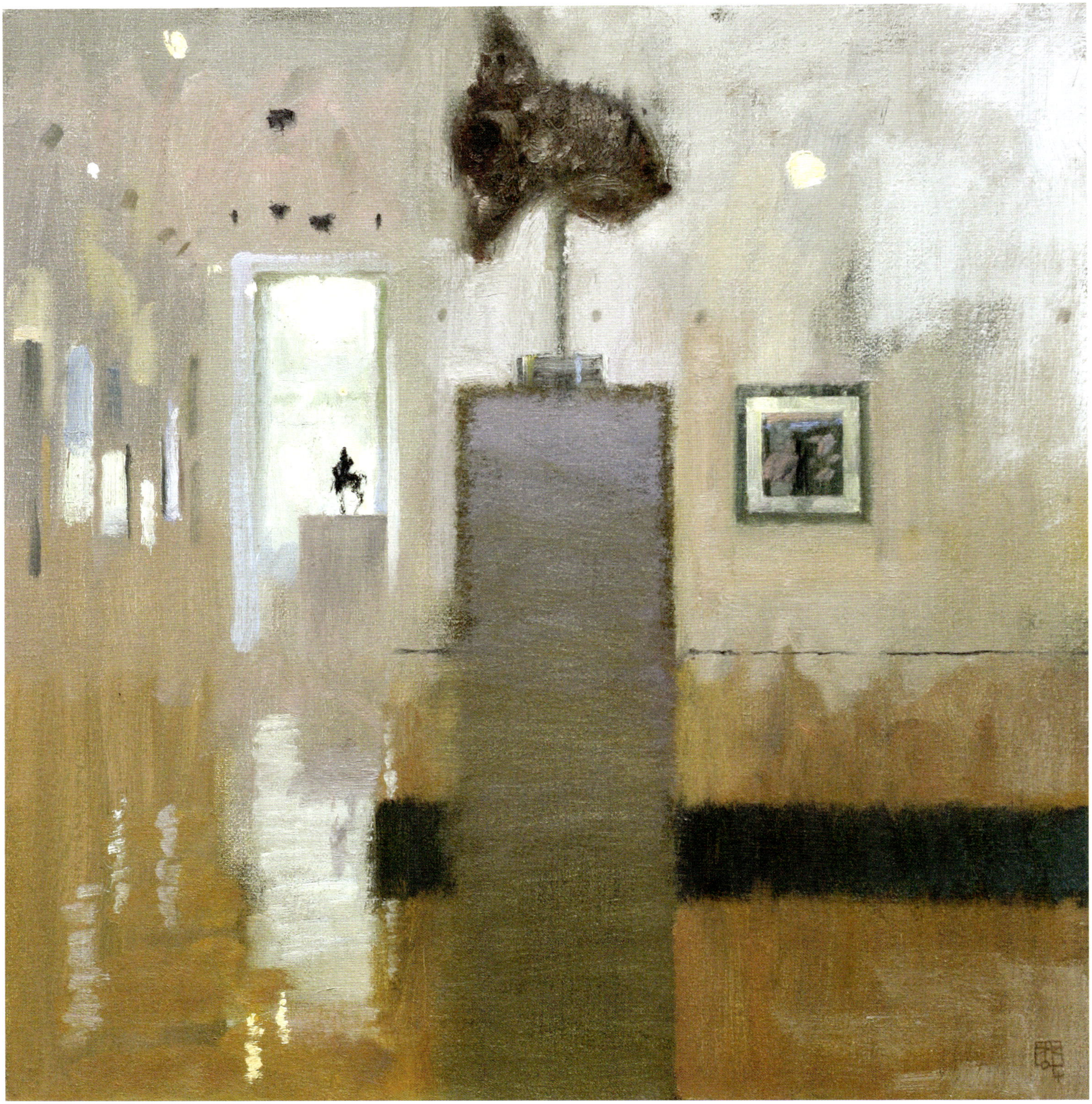

The Hotbath With Ned Kelly in the Distance | 2004 | oil on linen | 41 x 41 cm private collection

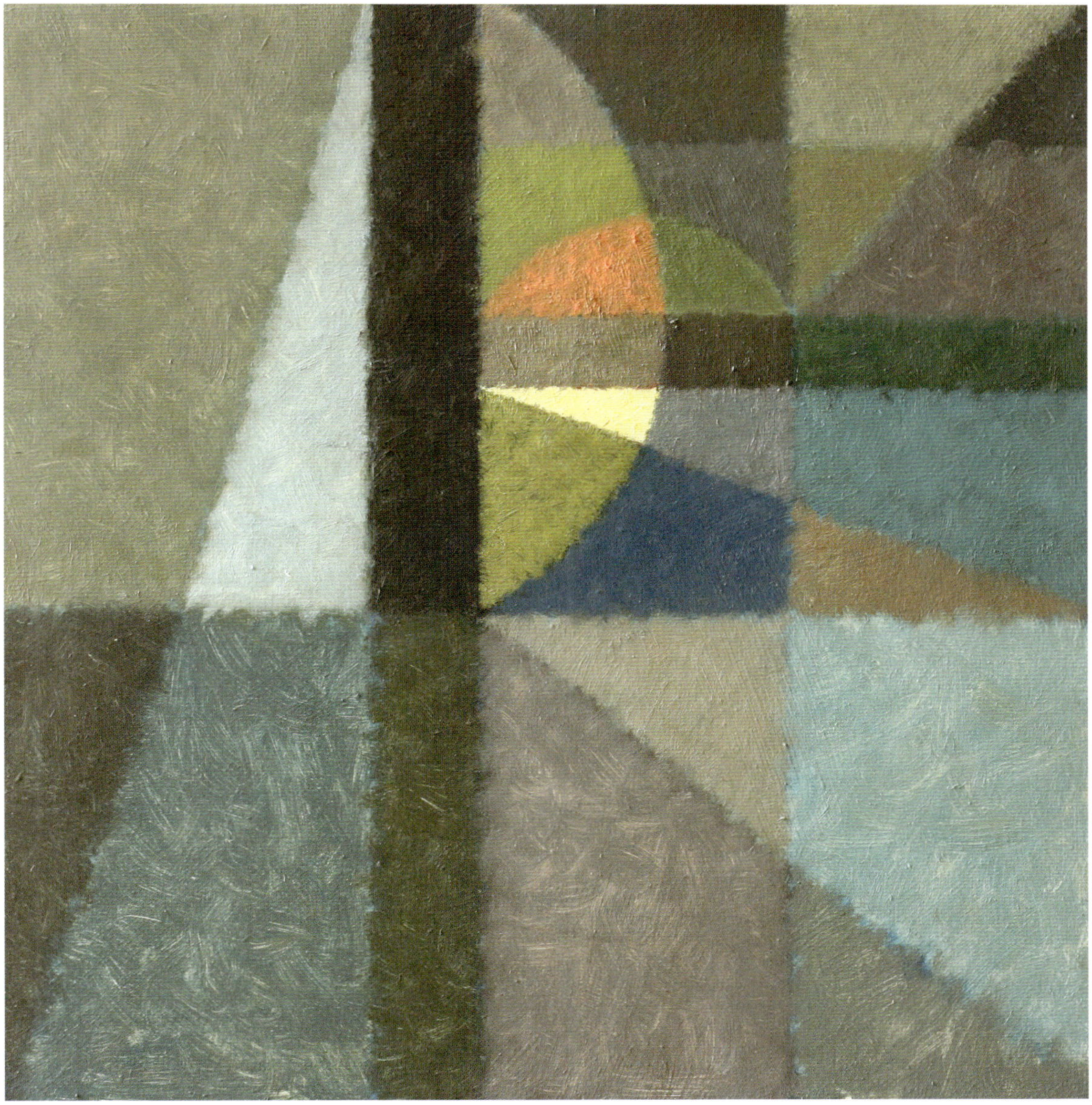

Art | 2010 | oil on linen | 30.5 x 30.5 cm

private collection

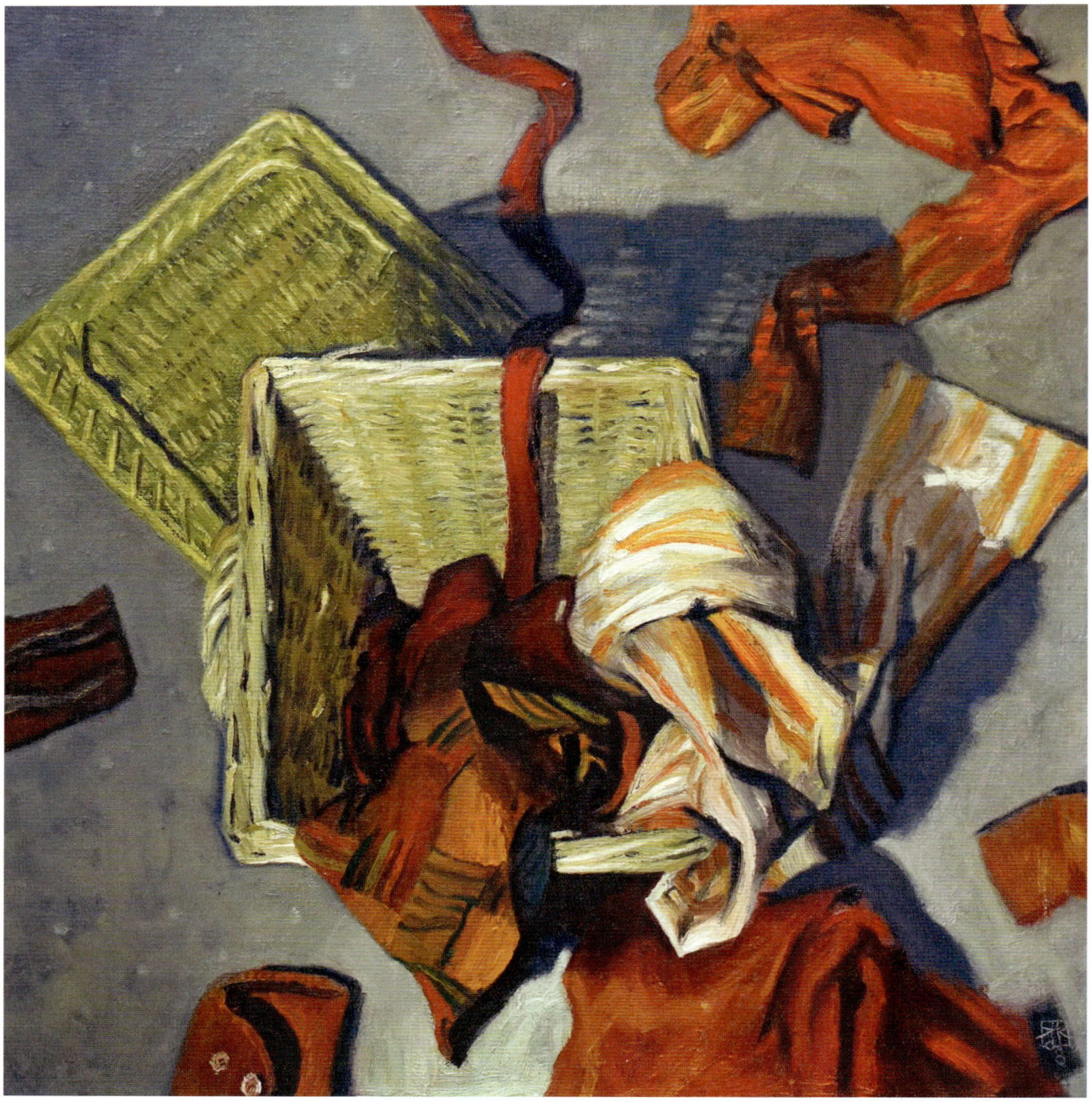

And So it Begins | 2008 | oil on linen | 45.5 x 45.5 cm collection of the artist

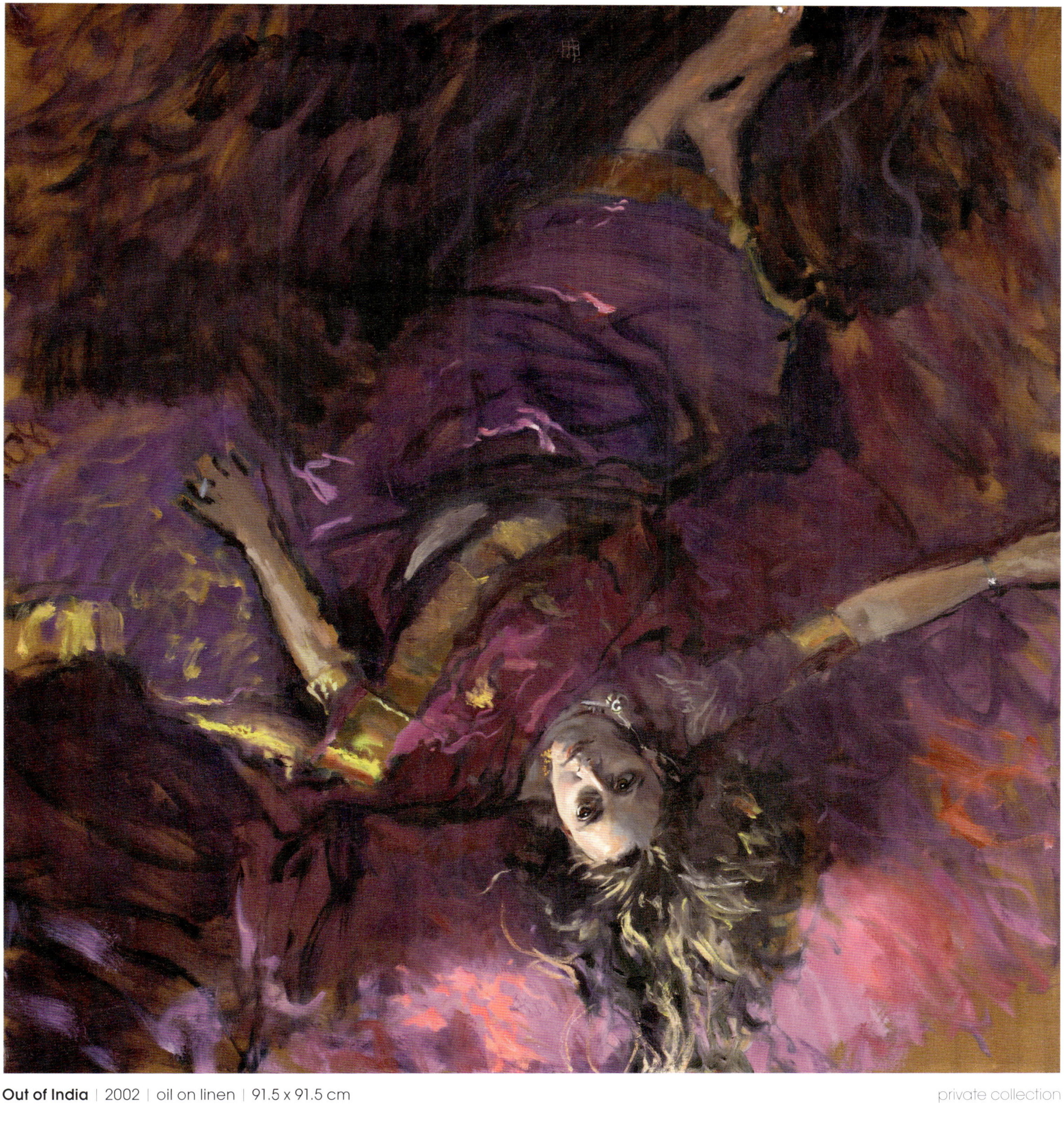

Out of India | 2002 | oil on linen | 91.5 x 91.5 cm   private collection

Spilt Milk
2005 | oil on linen | 91.5 x 91.5 cm
collection of the artist

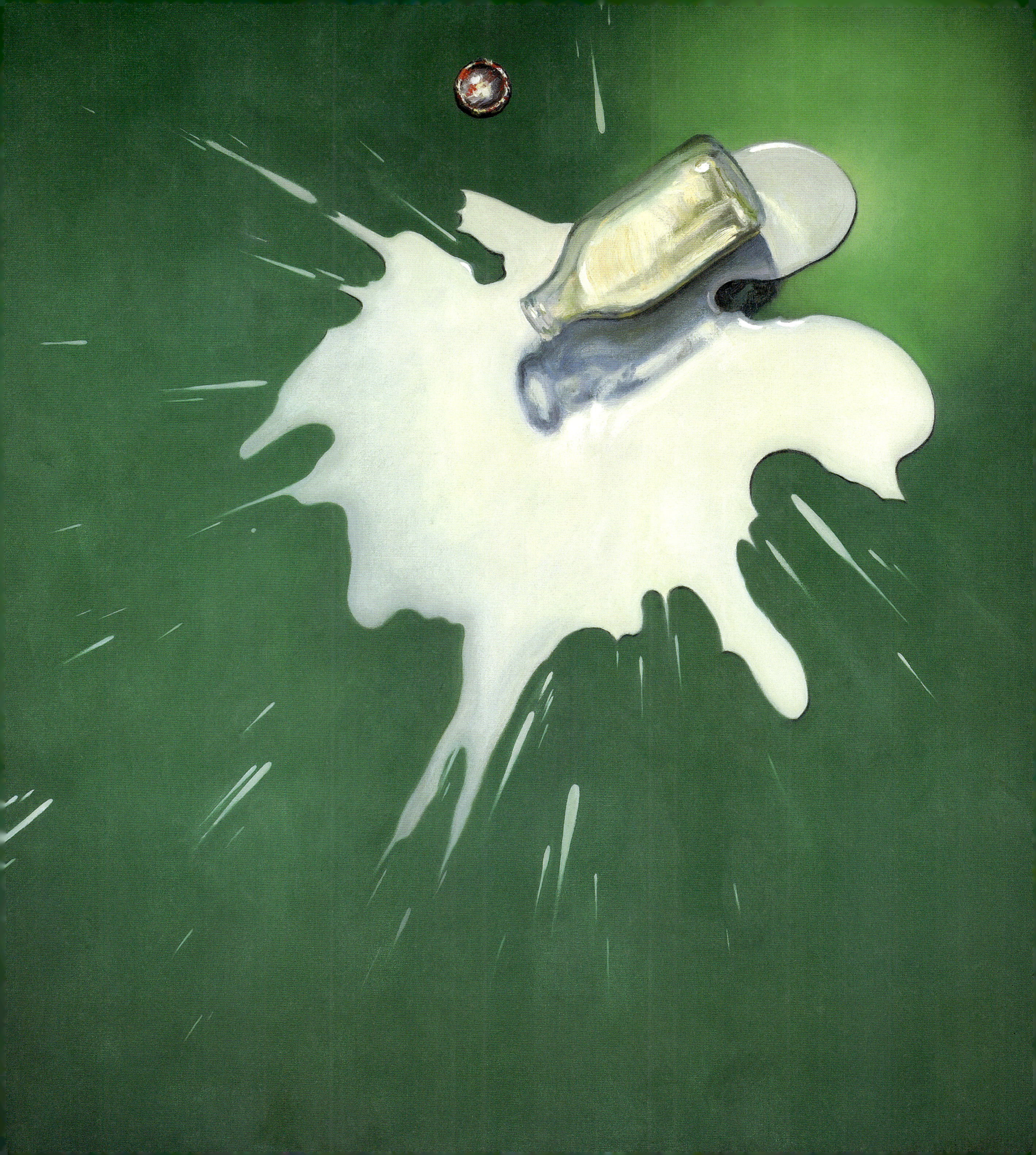

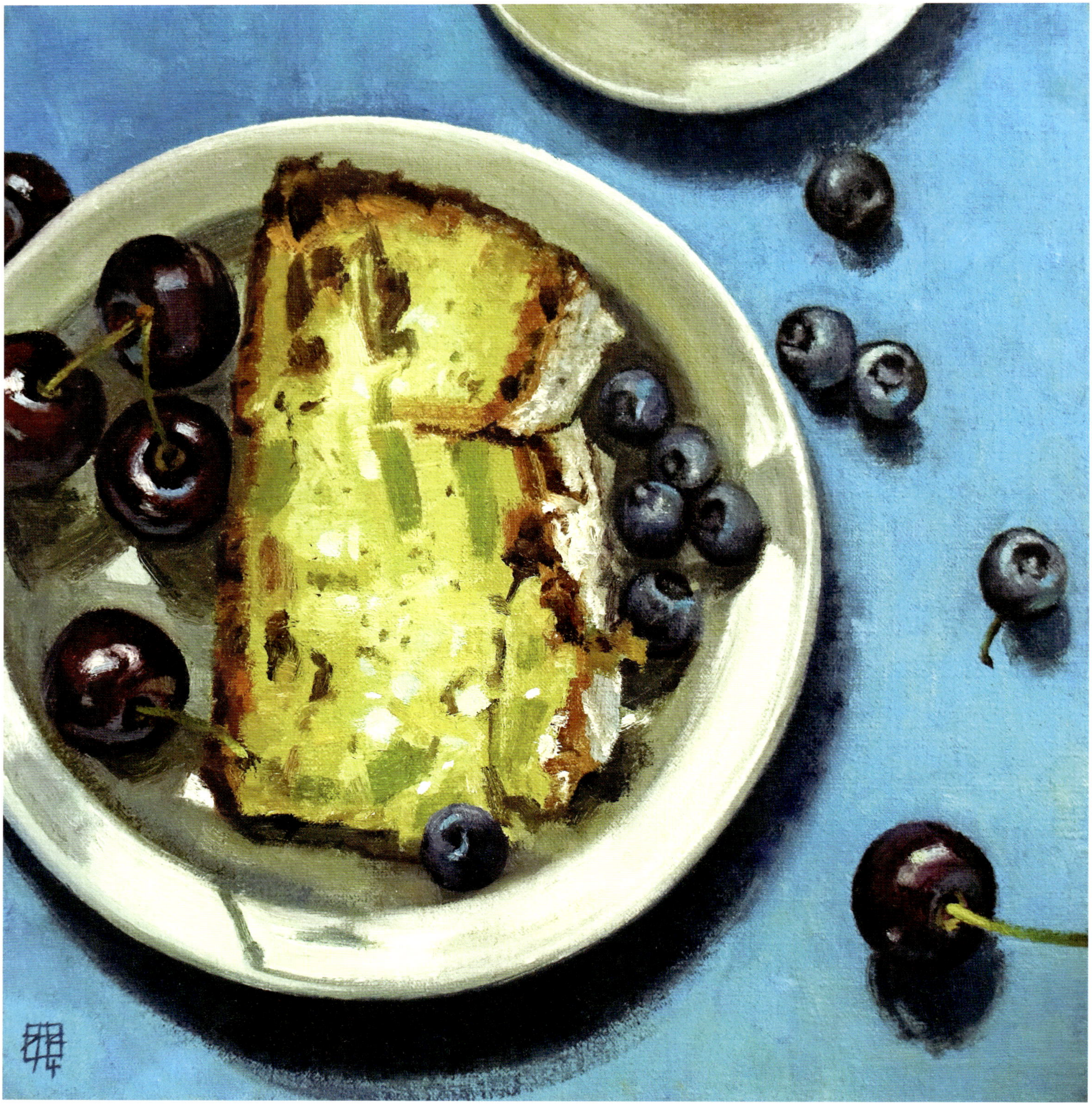

Dolcipani I | 2014 | oil on linen | 30.5 x 30.5 cm   collection of the artist

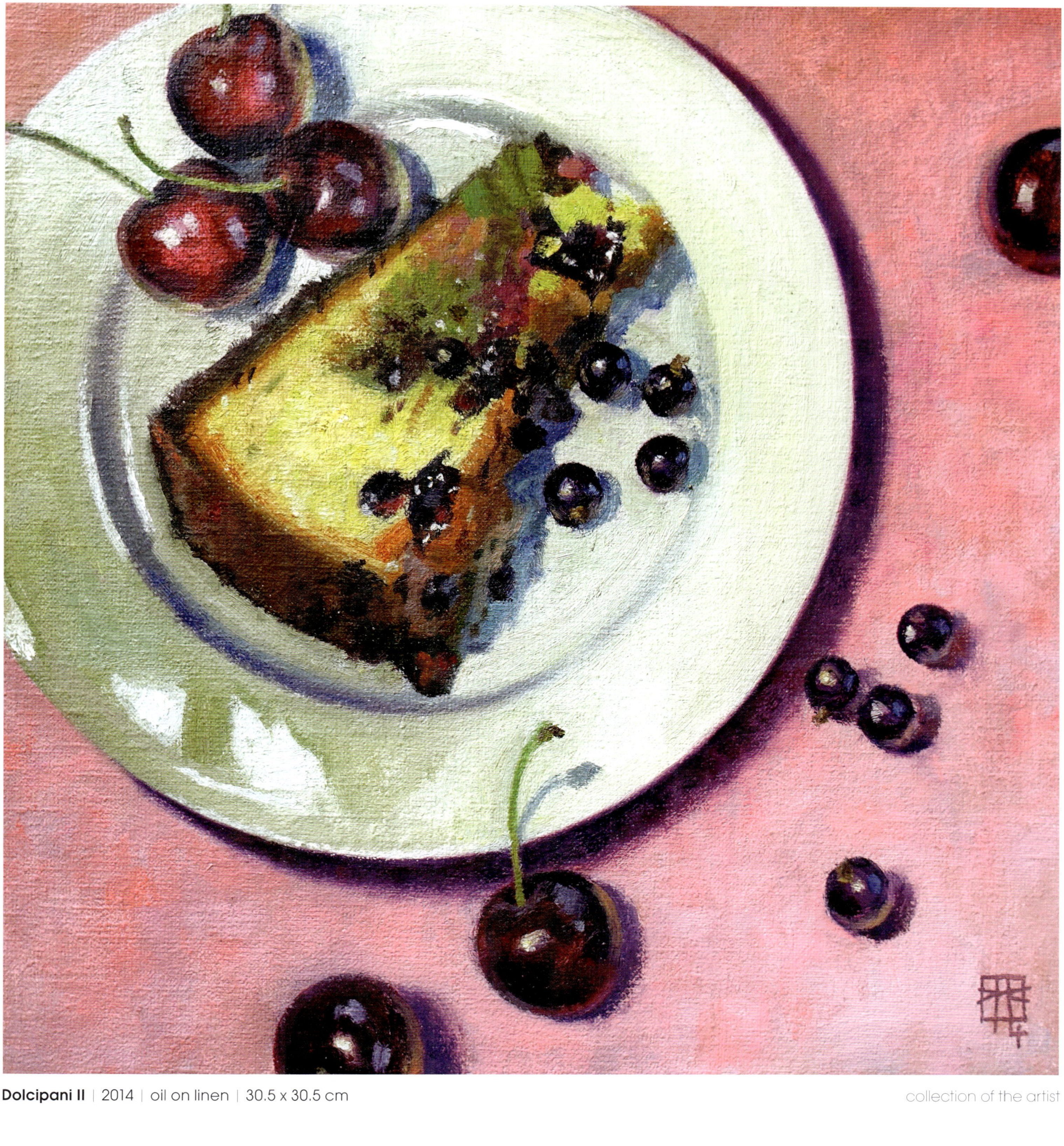

Dolcipani II | 2014 | oil on linen | 30.5 x 30.5 cm

collection of the artist

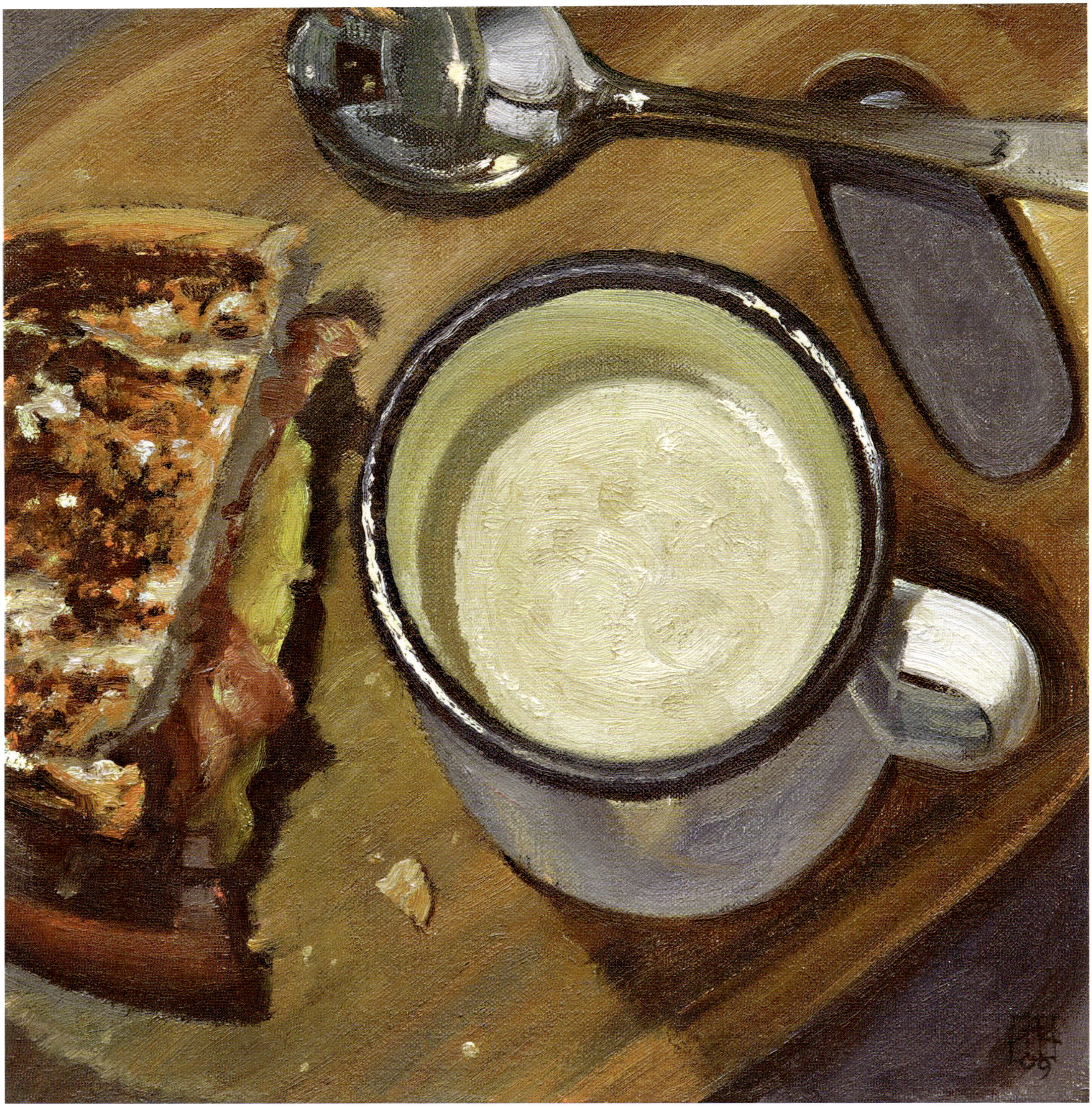

Pub Grub | 2005 | oil on linen | 30.5 x 30.5 cm

collection of the artist

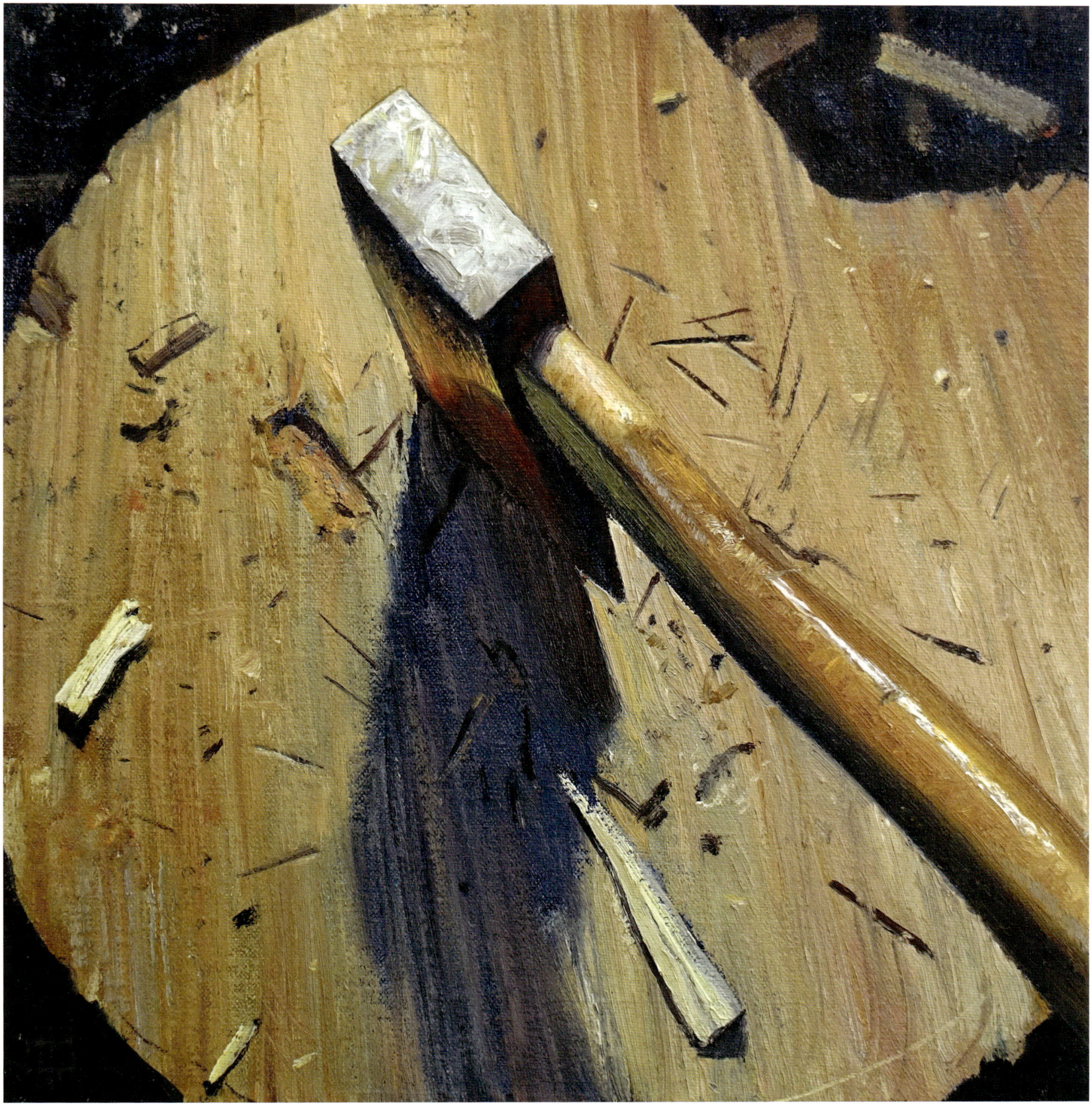

Chop Chop | 2005 | oil on linen | 30.5 x 30.5 cm collection of the artist

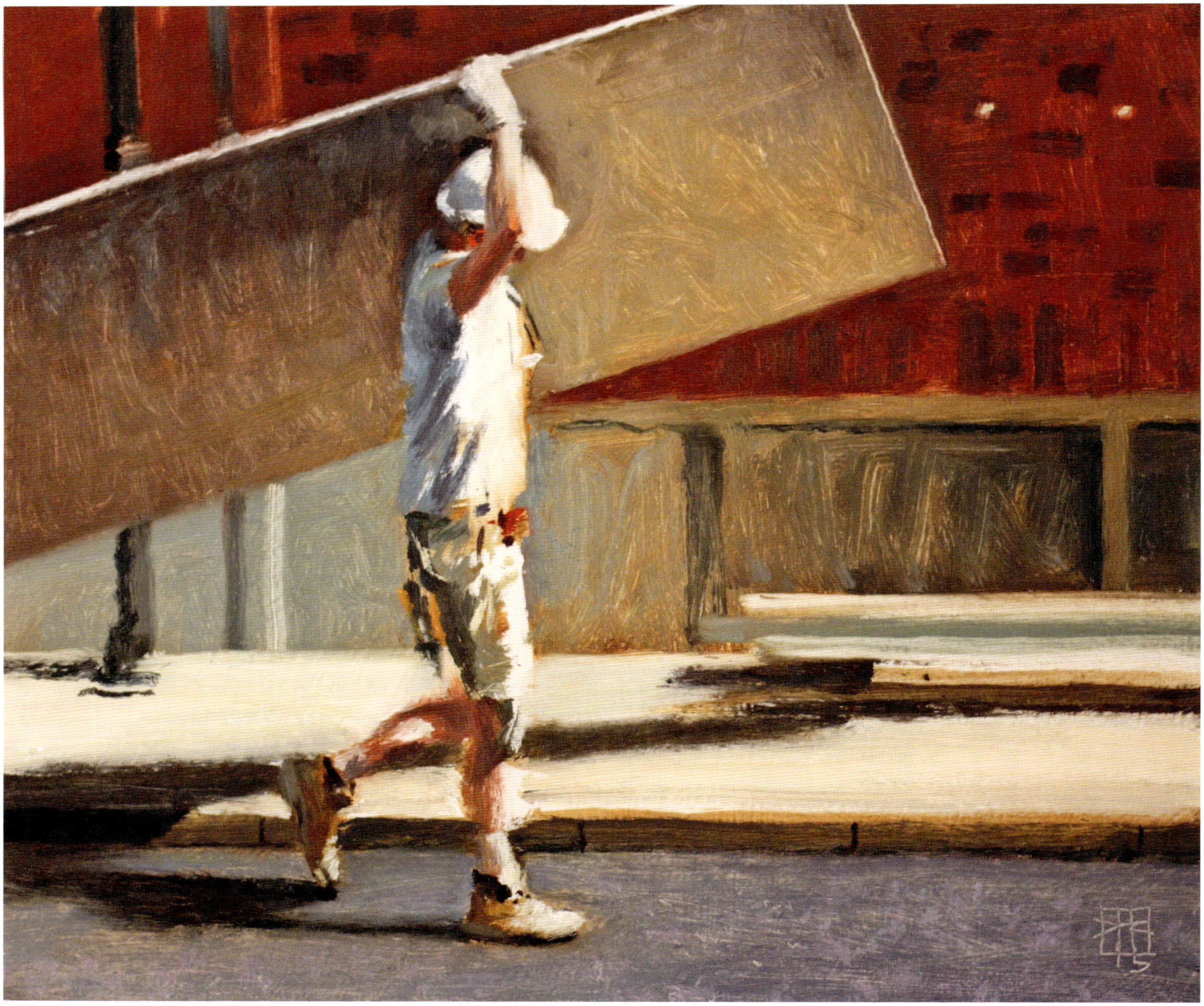

The Builder | 2015 | oil on panel | 20 x 24 cm private collection

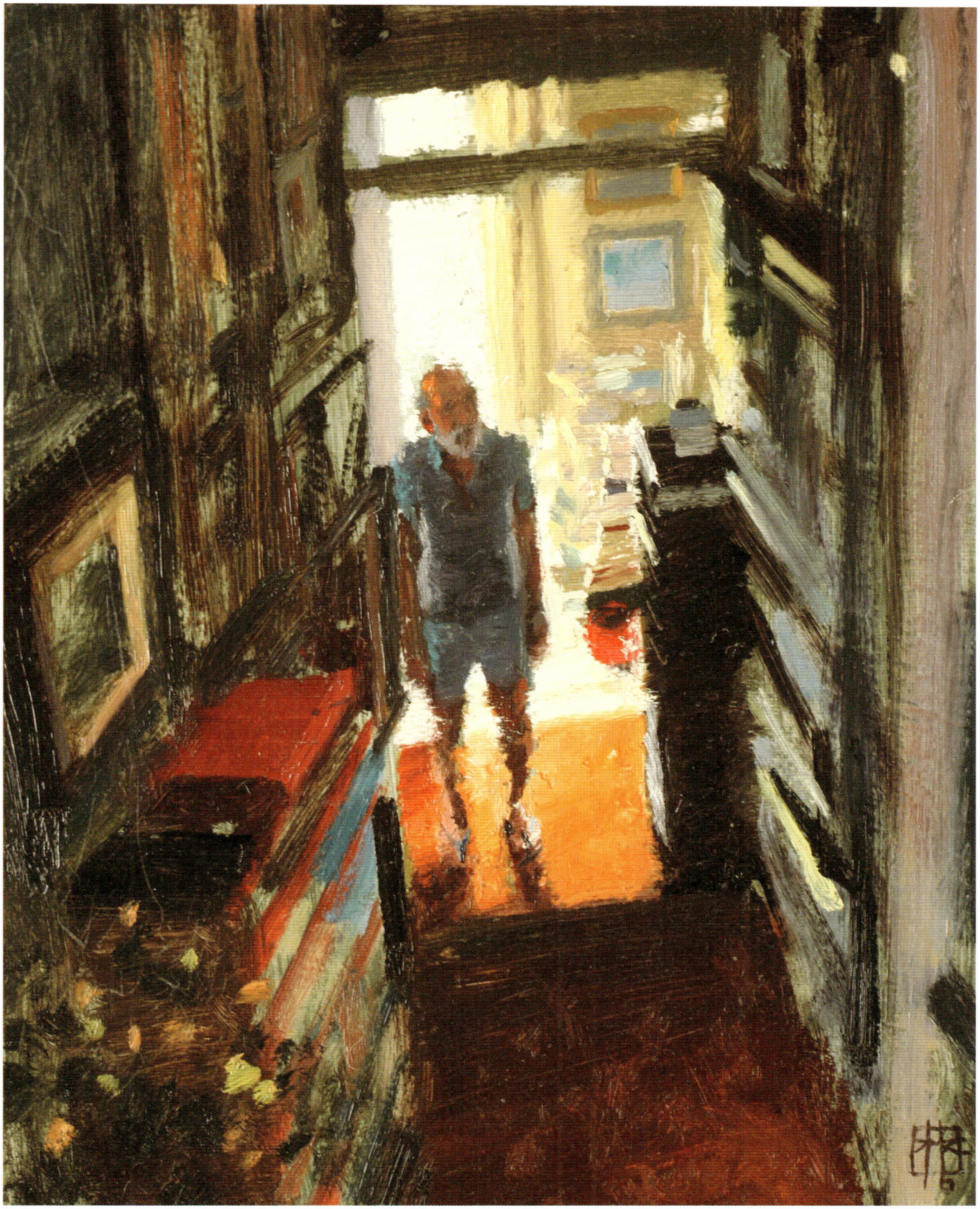

The Collector | 2016 | oil on panel | 24 x 20 cm   collection of the artist

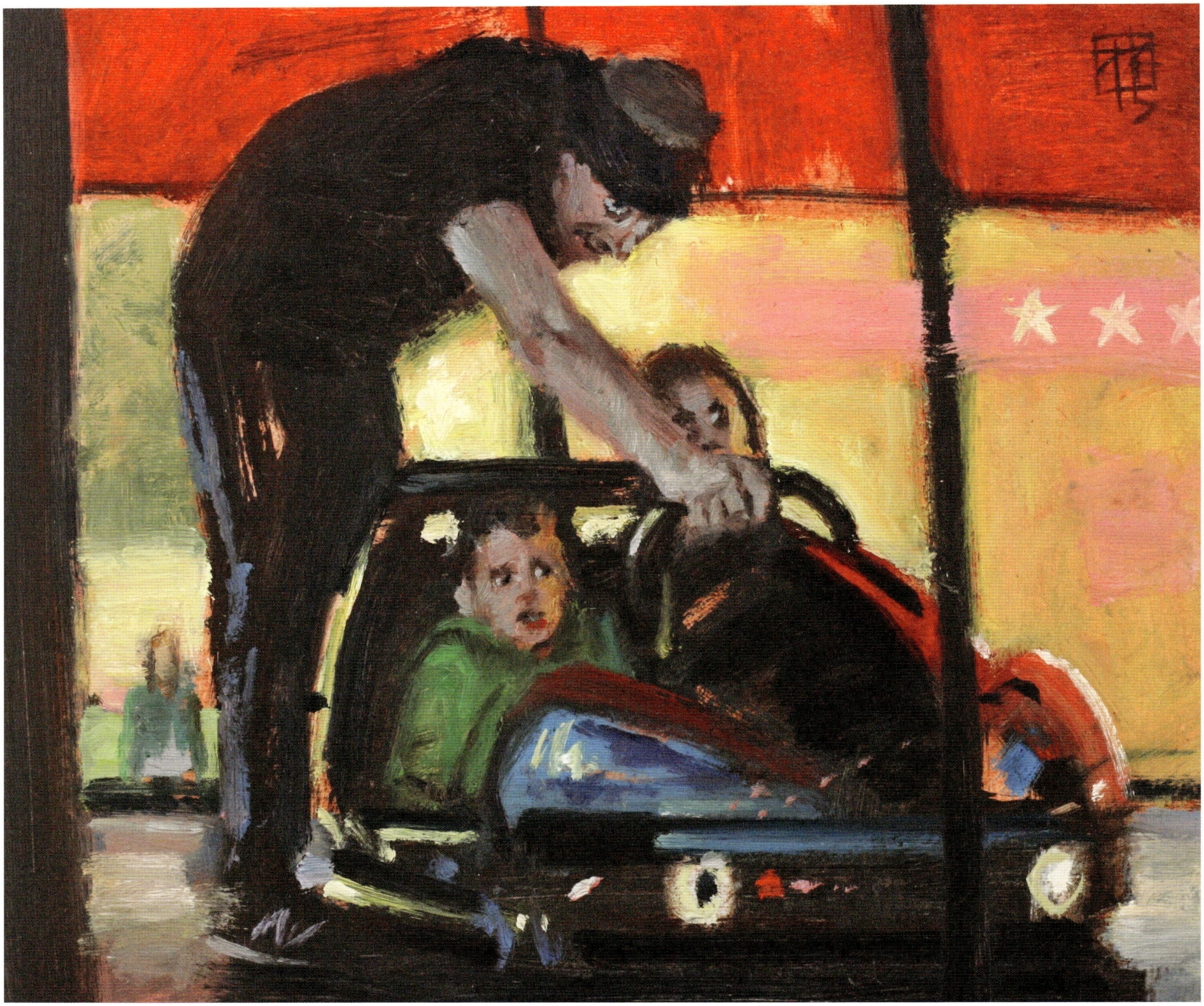

On the Dodgems | 2015 | oil on panel | 20 x 24 cm collection of the artist

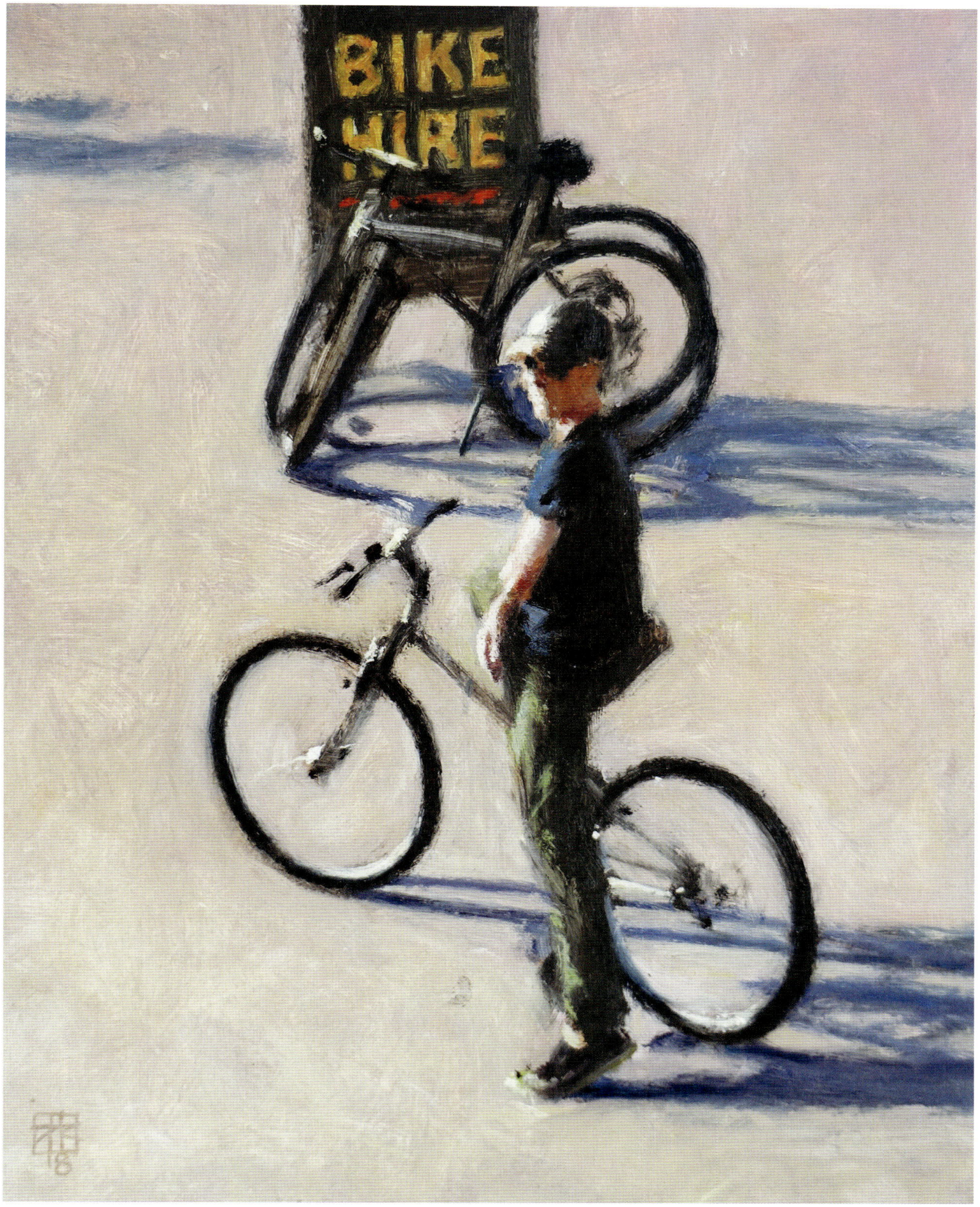

On Her Bike | 2018 | oil on panel | 24 x 20 cm

collection of the artist

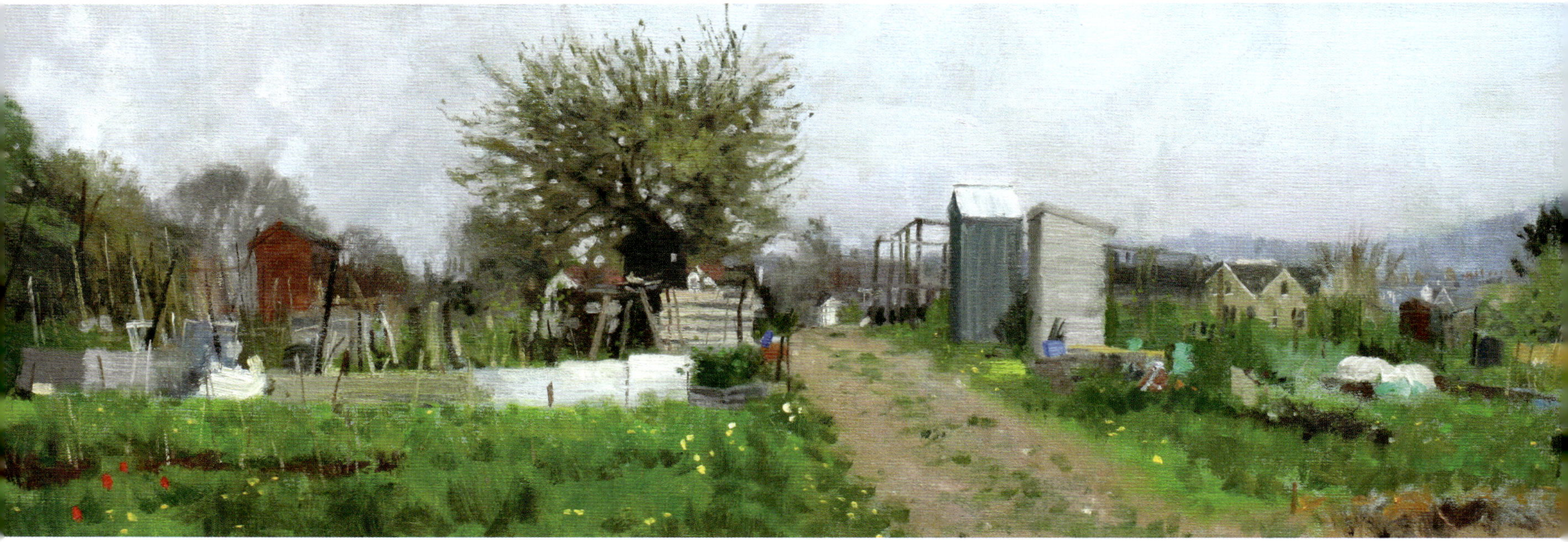

Allotment VI | 2006 | oil on linen | 30.5 x 91.5 cm collection of the artist

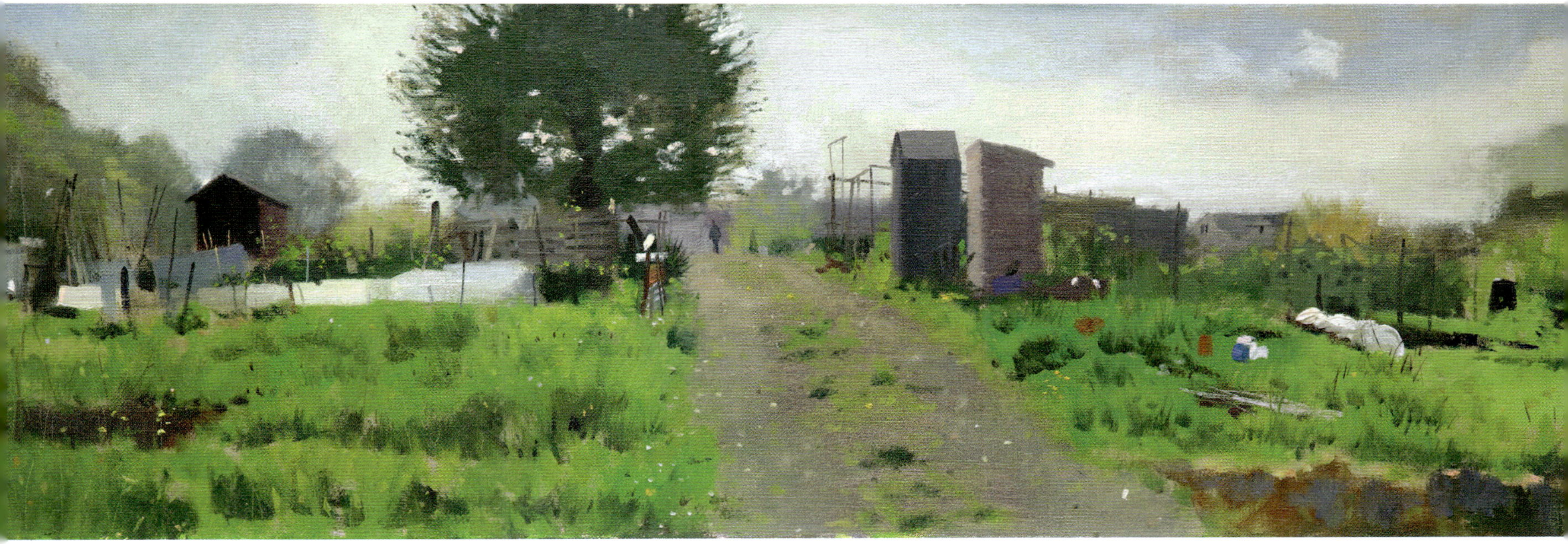

Allotment VII | 2009 | oil on linen | 30.5 x 91.5 cm collection of the artist

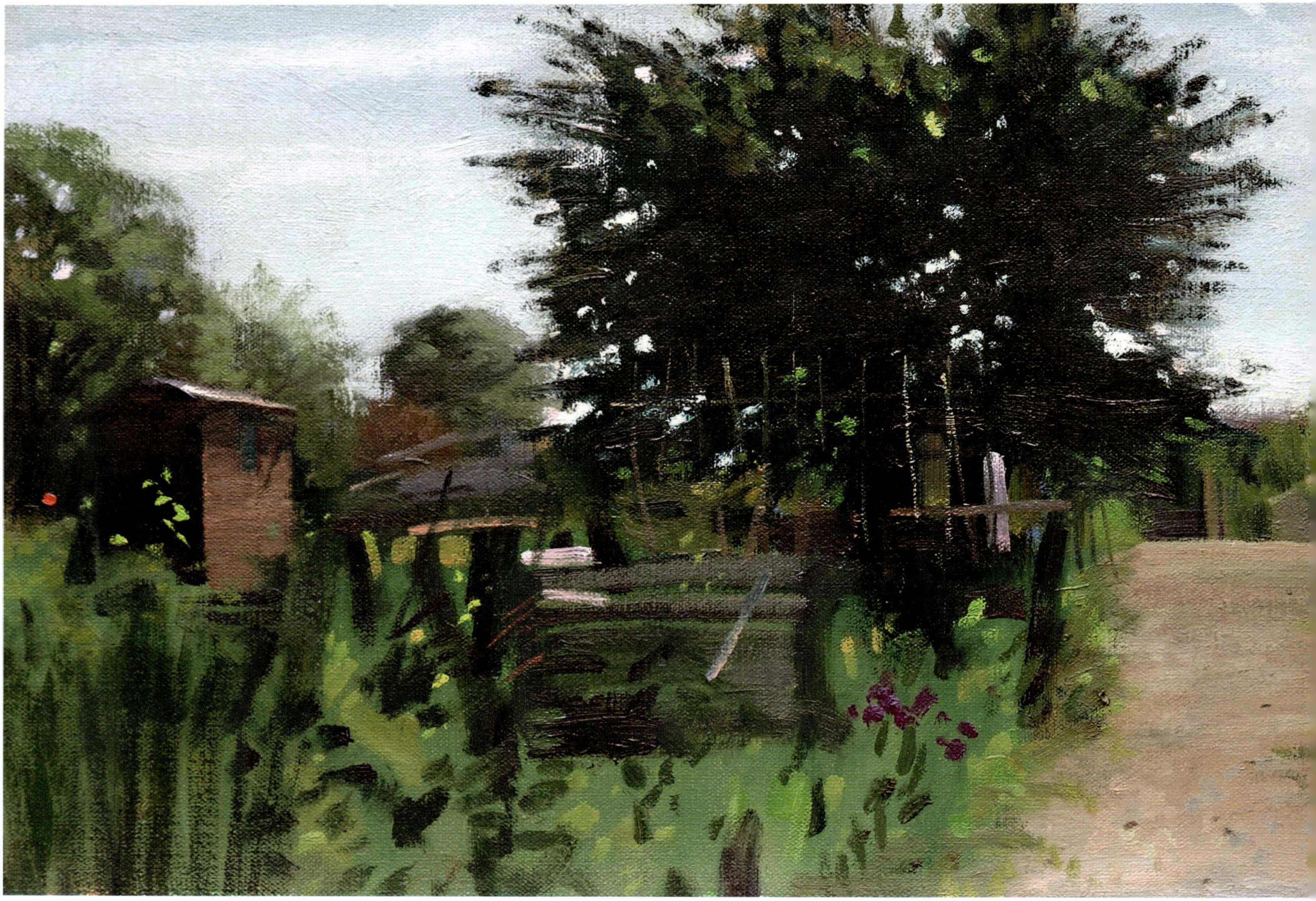

Allotment III | 2006 | oil on linen | 30.5 x 91.5 cm

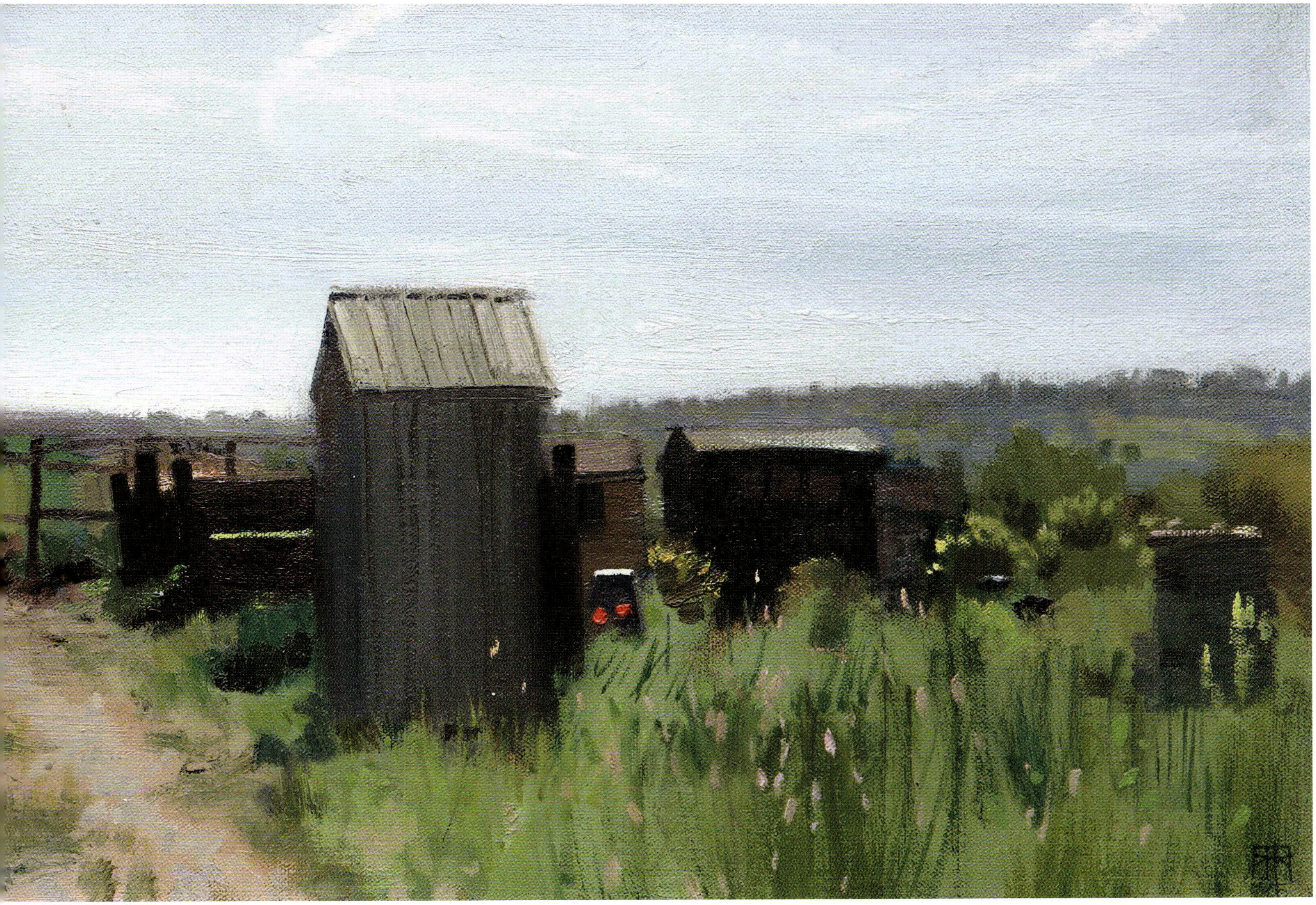

collection of the artist

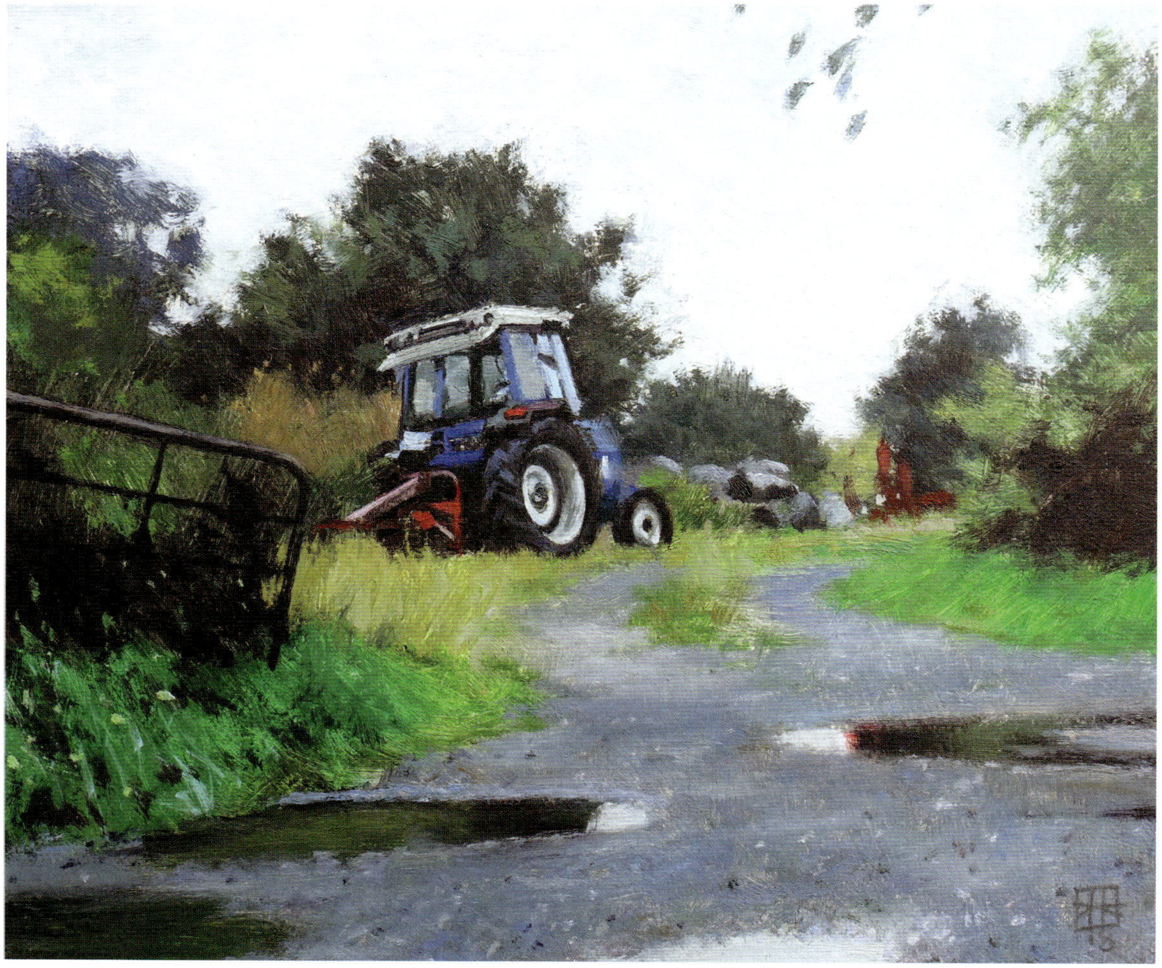

The Tractor | 2018 | oil on panel | 20 x 24 cm

collection of the artist

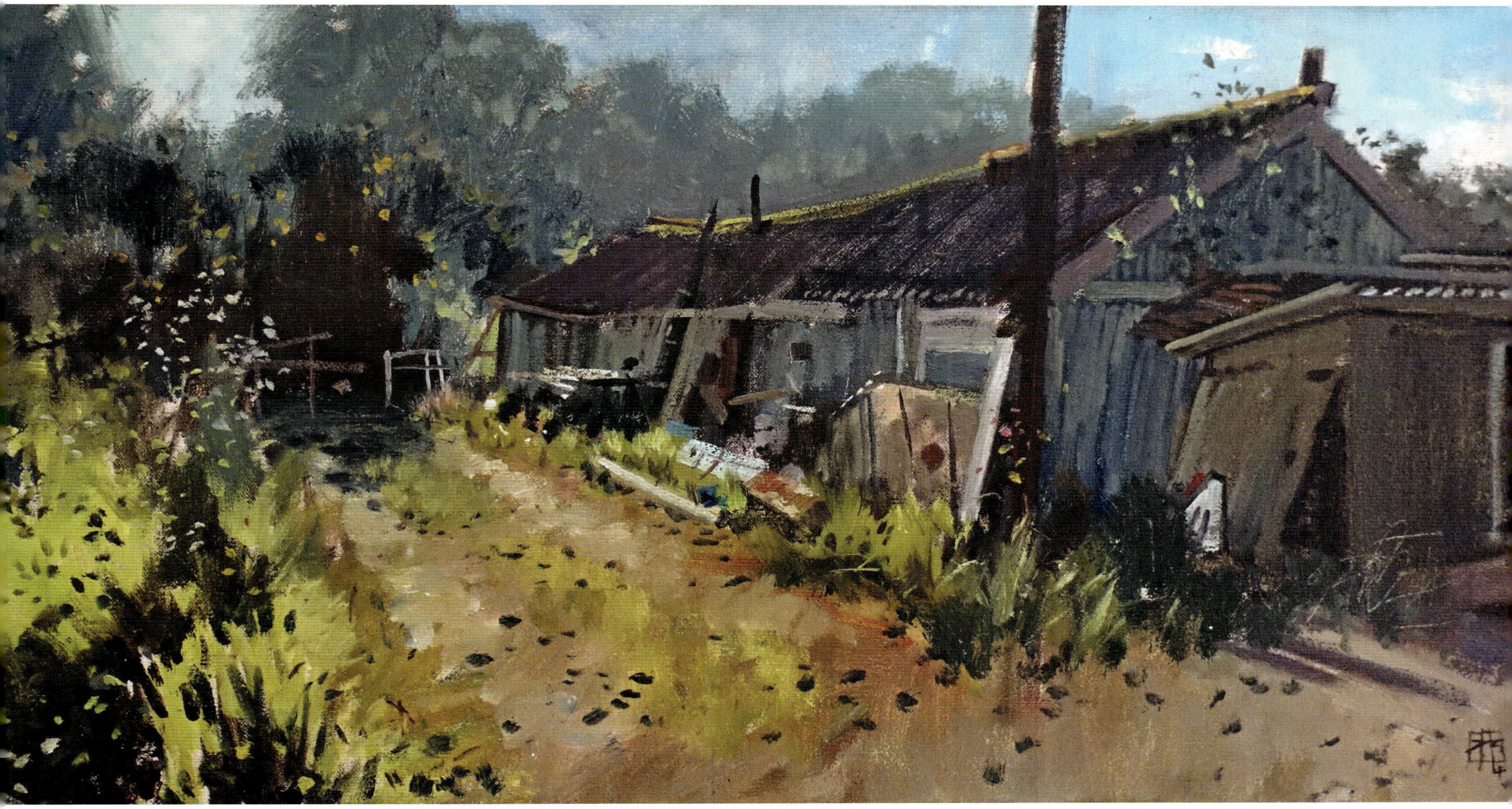

The Old Boathouse | 2014 | oil on linen | 30.5 x 61 cm

collection of the artist

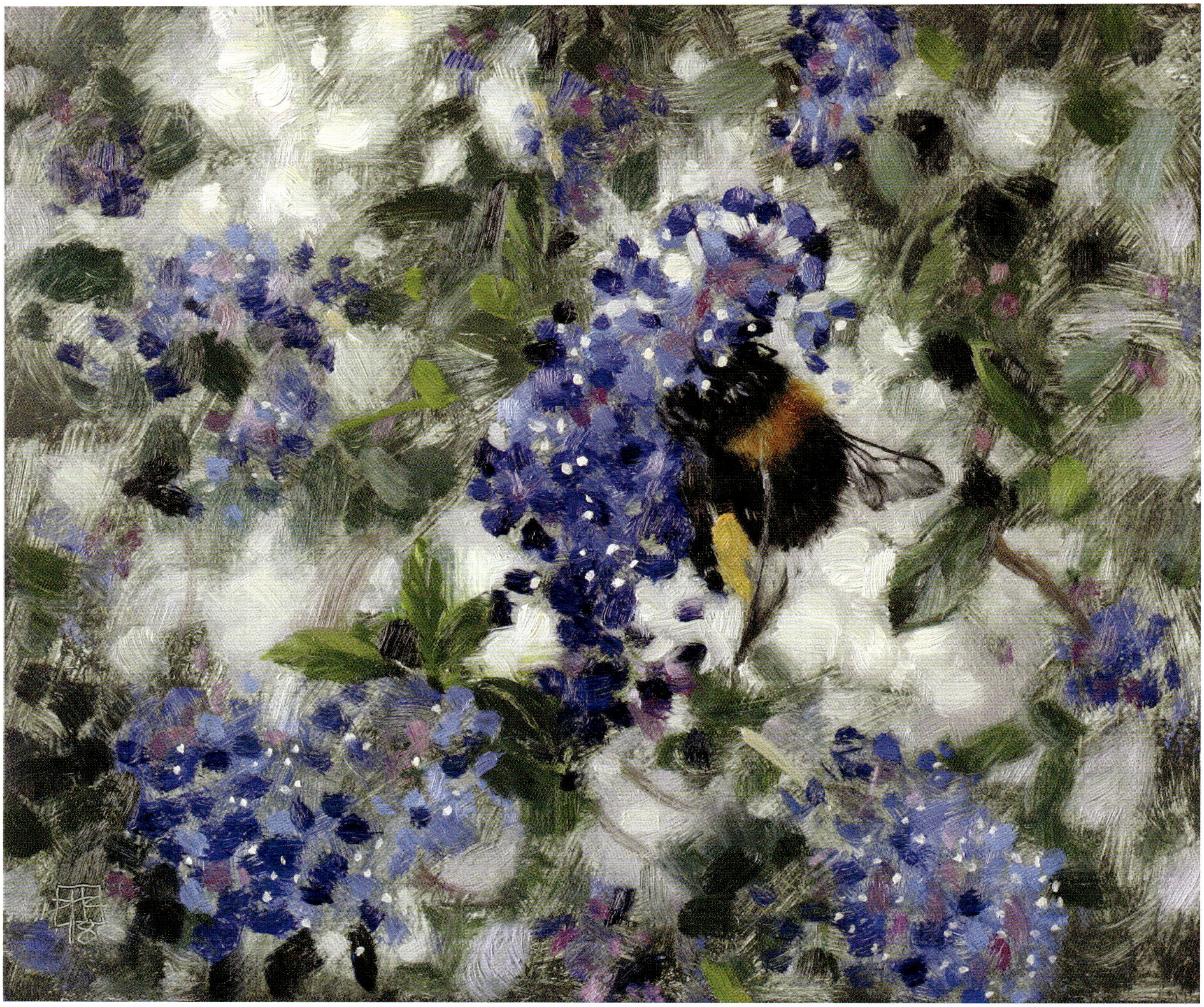

Bumble Bee | 2018 | oil on panel | 20 x 24 cm

private collection

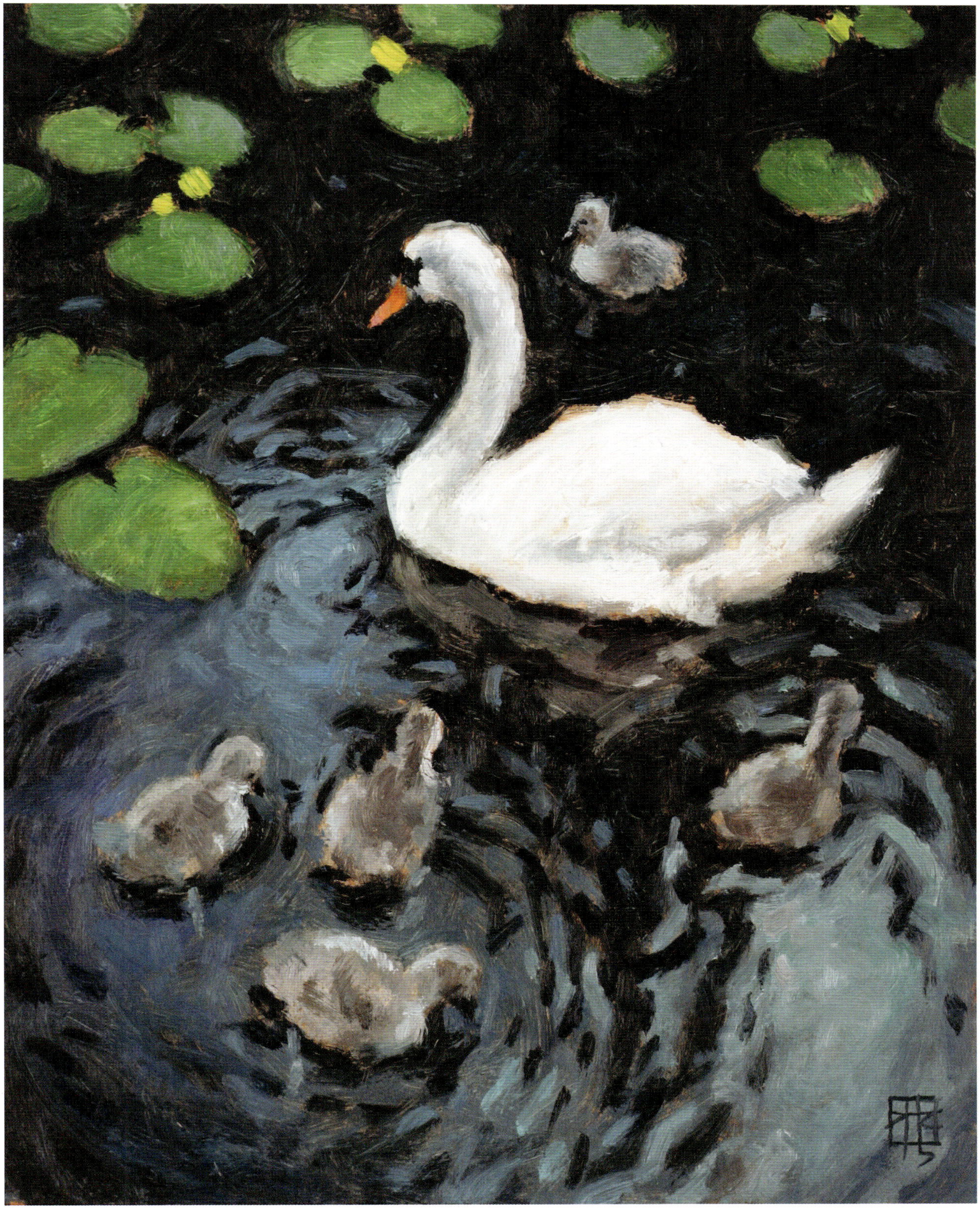

With Her Cygnets | 2015 | oil on panel | 24 x 20 cm private collection

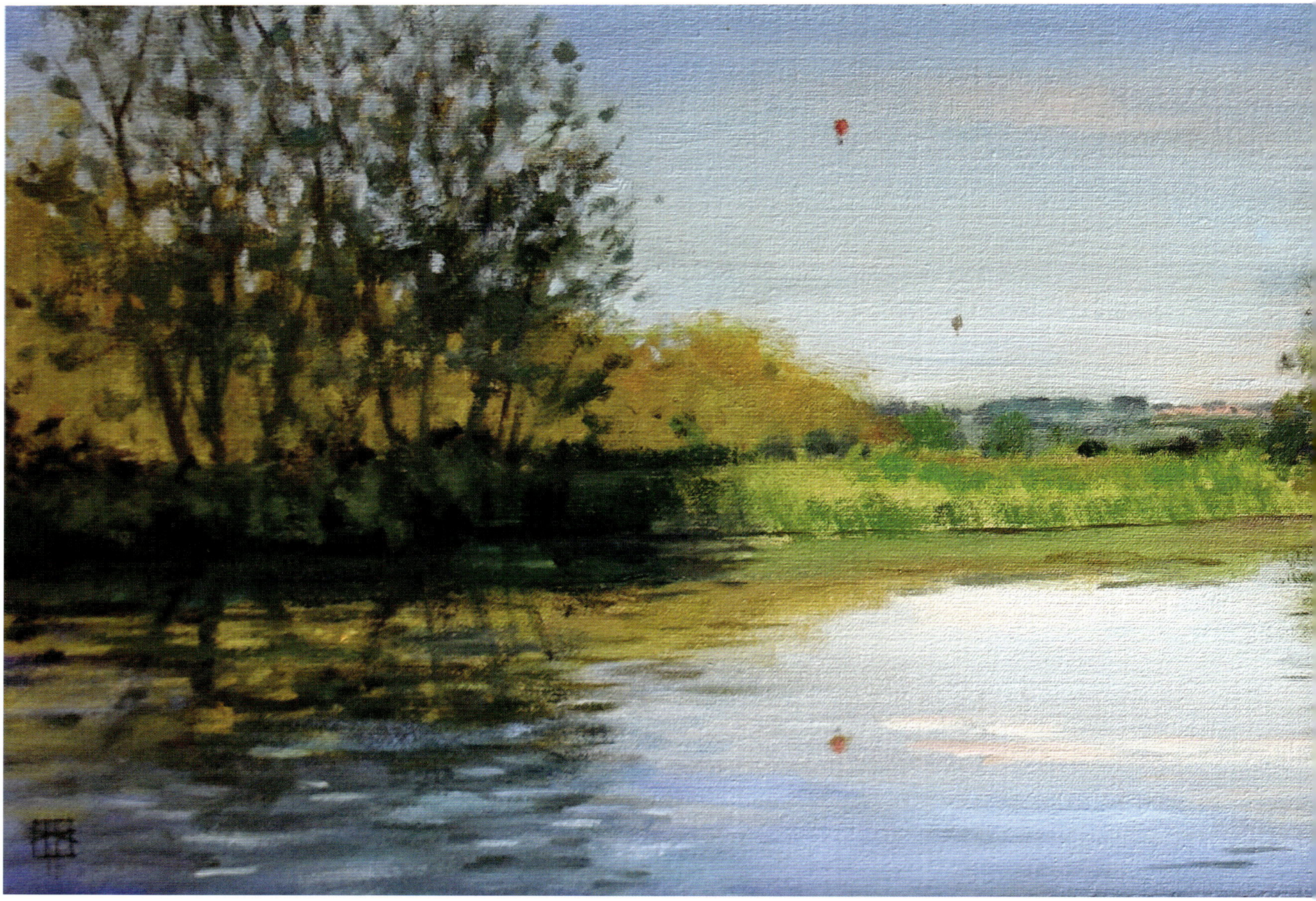

Sculling | 2011 | oil on linen | 30.5 x 91.5 cm

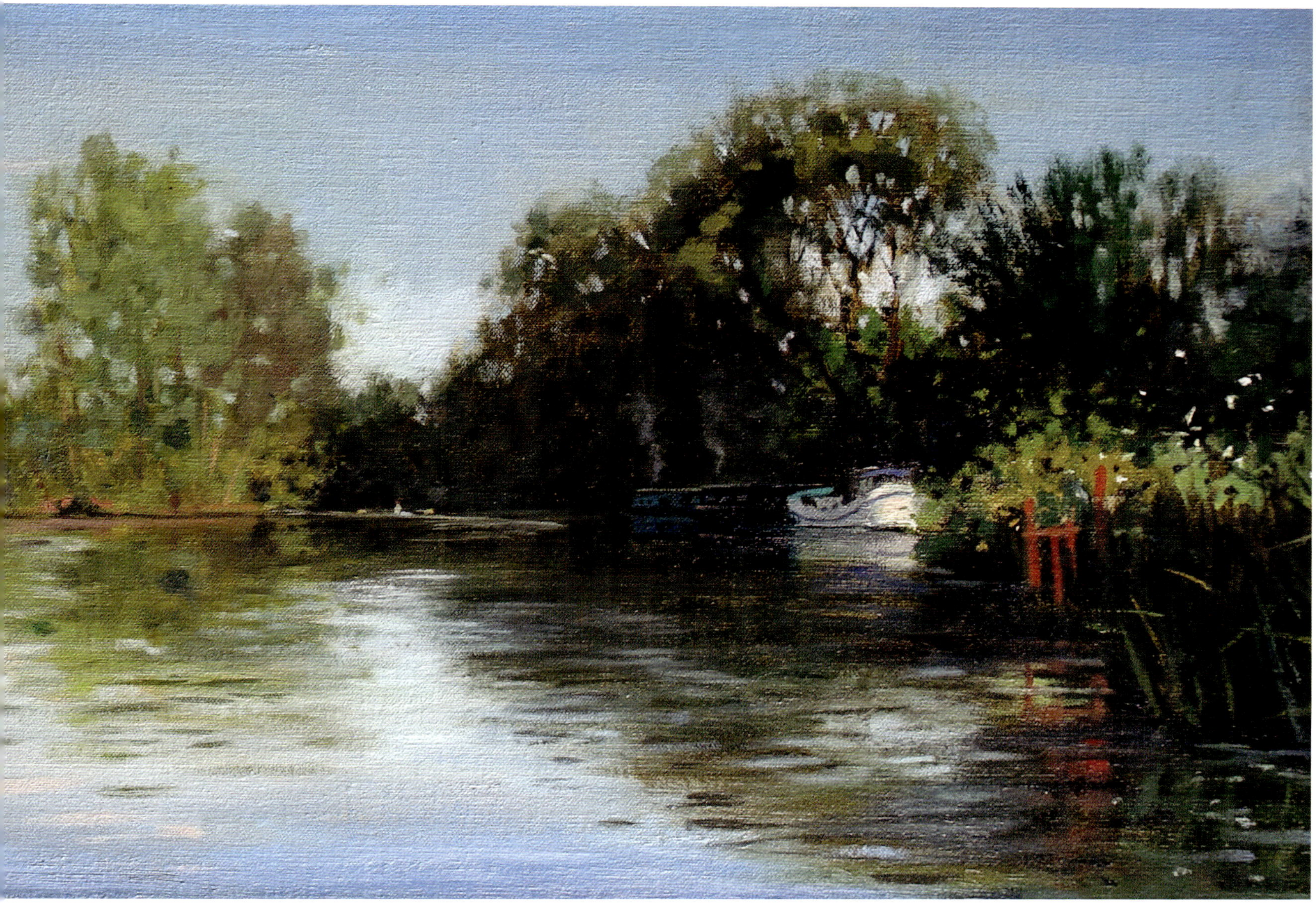

private collection

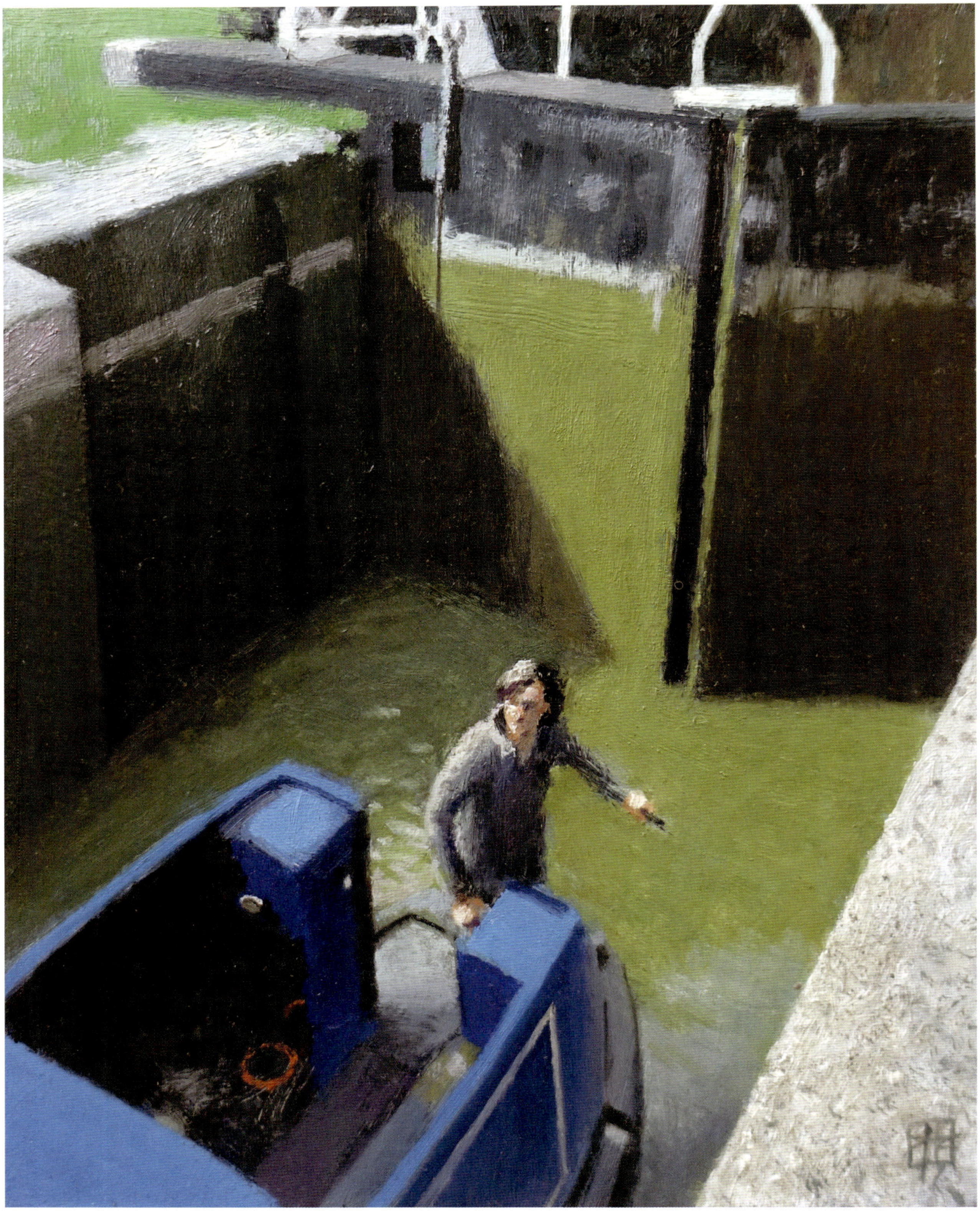

Towards Devizes | 2017 | oil on panel | 24 x 20 cm collection of the artist

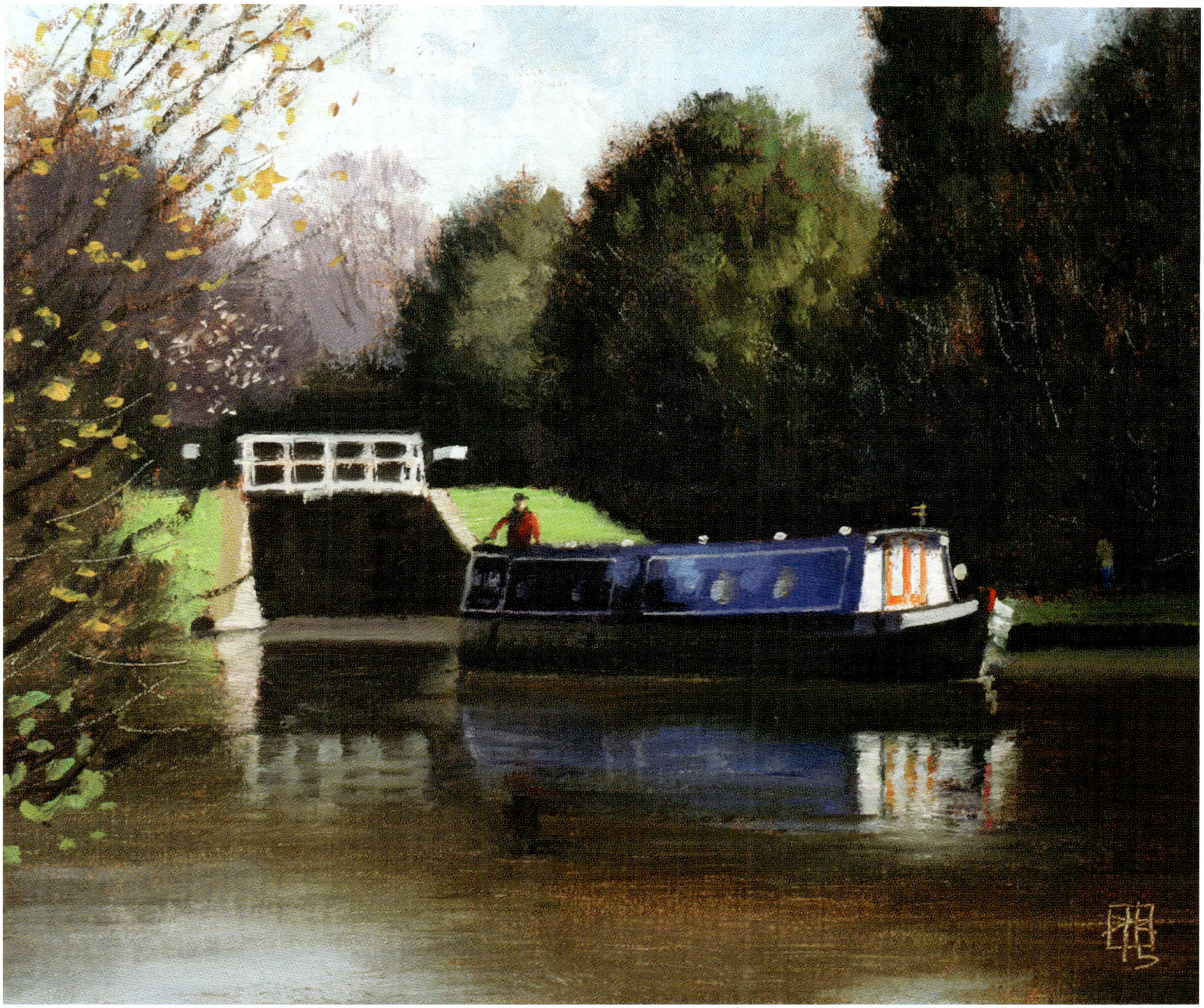

On His Way | 2015 | oil on panel | 20 x 24 cm collection of the artist

From the Bridge on Couch Lane
2019 | oil on linen | 61 x 61 cm
collection of the artist

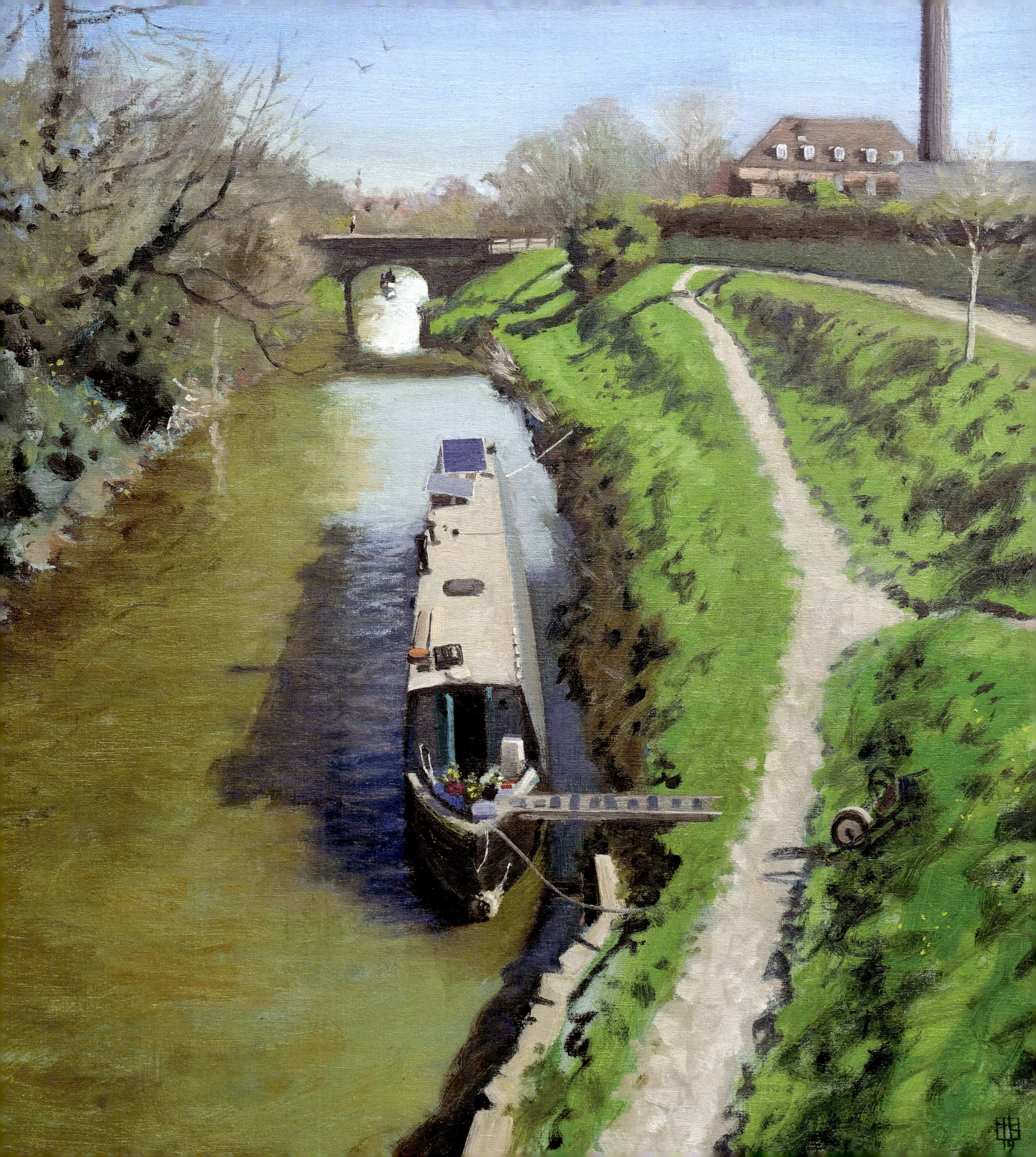

David Cobley RP NEAC

CHRONOLOGY

1954	Born 27 June, Northampton, England
1965–71	Wellingborough Grammar School
1971–2	Northampton College of Art, Foundation Course in Art and Design
1972	Liverpool College of Art, Diploma in Fine Art (incomplete). Joins the Unification Church
1975	Japan, with International One World Crusade
1978	Leaves the Unification Church
1978–81	Sophia University (Tokyo), BA in Comparative Culture
1981	Marries Masami Minagawa
1984	Returns to the UK to live in Pembrokeshire
1985	Moves to Wiltshire
1996	Sets up Widcombe Studios, Bath
1997	Elected a member of the Royal Society of Portrait Painters
2001	Elected a member of the Royal West of England Academy (RWA), Bristol
2007	Elected a member of the New English Art Club
2008–13	Lives on a houseboat at Bath Marina
2011	Divorces
2013	Moves to Devizes
2019	Still alive and kicking

AWARDS

1989	Shortlisted, John Player Portrait Award
1993	John Brandler Prize
1999	Daler-Rowney Prize; Tom Rice Gallery, Dublin, Award; RWA, Bristol, Public Prize
2001	Andrew Brownsword Prize
2002	Prosigns and Graphics Prize
2004	Llewellyn Alexander Award; Public Prize, Holburne Portrait Prize
2013	Public Prize, Bath Society of Artists
2017	Peter Ashley Framing Prize; Smallwood Architects Prize

EXHIBITIONS

1989	John Player Portrait Award
1995	BP Portrait Award; Hunting Art Prize
1998	'The Discerning Eye', Mall Galleries, London
2000	'People's Portraits' touring exhibition; 'The Discerning Eye', Mall Galleries, London
2001	'Summer Exhibition', Royal Academy of Arts; 'The Discerning Eye', Mall Galleries, London
2002	Solo exhibition, Beaux Arts, Bath; 'Summer Exhibition', Royal Academy of Arts; The Holburne Portrait Prize
2003	'Summer Exhibition', Royal Academy of Arts
2004	Solo exhibition, Beaux Arts, Bath; The Holburne Portrait Prize; 'Naked', RWA, Bristol
2005	Solo exhibition, Messum's, London; 'Summer Exhibition', Royal Academy of Arts; Hunting Art Prize
2007	'Inside and Out', Victoria Art Gallery, Bath
2018	'Sawdust and Sequins: The Art of the Circus', RWA, Bristol
2019	'David Cobley: All By Himself', Mall Galleries, London

PUBLIC COLLECTIONS

Brasenose College Oxford
Exeter College Oxford
Gonville & Caius College Cambridge
National Portrait Gallery, London
Sheffield Hallam University
Trinity College Cambridge
University College Oxford
University of Bath
Victoria Art Gallery, Bath